Louise Page
Plays : One

Tissue, Salonika, Real Estate, Golden Girls

Tissue: 'The tissue of the title is a left breast and a lymph node removed during Sally Bacon's mastectomy . . . Louise Page catalogues Sally's changing attitudes to what her mother calls her chest, her brother calls her tits, and what she calls her bosoms.'

Guardian

Salonika: 'There is in this strange and beautiful new play . . . a moment when the author crosses the boundaries of naturalism and the seaside sands of Salonika are literally parted and the dead past rises to life.'

Nicholas de Jongh, *Guardian*

Real Estate: 'Miss Page, by accurate, detailed, loving writing has created four real people, sensitive to the needs of others yet each, ultimately, with an instinct for self-preservation. These are "ordinary" people to whom nothing special happens. They become special, extraordinary because of the dignity their creator endows them with.'

Giles Gordon, *Spectator*

Golden Girls: 'Not only does this enthralling play take us into the world of women's athletics, it also raises any number of questions about the success ethic, the dubious role of sponsorship and the secondary status of nearly all women's sports.'

Guardian

LOUISE PAGE's stage plays include *Want-Ad* (Birmingham Arts Lab, 1977; ICA, 1979); *Lucy* (Bristol New Vic Studio, 1979); *Tissue* (Birmingham Repertory Theatre, 1978; ICA, 1978; adapted for Radio 4, 1979); *Hearing* (Birmingham Repertory Theatre, 1979); *Flaws* (Sheffield University Drama Studio, 1980); *Housewives* (Derby Playhouse, 1981 a Radio/Theatre production); *Salonika* (Royal Court Theatre Upstairs, 1982; winner of the George Devine Award); *Real Estate* (Tricycle Theatre, London, 1984) and *Golden Girls* (Royal Shakespeare Company, The Other Place, Stratford-upon-Avon, 1984); *Beauty and the Beast* (jointly commissioned by the The Women's Playhouse Trust and Methuen) opened at the Liverpool Playhouse in November 1985 before transferring to the Old Vic, London in December 1985; *Diplomatic Wives* (Palace Theatre, Watford, 1989). She was awarded the first J T Grein Award for Drama by the Critic's Circle. She has also written for radio and television.

authors in the World Dramatists series

Aeschylus (two volumes)
Jean Anouilh
John Arden
Peter Barnes
Brendan Behan
Aphra Behn
Edward Bond (four volumes)
Bertolt Brecht (three volumes)
Howard Brenton (two volumes)
Georg Büchner
Bulgakov
Calderón
Anton Chekhov
Caryl Churchill (two volumes)
Noël Coward (five volumes)
Margaretta D'Arcy
Sarah Daniels
Eduardo De Filippo
David Edgar (three volumes)
Euripides (three volumes)
Dario Fo
Michael Frayn (two volumes)
Max Frisch
Gorky
Henrik Ibsen (six volumes)
Lorca (three volumes)
Marivaux
Mustapha Matura
David Mercer
Arthur Miller (three volumes)
Anthony Minghella
Molière
Tom Murphy
Peter Nichols (two volumes)
Clifford Odets
Joe Orton
Louise Page
A. W. Pinero
Luigi Pirandello
Stephen Poliakoff
Terence Rattigan (two volumes)
Sophocles (two volumes)
Wole Soyinka
August Strindberg (three volumes)
J. M. Synge
Oscar Wilde

LOUISE PAGE

Plays: One

Tissue
Salonika
Real Estate
Golden Girls

with an introduction by the author

Methuen Drama

METHUEN WORLD DRAMATISTS

This edition first published in Great Britain in 1990
by Methuen Drama, Michelin House, 81 Fulham Road, London SW3 6RB
and distributed in the United States of America by
HEB Inc., 361 Hanover Street, Portsmouth, New Hampshire, NH 03801 3959
Reprinted 1992

A CIP catalogue record for this book is available from the British Library

ISBN 0-413-64500-2

The painting on the front cover is *Woman Seated* by Henry Moore.
© Henry Moore Foundation.
Reproduced by kind permission of the Henry Moore Foundation.
The photograph of the author on the back cover is by Sarah Ainslie.

Printed and bound in Great Britain
by Cox & Wyman Ltd, Cardiff Road, Reading

Contents

	page
Chronology	vii
Introduction	ix
TISSUE	1
SALONIKA	55
REAL ESTATE	131
GOLDEN GIRLS	215

A Chronology

Want Ad	1977
Tissue	1978
Lucy	1979
Hearing	1979
Flaws	1980
Housewives	1981
Salonika	1982
Real Estate	1984
Golden Girls	1984
Beauty and the Beast	1985
Diplomatic Wives	1989

Introduction

I'd written other plays before I wrote *Tissue*. I'd been writing them fairly consistently since the age of 13; before that I had written turgid novels about love even though I didn't know about love. It was a fascination with dialogue and the theatre which focused my attention on playwrighting. My earliest attempts were, of course, entirely derivative. The first three were in blank verse and rhyming couplets. Shakespeare was the only playwright I had ever read and I thought that was how plays had to be written. It wasn't until I read Wesker, who was the only contemporary playwright whose work was in the school library, that I realized you didn't have to write like Shakespeare, you could write with your own voice and make up your own rules.

I was very disciplined. I used to write for an hour a day when I got home from school, a treat before doing my homework. At school I was endlessly made to rewrite my essays because I can't spell. I was supposed to get the spellings right but I found improving the story much more interesting. Rewriting rather than respelling stopped it being ignominious (that is not the first word in this introduction I've had to get the dictionary out for) and taught me very early on not to be frightened of rewriting. The headmistress tried to show me the difference between weather and whether. My father promised me a career working in Woolworths. But I still knew I was going to be a writer: I've known that ever since I can remember.

I finished eleven other plays before I wrote *Tissue*; two of which had been performed. So these plays aren't quite the early plays they seem. With each play you learn a little more about the craft. *Golden Girls* taught me to write exit lines, for example. *Light Fantastic*, the play I have just finished, has taught me how to write argument. And the play I am about to begin will teach me something too.

Tissue had to be written in the way it was because I knew from the outset that the Birmingham Arts Lab who had commissioned it could only afford three actors and there was very little money to spend on the set. I wanted to explore as many aspects of the subject of breast cancer as possible and the only way to do it was to have one actor playing Sally and the others playing multiple male and female roles. Once you've escaped naturalism in the casting you also have to do so in the writing. Episodic writing demands a heightened impact: each of the 51 scenes in *Tissue* had to make its point in its own right and as part of the whole as quickly as possible. More than any other play I have written *Tissue* was shaped by the rehearsal process. I would sit outside the rehearsal room writing while inside the actors and director rehearsed the scene we had previously discussed and which I had just rewritten in the light of their comments.

I remember being ferocious about the language and punctuation. Sometimes the actors didn't like me for it. I may not have been writing blank verse but I do have an absolute sense of the rhythm of the lines I write. The easiest way for me to tell if an actor is off the lines is just to close my eyes and listen to the structure of the text; if the rhythm's wrong I usually open my eyes to discover that the actors have the lines wrong. Very often it is the finding of the right rhythm for a character that is the most important clue to the writing of that character. In the theatre characters are what they speak. This is true of all of us. We change our dialogue depending on our relationship to the people we are talking to. We are chameleons with words. That is the thrill of constructing character through dialogue.

I was paid £120 for *Tissue*. In the mistaken belief that the right equipment would make the writing better, and if not better at least easier, I bought an electric typewriter with the money.

Salonika was written easily. Some plays use so much of you that they eat you alive, but you can't tell before you start writing what they are going to demand. I wrote *Salonkia* very quickly, in less than two weeks, but those two weeks were the result of many months of thought about the play. My original idea had been to write a play about old age. At this stage I assumed that the finished play would be a naturalistic piece about the changing demography of the family. Starting to research the play (I was 26 at the time) I began to change my preconceptions. The more old people I met and talked to about their response to ageing, the more I realized that people's reaction to ageing and the way in which they aged was to do with a combination of internal and external circumstances. Most of my research was done while travelling by train between Sheffield, where I was living, Birmingham, where I was teaching, and London where I was going to the theatre. At the time British Rail were offering people over 60 the chance to travel anywhere in the country for a pound. I met elderly people undertaking journeys I would have hesitated to contemplate; going from London to Edinburgh for tea in one example. I decided that I had to write a play which expressed their immense vitality and zest for life. It became clear when talking to women how extraordinarily their lives had been altered by the First World War and I felt it would be dishonest of me not to acknowledge that experience in the play.

Having decided on the characters of Enid and Charlotte I began to write the play. Suddenly, after eight pages, I became terribly stuck and there seemed no way forward without introducing the character of Ben. His presence in the lives of Enid and Charlotte was so palpable that it demanded an expression, hence my decision to include a character from a completely different time. Ben is not a ghost. He is as real to Charlotte and Enid as if they'd seen him a week ago. His presence is as real as that of any other character on the stage. More real perhaps because the constant memory of him has expanded the women's relationship with Ben. Enid has only ever seen her father in photographs but recognizes him because he is the controlling force of her life. Ben is both her fate and her destiny. It is only when Peter proves that Ben did not die a hero's death that Ben's grip on his daughter is weakened. Enid has been living with an erroneous version of her father. It has distorted her life. It is only when she admits the truth of Ben's death and treats him as her equal that Enid becomes free to be herself. At the end of the play she can both literally and metaphorically look up and see the stars and envisage the other worlds they encompass.

Real Estate is a response to *Salonika*. Having written about a mother and daughter who had never been separated I wanted to write about a separated mother and daughter. I once knew someone who disappeared from her parents' life. I thought it was a cruel thing to do but the thought of it fascinated me. In the beginning I thought that *Real Estate* would be a two hander. But I needed Dick and Eric to be able to write *Real Estate* in the same way that I had needed Ben in *Salonika*. Everyone in the play is looking for love. When it is under their noses they don't recognize it, what they want are demonstrations of it. They try to manipulate one another to get love. In many ways Jenny's coming back is more cruel than her leaving. Reading the play now, I see it as far more autobiographical than I had thought at the time. I remember crying into the new electric typewriter whilst writing it.

Golden Girls, which was written for the RSC almost in tandem with *Real Estate*, was another response play. In the character of Jenny I had touched on the sticky subject of women's ambition: Jenny is ambitious but not to the exclusion of everything else in the world. The women in *Golden Girls* have become isolated inside their ambitions. The personal cost to themselves is massive. When Muriel (who I think is my favourite character in these plays), feels she can no longer pay the personal cost, she threatens the whole structure. It was exciting when writing Vivien's part to write a character who should be sympathetic but who actually is not. It's always strange rehearsing *Golden Girls* because it's the women's roles which give the play its dramatic thrust. The women control the action of the play. The male actors often find it very difficult to accept that they do not provide the motor for the play. We don't yet live in times when men will accept that they don't always have to control. If the men are fractious and difficult when rehearsing *Golden Girls* that is why. In many ways Sue, Pauline, Dorcas, Muriel, Janet, Vivien and Hilary are an antidote to all the Marianas, Juliets, Julias, Cordelias and Hermiones. Writing in this country you can never shake Shakespeare off your pen. And somehow he also seems to be in all the word processing packages.

My reaction to seeing any of these plays now is to be surprised by the fact that I could write them. The work seems wise and sensible. I never feel wise or sensible. But then the world you write in is a magical place. It's a place where as a writer you try and make order out of the world's chaos. It's a place where you are free to be wise and sensible. And it's a privilege to pass that on to an audience. Playwrighting is about the folly of talking to strangers.

Louise Page
30 July 1990

Tissue

Tissue was first presented at the Studio Theatre of the Belgrade, Coventry on 3 May 1978, with the following cast:

SALLY	Elizabeth Revil
MAN	Michael Cassidy
WOMAN	Kate Crutchley

Directed by Nancy Diuguid
Designed by James Helps
Stage manager Joanne Richler-Ostroff

Reset – Lx 1.

One

Lx 2.

SALLY. Why me? It is a question as unsolvable as why I am here? Why me?

MAN. It has to happen to someone you know.

WOMAN. All this fuss over a pound of flesh.

MAN. It's not a functional organ after all.

WOMAN. If you don't want children, why do you need a breast?

MAN. God moves in mysterious ways.

WOMAN. It's not as if you're married.

MAN. It's only a bit of tissue.

WOMAN. Did you ever notice that you had it in the first place?

MAN. Put a bit of cotton wool in it.

WOMAN. Don't talk about it here.

MAN. If it hadn't been you it would have been someone else.

SALLY. But it is me. And I am here.

Lx 3

Two *hospital*

SALLY. I'm wearing knickers, in bed.

MAN. You'll have to get yourself some frillies.

SALLY. Said doctor, pulling my gown up and the sheets down.

WOMAN. Can you get a friend to bring you in some briefs?

SALLY. Said sister, pulling my gown down and the sheets up.

So my mother sent me undies, first class, still in their bag without their bill.

So the problem of decency under the sheets is resolved. I've got knickers on.

MAN. You'll have to get yourself a nightie and a housecoat.

SALLY. This isn't mine. You've lost mine.

WOMAN. Can you manage that? Ask a friend to bring them in?

SALLY. I haven't got one.

And am so confused I don't know if I mean a nightie, a housecoat or a friend.

WOMAN. What do you wear?

SALLY. Nothing!

MAN. Pardon?

SALLY. He is as surprised as if I said I went to the door in my birthday suit.

Nothing!

WOMAN. What do you do if someone comes to the front door?

SALLY. Nothing!

MAN. Or the back?

SALLY. Nothing!

WOMAN. What?

SALLY. Nothing!

WOMAN. Oh!

SALLY. I don't answer. Not early in the morning.

Three Lx 4

WOMAN. Miss Bacon, Miss Bacon, time to wake up.

SALLY. What time is it?

WOMAN. Seven.

SALLY. Every morning here at seven, because they shake me to make me face the day –

WOMAN. Wakey, wakey, Miss Bacon –

SALLY. And do not allow me to slip back, not even to semi-fantasy, I see the shimmer of purple and green sea nylon with lace billows of the bathroom rush. In case someone rips the sheets from them and shoves a towel under and lathers.

I smell.

WOMAN. Not at all, you don't.

SALLY. The nurse, of course, denies it. They have to. But I stink.

WOMAN. We'll get every bit of you as clean as a new pin.

SALLY. In spite of perfect hygiene techniques, I am stronger than all the cleanliness put about me. More pungent than mattress disinfectant and –

WOMAN. Is this the talc I'm to use?

SALLY. Yes. Do I smell?

WOMAN. Yes. You're a blue gardenia!

Four Lx 5

WOMAN. Sally!

SALLY. What?

WOMAN. Sally, don't!

SALLY. What, Mum?

WOMAN. Do that.

SALLY. I'm washing myself.

WOMAN. Not like that though.

SALLY. Like what?

WOMAN. If you want to wash your – your chest – do it with your flannel. Put the soap on your flannel and then use your flannel.

SALLY. It's much quicker if you just put the soap on with your hands. If you do it like this it's much better.

WOMAN. Don't, Sally!

SALLY. Simon does!

WOMAN. Simon might. But that's different. Ladies don't.

SALLY. Does Dad? Does he put the soap on a flannel first? Or does he just put in straight on?

WOMAN. Sally, don't wash your face with that flannel. Not when you've used it there. That's a smelly thing to do.

Five   *LX 6*

SALLY. Do I smell?

WOMAN. That will pass.

SALLY. They say and –

WOMAN. Have another squirt of spray –

SALLY. Which mostly misses and stales on the sheets. It is true.

WOMAN. Of course she smells. The wound is septic. I try not to breathe in through my nose but through my mouth and have to keep swallowing more than I should because the saliva is flowing from the ducts of my mouth and drowning my tongue between my jaws. She has an infection in her wound which will swell with pus and burst.

Six LX 7

SALLY. A spurt. A dab behind the ears, on the wrists, the neck, behind the knees and between the breasts –

Don't!

MAN. Come on.

SALLY. Don't!

MAN. Sally?

SALLY. Don't!

MAN. Come on.

SALLY. Don't touch me.

MAN. God, you're tense.

SALLY. Don't touch me.

MAN. Why?

SALLY. I don't want you to.

MAN. So what's wrong?

SALLY. I don't know.

Pause.

You can't feel anything, can you? Not a lump?

MAN. Where?

SALLY. There.

MAN. There? In your tit?

SALLY. In my bosom. Is there a lump there?

MAN. You've knocked yourself somewhere.

SALLY. I know I haven't. I'd remember if I had.

MAN. Why?

SALLY. Come on. It's obvious.

MAN. Okay. You're not bruised. You didn't hit yourself hard.

SALLY. I know I didn't. Can you feel a lump?

MAN. If you haven't knocked yourself there can't be anything.

SALLY. I don't want to be told there's nothing. I want you to check that there isn't.

MAN. You do it.

SALLY. Why me?

MAN. It's your tit.

SALLY. I don't know what it's supposed to feel like.

MAN. Suppose I do?

SALLY. You bloody well ought to. You're the one who touches them.

MAN. Go to the doctor in the morning.
    Now come on.

SALLY. Go to the doctor?

MAN. Ask him to feel you.

SALLY. God, you're callous.

MAN. Get him to examine you.

SALLY. But he won't know.

MAN. They feel hundreds.

SALLY. But not mine. Please, I want to know if I've got a lump.

MAN. Don't get hysterical.

SALLY. I want you to tell me.

MAN. Okay.

SALLY. What if I have?

MAN. You know why it happens? Because frigid women want it to. There's nothing there.

SALLY. Isn't there?

MAN. No.

SALLY. Are you sure?

MAN. There? Feel. There's nothing.

SALLY. No. Perhaps it's muscular.

Seven LX 8

WOMAN. As Sally's mother I watched her changing and becoming a woman. Her body taking on contours. I watched her as her body tried to copy mine as I had tried to copy my mother's. I watched her as she began to look in the mirror closely. Then –

Sally?

SALLY. What, Mum?

WOMAN. Can I come in?

SALLY. No.

WOMAN. Only quickly, I want a vest for Simon.

SALLY. No.

WOMAN. Come on, Sally. Why not?

SALLY. It's engaged.

WOMAN. Why?

SALLY. I've formed.

Eight LX 9

SALLY. Doctor, I smell.

MAN. Of course. You've got an infection. If you were an animal you would have licked yourself to rid yourself of the smell, thus keeping the wound free from infection. Very crafty, nature. But we've invented antiseptics now. Very clever, men.

SALLY. In former days he would have come to me, knowing of my wound, drawn to it with the same power as a hound on the scent of a fox, but not to tear me to pieces but to lick me clean.

MAN. Or any animal of the flock would have come, as ready as the others and as willing with its tongue.

SALLY. Or I would have licked myself alone.

Nine   L𝗑 10

SALLY. At school we were taught—

WOMAN. If you prick your finger and get blood on your sewing, the only way to take out the mark is to spit on your finger, a clean finger — then rub the mark with your spittle until it goes.

SALLY. In needlework we made cookery aprons and nightdresses.

MAN. Can you get a nightie?

SALLY. Said doctor.

It was brushed cotton, pink, with sprigs of yellow flowers and blue ribbons. My mother's still using it for cleaning rags. She's been using it for rags since—

WOMAN. Sally is not neat.

SALLY. Appeared on my report. The end of term had come and I was still taking out—

WOMAN. Those tacking stitches because they are too large and not straight.

SALLY. I gave up domestic arts for language. A surgeon is a man who must like cutting and stitching.

Ten   L𝗑 11

WOMAN. Can I help you?

SALLY. I want to see the doctor.

WOMAN. Yes? Name?

SALLY. Bacon.

WOMAN. As in egg?

SALLY. Yes.

WOMAN. And the initials?

SALLY. S.

WOMAN. Wait here.

SALLY. Thank you.

WOMAN. Forename?

SALLY. Sally.

WOMAN. Is that short for Sarah?

SALLY. No. It's my name.

WOMAN. And the surname?

SALLY. Bacon. As in egg.

WOMAN. Thank you.

We've not got a card for you. Are you registered here?

SALLY. Pardon?

WOMAN. Have you seen a doctor here before?

SALLY. Here? No.

WOMAN. Well, no wonder I can't find a card for you. If you're not a patient you should have said. Are you a temporary?

SALLY. What?

WOMAN. Are you in the district temporarily?

SALLY. How long is temporary?

WOMAN. Will you be in the district for longer than three months?

SALLY. I don't know.

WOMAN. Umh –

SALLY. Please, can I register?

WOMAN. Yes – well, I'll give you a temporary form to fill in. Is it an emergency?

SALLY. An emergency?

WOMAN. Doctor doesn't have to take you on unless it's an emergency.

SALLY. I'm not sure.

WOMAN. What are your symptoms?

SALLY. I've – are you a nurse?

WOMAN. Not trained but I've picked up a lot working here.

SALLY. I have to see a doctor.

WOMAN. Doctor doesn't have to treat you unless it's an emergency.

SALLY. But I need to see one.

WOMAN. I should try another practice.

SALLY. But –

WOMAN. Why don't you try a couple of aspirins and a day in bed with a hot water bottle? You don't need a sick note for a day.

SALLY. I don't want a sick note. I want a proper physical examination.

WOMAN. The doctors here are very busy people. I wouldn't trouble them unless it's really necessary.

SALLY. Where do I find another doctor? Where do you recommend?

WOMAN. The doctors here are very good.

SALLY. Where do I find a surgery?

WOMAN. How did you find this one?

SALLY. I looked at doors until I came across it.

WOMAN. Then I should try the same again.

Eleven LX 12

SALLY. That's real rejection for you, Simon.

MAN. Find another doctor.

SALLY. I suppose so.

MAN. If you think something's wrong.

SALLY. I can't be bothered.

MAN. How do you feel?

SALLY. Fine but I think I can feel a lump.

MAN. Ask Mum what she thinks.

SALLY. She thinks it's the fibres in my bust sinking because I don't wear a bra.

MAN. They say you need up-lift.

SALLY. Who do?

MAN. Well –

SALLY. Come on, Simon, who do?

MAN. All the adverts you ever see for bras.

SALLY. I've been wearing mine solidly for the past two weeks, even in bed in case it made it go away. It doesn't make any difference.

MAN. Perhaps you haven't got the right sort.

SALLY. How come you're such an expert?

MAN. I read the bra ads.

SALLY. Do you read the ads or do you look at the bras?

MAN. What's in them, perhaps.

SALLY. I never think of you doing that, Si.

He said it was because I was frigid, that I wanted something wrong. An excuse. Women can have psychosomatic pregnancies.

MAN. More believable than breast lumps.

SALLY. But what if I have, Simon? What if it is cancer?

MAN. You have to be at least forty to get it.

SALLY. I read it can happen when you're younger.

MAN. Your chances must be pretty remote.

SALLY. How remote?

MAN. As winning the pools or something.

SALLY. People do win.

MAN. They aren't likely to be you.

SALLY. I suppose not.

Twelve   Lx 13

WOMAN. I must, I must, I must increase my bust.

SALLY. I must, I must, I must increase my bust.

WOMAN. I must, I must, I must increase my bust.

SALLY. It's a bit exhausting.

WOMAN. It's worth it.

SALLY. It had better be.

WOMAN. It really is.

SALLY. How many times do you have to do it?

WOMAN. Millions.

SALLY. We'll be worn out.

WOMAN. Don't you want to grow?

SALLY. Yes.

WOMAN. Then you have to do it. You have to do it a million times for every inch!

SALLY. One million?

WOMAN. Yes. But the results are amazing.

SALLY. That means if I want six inches I'll have to do six million!

WOMAN. I must, I must, I must increase my bust.

SALLY. I've only done about twenty.

WOMAN. It doesn't show until you've done half a million.

SALLY. Oh gosh.

WOMAN. And you mustn't lie on them in the night in between.

SALLY. Why not?

WOMAN. They get squashed in.

SALLY. Do they?

WOMAN. They get squashed right in.

SALLY. Then what happens?

WOMAN. I don't know.

SALLY. Don't they come out again?

WOMAN. No.

SALLY. How horrible.

WOMAN. They get ingrown like toenails.

SALLY. What do you do?

WOMAN. You have to put lots of pillows in your bed to sleep on.

SALLY. You can't do that.

WOMAN. Why?

SALLY. It makes your mouth come open when you're sleeping.

WOMAN. What difference does that make?

SALLY. It gives you double chins.

WOMAN. You've got them already.

SALLY. I haven't.

WOMAN. I've done nearly three thousand this week. Which means I'll get a bra first.

BOTH. I must, I must, I must increase my bust.

WOMAN. I can feel mine growing.

SALLY. Can you?

WOMAN. Yes.

SALLY. I can feel mine too.

Thirteen LX 14

WOMAN. Miss Bacon, Sally –

SALLY. I heard them calling me as I came back from the theatre –

WOMAN. Sally –

SALLY. I could hear them calling me as I floated back and made my way through thick grass —

WOMAN. Sally —

SALLY. Which swished as I walked and I felt that they couldn't see my head as I parted the green hay and scarlet poppies.

Oh Sally go and call the cattle home,
and call the cattle home,
and call the cattle home,
Across the sands of Dee:
The western wind was wild and dank with foam
And all alone went she.

I wouldn't open my eyes but I could hear them calling me.

WOMAN. Miss Bacon, Sally, Miss Bacon —

SALLY. Every morning here at seven, because they shake me to make me face the day —

WOMAN. Wakey, wakey, Miss Bacon —

SALLY. And do not allow me to slip back —

WOMAN. Open your eyes.

SALLY. Even to semi-fantasy —

WOMAN. That's a good girl —

SALLY. I see a shimmer of purple and green sea. I knew I was still alive and felt a moment of great elation. I wanted to stand on my bed in my white gown and shout, 'I am alive!' I will open my eyes.

WOMAN. They've had to take it.

SALLY. What — ?

WOMAN. They're sorry but they've had to take it off.

SALLY. No.

WOMAN. Shush. You're all right. It's gone to make you better. It was a malignant tumour.

SALLY. Have they got it all?

WOMAN. Yes.

SALLY. Is it all gone?

WOMAN. Yes.

SALLY. Have they got all of it? They haven't left any, have they?

WOMAN. No.

SALLY. I'm all right?

WOMAN. Right as rain. Would you like something to send you back to sleep?

SALLY. They said –

MAN. You will feel some discomfort. Perhaps a little aching and a sense of loss. But that will pass.

SALLY. Are you sure they've got it all?

WOMAN. Yes. That's why you can't feel anything. There's nothing there. That's it – you go back to sleep – that's it.

SALLY. I shut my eyes and there are no colours. No one has told me what they have done with it. Whether it collapsed itself to be accommodated, nipple upwards in one of those dishes, stainless steel and shaped like a kidney, or was it just put down somewhere, on some convenient surface after its nature of a pink blancmange with a cherry on top –

Sally no longer calls the cattle home,
calls the cattle home,
calls the cattle home,
Across the sands of Dee:
The western wind was wild and dank with foam
And all alone went she.

Fourteen   LX 15

WOMAN. Yes?

SALLY. I've a lump.

WOMAN. Where?

SALLY. Here.

WOMAN. There?

SALLY. Yes. I've a lump.

MAN. Where?

SALLY. Here.

MAN. There?

SALLY. Yes. I've a lump.

WOMAN. Where?

SALLY. Here.

WOMAN. There?

SALLY. Yes. I've a lump.

MAN. Here?

SALLY. There!

WOMAN. Where?

SALLY. Here.

MAN. There?

SALLY. Where?

WOMAN. There?

SALLY. I've

BOTH. a lump—

MAN. Where?

WOMAN. There.

SALLY. Here!

Fifteen   Lx 16

SALLY. It's still there.

WOMAN. No it isn't, love. That's just the strapping and the bandages.

SALLY. Are you sure?

WOMAN. I promise you. You'll be able to have a look when we take
the bandages off.

SALLY. I don't want to.

WOMAN. You'll have to look some time.

SALLY. I don't.

WOMAN. If you see it while it's really nasty you'll think it that much
nicer when it heals.

SALLY. Is it horrid?

WOMAN. I expect it's a bit messy just at the moment.

SALLY. I never want to look at it.

WOMAN. You will – in time. *LX 17*

  I find it hard to nurse these women, who remind me of my mother
  and my sisters. And wonder how I would feel lying there. For all I
  feel pity and sorrow but with these women I feel guilty – and
  wonder if it will ever be me.

Sixteen *LX 18*

MAN. I'm worried for Sally, my daughter. I want to help.

  Sally, if there's anything –

SALLY. My father has found a time for us to be alone.

MAN. Anything.

SALLY. And I notice that my father is growing old.

MAN. Tell me.

SALLY. And I think perhaps I have always been close to this man who
turns his coins over in his pockets.

MAN. Do you want it done privately?

SALLY. I was uneasy when my father said –

MAN. I can pay for you.

SALLY. I said 'Dad' and let him continue.

MAN. We can afford it. Would you feel better if I did that?

SALLY. The subject is so awkward I can say nothing about it.

MAN. You'd get it done at once.

SALLY. They do it as quickly as they can.

MAN. Can you be sure?

SALLY. They do, Dad.

MAN. I suppose so. You'd get good nursing.

SALLY. It's okay, Dad.

MAN. And the privacy. You might want to be private.

SALLY. Yes.

MAN. There are advantages.

SALLY. I know. Matching cups and saucers and lunch in bed and not being woken in the morning and being able to have coffee at tea time and being able to sleep with flowers in my room at night.

MAN. It's the treatment you get.

SALLY. The surgeon you had used to operate at the General in the mornings.

MAN. Let me help.

SALLY. They're expecting me at the General.

MAN. I could change it.

SALLY. No, Dad. I need to be with other women.

   Pause.

   I didn't want Simon to tell you. A cyst isn't serious, Dad.

MAN. Are they sure it's a cyst?

   Pause.

SALLY. No.

MAN. Life isn't fair.

SALLY. No.

MAN. I look at this strange woman who sits with her eyes on the road. It is dark. I watch my daughter who will not look but stares at the road and knows I am watching her.

SALLY. I rang my father late in the evening.

MAN. I found my daugher that night. With her flat door shut behind her and her keys in her bag. She put her case in the boot and sat in the car. We did not touch each other and she said –

SALLY. Will Mum make me cocoa?

WOMAN. On paper Sally's breasts are minutely complicated. Their components interlaced like a clump of trees on the skyline before the dawn. Blue, blues and bluish. The first mammogram I saw I was astonished that women are like that inside.

SALLY. I look at the dark.

WOMAN. In one there is a blue shadow like the moon behind thick clouds.

Seventeen $L \times 19$,

SALLY. Oh Zoey –

WOMAN. I am a friend. Because I am a friend I went to Sainsbury's to buy fruit. I was going to buy chocolate, but if I, Zoey am expected to share, I had rather be indulged in grapes. I wanted to bring black ones or the tiny seedless ones. I notice some have fallen off the stem and crushed. Always select.

I'm sorry.

SALLY. I wouldn't recognise it.

WOMAN. What?

SALLY. My boob. I wouldn't know that it was mine. I wouldn't.

WOMAN. Have a good cry about it. Afterwards you'll feel better.

SALLY. Why do people keep telling me that I'll feel better after crying?

WOMAN. You always do.

SALLY. I've cried a lot. And every time I dry my eyes I think – that's it. All over. It isn't.

WOMAN. Look, you have a cry about it.

SALLY. This woman, though not my closest or most amusing, is my oldest friend. She is the most flat-chested.

L ⟩ 20

Eighteen

SALLY. What are you doing?

WOMAN. What's it look like?

SALLY. I don't know.

WOMAN. Bet you do.

SALLY. They're your socks. Why are you putting knots in your socks?

WOMAN. I'm making nipples.

SALLY. Are you?

WOMAN. When I get them knotted right.

SALLY. Really?

WOMAN. See.

SALLY. They're too big!

WOMAN. How do you know?

SALLY. Nobody has nipples like that!

WOMAN. Ladies with real bosoms do.

SALLY. They don't.

WOMAN. How do you know?

SALLY. My Mum doesn't.

WOMAN. Have you seen your Mum's?

SALLY. Yes.

WOMAN. When?

SALLY. Sometimes.

WOMAN. How many times?

SALLY. Often.

WOMAN. Is often more times than lots?

SALLY. Lots. Her's aren't like that.

WOMAN. That's because your mother hasn't got proper ones.

SALLY. Zoey was the only one who had the style to venture out with nipples. I have never seen my mother's breasts.

Nineteen

MAN. Next please. Yes?

SALLY. I've got a lump. In my breast.

MAN. Are you pre-menstrual?

SALLY. No.

MAN. Any pain?

SALLY. No. Why?

MAN. Pain usually means it's mastitis.

SALLY. Will you examine me?

MAN. Of course. Just slip your top things off.

Which breast?

SALLY. My left one.

MAN. Where?

SALLY. Here.

MAN. There?

SALLY. Can you feel it? That's where it is.

MAN. I see.

SALLY. It's not the same as the other one, is it?

MAN. No. I'm afraid I don't think it is.

SALLY. It's a lump?

MAN. There is something there.   LX 23

SALLY. Oh God!

MAN. Most probably a cyst.

SALLY. That's what everybody says.

MAN. Everybody?

SALLY. People – when I tell them I've got a lump.

MAN. Why tell them and not seek proper medical advice?

SALLY. I have. But no one's taken me seriously. Now I'm frightened.

MAN. You are, aren't you?

SALLY. Wouldn't you be?

MAN. In your position? Yes, I think I'd be terrified. How long's it been troubling you?

SALLY. I'm not sure.

MAN. You must have some idea?

SALLY. I first thought I found it about four months ago.

MAN. Has it increased in size since then?

SALLY. I don't know. I didn't think it had.

MAN. Wishful thinking?

SALLY. Everybody said it was mastitis or nothing. That I was going through a bad time and imagining it.

MAN. And you took their word for it?

SALLY. I thought they'd find it at the FPA.

MAN. I might not have found it if you hadn't pinpointed it so accurately.

SALLY. Then am I right?

MAN. Let's let the dog see the rabbit.

SALLY. What?

MAN. Shine a bright light through it. Anything hollow, like a fluid filled cyst will show up as a shadow and we'll be able to aspirate it.

I'm afraid it looks pretty solid.

SALLY. More serious?

MAN. Not necessarily. We'll just have to look further into it.

SALLY. Operate on it?

MAN. My jokes aren't that bad. We might, as a very last resort, we
might have to biopsy it.

SALLY. Biopsy?

MAN. We remove a bit of tissue for examination. But that's unlikely.
I'll send you up to outpatients for a mammogram.

SALLY. A what?

MAN. It's a technique of x-raying the breast, only the print appears on
paper and not on film.

SALLY. What's it called?

MAN. The technique? A mammogram. Don't worry, it's perfectly
painless. I'll get an appointment made as soon as possible.

SALLY. Thank you.

Twenty L X 24

SALLY. I have a scene where a lover comes to me in tears and buries
his face between my breasts and cries.

MAN. I am an ex-lover. Because I am an ex-lover and therefore no
longer care about her putting on weight and having to secure her
jeans with safety pins, I have brought her chocolates. Because I am
an ex-lover and not quite a friend, I have bought a box without a
ribbon, not soft centres. Choosing in a shop which graded its
goodies towards the ceiling and in a state of financial cut back, I
chose the level just above the jelly fruits.

She looks ghastly and I ask her if she is OK.

SALLY. Because he is my ex-lover I am embarrassed by him being
here. His seeing me like this. I tell him I am fine, remember to smile
and ask him how he is.

MAN. I tell her that I'm well and that she's looking good.

SALLY. I tell him I'm feeling better than I thought I would and isn't it a lovely day?

MAN. I tell her it's colder than it looks and that I'm sorry I didn't bring her flowers.

SALLY. I tell him it's a bad time of the year for cut flowers, but chocolates, he shouldn't have, how lovely.

MAN. I tell her it's a pleasure.

SALLY. I tell him I'll get fat.

MAN. I tell her I expect the food here is dreadful.

SALLY. I tell him it isn't that bad.

MAN. I tell her that —

SALLY. I tell him that —

MAN. I tell her —

SALLY. I tell him —

MAN. I tell —

SALLY. I tell —

MAN. I —

SALLY. I —

MAN. I kiss her goodbye when I leave and say nothing about coming again. There are no promises made about seeing each other and I don't know why I came unless it was to see I left a box of chocolates by her bed. I wonder what will become of her.

SALLY. For the first time, I look.

Lx 25

Twenty-one

MAN. Bags I be doctor.

WOMAN. I'm the nurse.

MAN. You're the patient.

SALLY. Why?

MAN. Because I'm the doctor and she's the nurse so you've got to be.

SALLY. I don't want to be.

WOMAN. You didn't bags.

SALLY. I didn't know we had to.

WOMAN. That's your fault. I've got to be a nurse because I've got a nurse's uniform.

SALLY. Can we bags again?

MAN. No.

SALLY. Let's do something different.

MAN. We're doing this. I'm going to do an operation.

SALLY. No.

WOMAN. Are you going to cut her open, doctor?

MAN. Yes.

WOMAN. Then she's got to take her vest off.

SALLY. Leave me alone.

WOMAN. Doctors have to look.

SALLY. For the first time, I look.

MAN. I'm going to cut you open and take all the badness out of you.

SALLY. It's still there!

WOMAN. No love, it's just the strappings and the bandages.

Twenty-two Lx 26

MAN. Hello, Sliced Bacon.

WOMAN. Simon!

SALLY. It's okay, Mum.

WOMAN. How are you, darling?

SALLY. I'm fine.

MAN. Shall I leave you and come back?

SALLY. Stay.

WOMAN. Please, I've brought you this and these and I thought you'd like this and these and Simon's got this for you.

SALLY. Mum, you shouldn't have.

WOMAN. Is that everything, Simon?

MAN. I think so.

WOMAN. We forgot the flowers.

SALLY. It doesn't matter, Mum.

MAN. I could go back for them.

SALLY. There's no need. Bring me them tomorrow.

WOMAN. Is there anything else you need?

SALLY. Nothing.

WOMAN. I wish you could come home.

SALLY. So do I, Mum. I want to sit in the garden and talk.

Twenty-three LX 27

SALLY. Fleur, they won't believe me.

WOMAN. You'll have to go back again, Sal.

SALLY. Again? I do nothing but, and still nobody does anything.

WOMAN. They can't stop you going back as many times as you want.

SALLY. It's getting to the stage when I think I daren't show my face again.

WOMAN. Sally, it's your body, you've got to take yourself seriously.

SALLY. I do but they won't. Officially this time its nerves. I've got the tranquillisers to prove it.

WOMAN. You taking them?

SALLY. No.

WOMAN. It's the same old story. Give her something, she'll be OK. Look at the way they fobbed me off with my cyst. Have you had a physical examination?

SALLY. No. That's what I can't understand; I go in and they ask me what's wrong and I tell them and they write out another prescription. The last one told me I was imagining it. Four months, imagining!

WOMAN. Has it got bigger since the last time you checked?

SALLY. I daren't check. I can't bring myself to.

WOMAN. Come on, it's every month. Every single month.

SALLY. Do you check every month?

WOMAN. Listen Sal, it's probably nothing serious – most breast lumps are benign, but you've got to make certain.

SALLY. I'm scared, Fleur.

WOMAN. I know, I dread checking. Every month I think 'What if I find another?' I do it when everyone else is out. I always have to look in the mirror first, just in case there's something obvious like puckering or the nipple inverting. I'm so nervous and my fingers are tense. I have to make myself touch them. It's like that every month, Sal. It has to be. Those moments of being frightened of your own body. Do you know how to check?

SALLY. Yes. Like this.

WOMAN. No, you must do it properly. That way you're going to pick up all the natural masses in the breast. Watch, it's like this, with your hand flat and the fingers gently together. In the bath with soap on your hands is much the best time. That way your hand just glides over the breast and the fingers will pick up any lumps that are there. Like this. Two sweeps then down and part the fingers as you pass the hand over the nipple.

SALLY. It's so awkward.

WOMAN. No, it's simple and it's quick. How could you forget to do something so easy?

I should have offered to check my friend's breasts. After Line LX 28.

Twenty-four

SALLY. Suddenly I am certain.

WOMAN. Name?

SALLY. Bacon.

WOMAN. Forenames?

SALLY. Sally Deborah.

WOMAN. Age?

SALLY. Twenty-nine.

WOMAN. Religion?

SALLY. None.

WOMAN. Next of kin?

SALLY. Simon Bacon.

WOMAN. Relationship?

SALLY. Brother.

Twenty-five L × 29

MAN. Because she has asked me to, I am the one who copes. Sally is my responsibility. I am the one who goes to the hospital and waits like an expectant father.

WOMAN. Mr Bacon?

MAN. Yes?

WOMAN. You're Miss Bacon's brother?

MAN. Yes, is she all right?

WOMAN. I'm sorry, it was malignant. We've had to take the breast.

MAN. That's what she was frightened of. Losing it.

WOMAN. What's important is that we've caught the cancer.

MAN. Can I see her? I want to tell her.

WOMAN. It's best that we tell her. You come this evening.

MAN. Yes.

WOMAN. Help her get back to normal.

MAN. Normal. What is normal after losing a breast? I don't know. What is it like without a breast? What does it feel like? How does she feel? Is it a loss or a change? Is she different? Is there a difference?

Twenty-six Lx 30

WOMAN. OK?

SALLY. I just sign it?

WOMAN. You just sign your normal signature there and that gives us your permission to do the operation.

SALLY. I sign.

Twenty-seven Lx 31

MAN. 'Scuse me love, can I fix the headset?

SALLY. What?

MAN. Headset?

SALLY. Oh, yes.

MAN. You're looking lovely this morning. Gorgeous day.

SALLY. Yes.

MAN. What you in for?

SALLY. Check up.

MAN. Days in bed, nice and cosy. Perhaps I ought to get checked.

SALLY. What's wrong with it?

MAN. Got pulled out of the wall. Got brute strength some of them in here.

SALLY. Yes.

MAN. You weren't the one? Pulled it out?

SALLY. I've only been in four days.

MAN. Teasing you, love. Know the sort of pulling you do with a body like yours. I like voluptuous women.

SALLY. Me. Why me? Me. Why me? Why me? Why me? Why me?

Twenty-eight $Lx\ 32$

SALLY. My TB test?

MAN. You banged your breast.

SALLY. From too much sport?

WOMAN. Lack of support.

SALLY. From being caressed?

MAN. You're overstressed.

SALLY. Some childhood ill?

WOMAN. You're on the pill.

SALLY. From over eating?

MAN. Hormone secreting.

SALLY. Some unknown pest?

WOMAN. Bra wearing's best.

SALLY. From carrying bags?

MAN. From smoking fags?

SALLY. The drugs I've had?

WOMAN. From being bad.

Twenty-nine $Lx\ 33$

MAN. Peep, peep, peep.

  You're getting bosoms!

SALLY. I'm not!

MAN. You are. Girls always do.

SALLY. I'm not.

MAN. Don't you want to have bosoms?

SALLY. No!

MAN. I thought girls wanted to?

SALLY. I don't.

MAN. But you will.

SALLY. I won't.

MAN. How do you know?

SALLY. I just won't.

MAN. Bet you do.

SALLY. Bet I don't.

MAN. Go on then, bet.

MAN. When you get bosoms, you'll get like Mum.

SALLY. Will I?

   Peep, peep, peep, peep.

Thirty Lx 34

MAN. Hello?

SALLY. Hello?

MAN. Sally?

SALLY. Simon?

MAN. Yes?

SALLY. It's me.

MAN. Sally? Is something wrong?

SALLY. Something's terrible.

MAN. OK, OK, I'm listening.

SALLY. I've got something wrong. I've got a lump in my breast – and so it could be –

MAN. Peep, peep, peep, peep.

What?

SALLY. Cancer.

MAN. Crabs?

SALLY. Cancer, Simon. Don't tell mother.

MAN. Why?

SALLY. Don't.

MAN. It's not a secret I can store up about my sister.

Thirty-one $L \times 35$

WOMAN. 'Morning, Simon.

MAN. 'Morning, Mum.

WOMAN. Was that Sally ringing last night?

MAN. Why?

WOMAN. She always rings so late to talk to you.

MAN. Yes.

WOMAN. Well, what did she say?

MAN. Nothing.

WOMAN. You were on the 'phone for hours.

MAN. She didn't say anything.

WOMAN. Is she well?

MAN. She's got a lump – they've found a lump. In her breast.

WOMAN. Sally's?

MAN. Yes.

WOMAN. Oh Simon –

MAN. I was silly about it. Mum, I just couldn't think what to say.

WOMAN. She said she thought she felt something – I thought – you know. You never know what's supposed to be there or not. You just don't know.

MAN. She said it's probably nothing.

WOMAN. What's going to happen?

MAN. She's got to go into hospital for a biopsy. Mum, she didn't want me to tell you. She's going to write you and Dad a letter.

WOMAN. I want to know.

MAN. So I tell my mother and she tells my father and we don't talk about it at supper that night.

Why Sally?

SALLY. Why me?

WOMAN. Why my daughter?

SALLY. I am not aware of being happy, or content or unhappy. Why me?

WOMAN. As Sally's mother I watched her changing and becoming a woman. Her body taking on contours.

Thirty-two *Lx 36*

WOMAN. Why Sally?

SALLY. Why can't I have a bra?

WOMAN. You don't need one.

SALLY. Everybody else has got them.

WOMAN. But you haven't got anything to put in it.

SALLY. I have.

WOMAN. I didn't have a bra until I was sixteen.

SALLY. Mum, please. All my friends have got them.

WOMAN. All your friends?

SALLY. Lots of them.

WOMAN. I suppose Zoey has?

SALLY. Yes.

WOMAN. Zoey's chest is practically a hollow.

SALLY. So if she's got one I ought to have.

WOMAN. You don't have to have everything Zoey has.

SALLY. Please, Mum.

WOMAN. You've got vests.

SALLY. Vests aren't grown up.

WOMAN. I wear a vest.

SALLY. You have a bra under it. I flop about. Look, see! See me flopping!

WOMAN. You haven't got anything to flop.

SALLY. Yes, I have. Flop, flop.

WOMAN. The only thing that's flopping is your jumper because you've pulled it off by the sleeves and stretched it.

SALLY. Mum, I've got to have one.

WOMAN. Why?

SALLY. I've got nipples.

WOMAN. Ladies are born with those.

SALLY. But Zoey says that you've got to cover them up.

WOMAN. Zoey talks a lot of rubbish.

SALLY. But you've got to have uplift. It says on the packets that they give uplift. Zoey says that if you don't have uplift they just grow until they reach the floor.

WOMAN. I'm not buying you a bra until you need one.

SALLY. Then I'll ask Dad to buy me one.

WOMAN. Sally, you don't talk to men about things like that. Not if you're old enough to have a bra.

SALLY. Will you buy me one then.

WOMAN. You won't like it.

SALLY. 'Cos if you do, Mum, then I won't have to ask Dad, will I?

WOMAN. OK, you win.

SALLY. You've promised. Do you think it will make me look nice?

Thirty-three ⟨× 37

SALLY. I think I will never again feel good because of it. Because if any one says —

MAN. You look good.

SALLY. I will think of this scar, curling across me. Buried in my skin. The vivid crest of the knife gash and the speckling of stitches. When I look in the mirror and think I am looking thinner it will always be right shoulder to the mirror.

Then I will turn full frontal and see one breast approaching opulence, I will always notice it curving round me and marking 'It was here'. I am disgusted. My mark of degradation. It is so humiliating and demanding of attention. I can't think that if I forget it — the fear will go away.

Thirty-four ⟨× 38

SALLY. Simon, would you sleep with a woman without a breast?

MAN. I suppose so.

SALLY. How do you mean, I suppose?

MAN. I suppose I could.

SALLY. You could bring yourself to.

MAN. It's not a question of bringing yourself to.

SALLY. So you could?

MAN. I would if she turned me on.

SALLY. Would she still turn you on?

MAN. If we'd got that far I don't suppose it would turn me off.

SALLY. Would it be the same?

MAN. I don't know.

SALLY. Think!

MAN. I don't suppose it would be different.

SALLY. It wouldn't be the same?

MAN. It's never the same.

SALLY. Don't you think? If she only had one?

MAN. That's not what it's all about.

SALLY. Isn't it?

MAN. It's about people not breasts.

SALLY. But if it came to it?

MAN. It's not the sort of thing you think about.

SALLY. Never?

MAN. I've never thought about it.

SALLY. I have. Often. Of loving men who have been mutilated. Because they were. Women can love men who are wrecks, it's traditional.

MAN. Women can be loved too.

SALLY. Can a lover bury his face between a lone breast?

Thirty-five ⫦X 39

WOMAN. Mastectomy, isn't it?

Can tell by the way you use your arm.

SALLY. It's sore.

WOMAN. Will be for a bit. Mine was.

SALLY. Have you had it done?

WOMAN. Twice. It spread. I've got secondaries. Makes you wonder why they do it if they don't stop it. They said if nothing happened for five years they thought I'd be OK. Four and a half years I'd gone.

SALLY. I'm sorry.

WOMAN. Didn't think it could happen. Not after everything else. I thought if anything else happened I'd go out of my mind. I haven't, I go on. He went after the first one. Thought he'd caused it at first, being a bit rough with me there. But they say it didn't. Couldn't have the second time. Our marriage wasn't much good before, just worse after. Wonder who'll want me with none?

SALLY. No one will be able to tell.

WOMAN. I've got four boys, they'll think we're a scout group. They did a radical the first time. Cut from here to here. They said it was a shame they didn't find it earlier. I wasn't to know, was I? I did this time though. This one's a simple. It is neater.

SALLY. Mine's a simple. They call it a simple.

WOMAN. It might be for them. It isn't for us. Not if you have to explain it – especially to the kids. First time I told them it had gone to make Mummy better. What am I going to tell them this time? It must have happened for a reason. Least that's what I keep telling myself. But I can't see one. Can you?

SALLY. It just happens.

WOMAN. I could understand if there was a reason. I could try.

SALLY. You have to be brave.

WOMAN. What's being brave? You have it, what else can you do? I don't want to die. I'm not frightened of it now but I don't want to. Not until the children – you see that's what frightens me. What happens to them. For them it's not how you look, is it? It's being there. That's all I want. Didn't have time to worry, not until I got here. Just rushing round trying to get everything ready. All I wanted was just to get here, get it done, get out and get back to looking after them. I'm so tired that I think I can't go on. You do. You get so strong. And if you're busy you don't have time to think.

SALLY. I touch myself in search of cancer for two minutes out of the thirty-five thousand, four hundred and twenty there are in each month of the moon. I spend five minutes a day making sure I cross roads properly. More women die of cancer of the breast when it spreads into secondaries than are killed every year on the road. More women than all the people I will ever meet.

Thirty-six LX 40

MAN. Sal, can I see your tits?

SALLY. Simon, they're bosoms.

MAN. Why aren't they tits?

SALLY. Tits is crude.

MAN. Who says tits is crude?

SALLY. Mum does.

MAN. You mean rude!

SALLY. Crude is nastier than rude.

MAN. What's the difference?

SALLY. Ask Mum.

MAN. Can I see your bosoms, then?

SALLY. No.

MAN. But I want to see some real ones.

SALLY. Why?

MAN. I just do.

SALLY. They're just the same.

MAN. They aren't.

SALLY. How do you know if you haven't seen any?

MAN. We found this magazine in the park. It was all torn up and we
    had to find all the bits and it was full of ladies with no clothes on.
    And I said I'd ask you if I could see yours because I'm the only one
    who's got a sister. And if you show them to Terry King he'll give me
    his United scarf. Will you, Sally?

SALLY. No.

MAN. Why not?

SALLY. It's not nice!

MAN. These ladies haven't got any clothes on.

SALLY. None at all?

MAN. Here. I'm sorry they're all torn up.

SALLY. I don't look like that!

MAN. I didn't think you did. I told them you didn't.

SALLY. That wasn't fair.

MAN. Well you don't.

SALLY. I'm still developing.

MAN. I don't think she looks very nice.

SALLY. No, they don't look real.

MAN. Do you think you'll develop as big as that?

SALLY. I don't know. You can't tell.

Thirty-seven $L \times 41$

SALLY. Afterwards they said –

MAN. You will feel some aching and a sense of loss.

SALLY. I do not go out and buy myself dresses or pamper myself in the
bath because I am ashamed. I think of the hospital as warm and safe
and the place where I was comforted.

　You can't tell?

WOMAN. No and that's only a temporary prosthesis to protect the
wound.

SALLY. I know the second I lay my hand about it I will cry.

　Hold me tightly, please. Hold me tightly. Hold me.

WOMAN. Is that tight enough.

SALLY. Tighter, please, tighter.

　I cry between two warm breasts and wish they were those of my
mother. I'm so alone.

WOMAN. Not here. There's me. The nurses, the doctors, everyone
else here, all your family and your friends. There are so many
women who come here more alone than you and who are twice as

lonely when they leave. There are some women here who make a fuss, because here at least they know the fuss will be listened to. Those aren't lonely women, they are isolated.

SALLY. I want to go home.

WOMAN. Of course you do. But we can't discharge you until you're ready. You'll feel better, you know. Once you're dressed. More like the real you.

SALLY. Yes.

When Danni moves
LX 42

Who does she mean by that? I want to be held until the fingers bruise the skin on my arm until I shake with being held and holding.

Thirty-eight

SALLY. Don't!

MAN. Come on.

SALLY. Don't!

MAN. Come on.

God – you're tense.

SALLY. Don't touch me! Please.

MAN. I'm sorry.

SALLY. You mustn't touch me.

MAN. OK, Sal.

SALLY. I'm sorry.

MAN. It's OK.

SALLY. I have prepared speeches for this moment. It's false.

MAN. Let me.

SALLY. No.

MAN. Kiss me.

SALLY. I have a lover.

Thirty-nine   Lx 43

WOMAN. Did sister give you your outpatients card?

SALLY. Yes.

   I can't carry this.

MAN. I'll take it.

SALLY. When I stand up my father holds my coat open for me. I
   fumble with the buttons and the nurse has already stripped the bed
   and I learn that all mattresses are disinfected, not only those of the
   dead.

WOMAN. Goodbye. Take care.

SALLY. Neither she nor I know whether or not we are supposed to
   shake hands and I can't remember if there is a protocol. From
   hospital drama slots I have a notion that now the closing credits
   should come upon the screen as we walk towards the entrance of
   the ward and do not look back.

MAN. Should I have brought them something?

SALLY. Why, Dad?

MAN. You know, a little present. Just to say thank you.

SALLY. There are so many.

MAN. Yes.

SALLY. They've been very good to me.

MAN. Come on. The car's just round the corner.

SALLY. I can't, Dad.

MAN. Sally?

SALLY. I can't go out there.

MAN. Yes, you can. Just round the corner down the steps.

SALLY. They'll look at me.

MAN. They won't.

SALLY. They will. They'll all be looking.

MAN. I thought you wanted to get out.

SALLY. They'll all know.

MAN. They won't.

SALLY. Everybody's staring at me.

MAN. Why should they be looking at you?

SALLY. They will.

MAN. You've got to get used to it. Your mother's waiting.

SALLY. Can I take your arm? I have learnt to be dependent.

Bosom implies the corporate identity of the mammary glands. Corresponding nerves, blood vessels et al. Two.

Forty Lx 44

WOMAN. I am a mother expecting her daughter home.

SALLY. I am a daughter arriving home.

WOMAN. Sally, darling!

SALLY. Hello, Mum.

WOMAN. On the outside there is no sign. I wonder if my daughter has lost her chances.

Did you have a good journey?

SALLY. Fine, thanks.

WOMAN. I've aired your bed. Do you want to get in?

SALLY. No.

WOMAN. A little rest?

SALLY. I'm not ill!

WOMAN. I know. But half an hour with your feet up? You needn't get in.

SALLY. She pulls back the bedspread, indicating it must be half an hour with my feet up, between the sheets. I have come home because they care.

WOMAN. I am glad to have my daughter home.

SALLY. She puts my underwear away and does not comment on it, although she is not familiar with it as she was when I lived at home and she did my washing and I liked her to. She puts things in exactly the same places in the drawers as she did when I was younger. It is the same system as my grandmother's. It has been passed down amongst the women of the family. She sits on my bed as she did when I was a child and slept with the door open and the light on in the night.

WOMAN. My mother said her mother died of a wasting disease.

SALLY. Was it cancer?

WOMAN. I don't know. We didn't talk about it. Are the risks of having it in your breast higher if it runs in the family? In the mother's line?

SALLY. They don't say so.

WOMAN. Is it because of me? Something in me. Is it my fault? Tell me.

SALLY. Even if it were known I could not acknowledge the blame on this woman.

WOMAN. It's too close for comfort.

SALLY. Do you check?

WOMAN. I never have.

SALLY. Not checking doesn't mean you never get it.

WOMAN. Do it for me.

SALLY. I place my skin on the flesh from which it came and can feel her heart beating under my pulse.

In the night it is worst. Sometimes in the night I can't go to sleep in case I am dead when I wake up. I am more afraid of that than I am of being followed at night on a dark street. I do not want to be a victim without a struggle.

Forty-one Lx 45

MAN. Do you want sympathy?

SALLY. My boss makes me coffee and offers me a biscuit.

MAN. My wife doesn't eat to compensate. She can't.

SALLY. He says.

MAN. My wife's arms are useless. They didn't catch hers in time. She doesn't have any breasts. After they treated her with chemotherapy she lost her hair.

SALLY. I have never seen his wife. I know she is a cripple and many times we have discussed between ourselves behind his back whether he is still faithful.

MAN. You are one of the lucky ones. What have you really lost?

SALLY. He offers me a biscuit and I refuse.

MAN. Nothing. It's in her bones. She is waiting for the cancer to creep over her and through her until she can't resist it. Until she becomes it. My wife will die of cancer slowly.

SALLY. The place which is empty aches.

MAN. I have to dress my wife in the morning. I have to undress her at night. Soon I won't be able to and someone else will have to manage, and someone else after that until her body becomes universal.

SALLY. I am a breast and a lymph node lighter.

MAN. It is the thoughts that weigh you down, whether she thought because I had admired her body that I meant it must be complete. She says there is no one to blame. But if there is no blame I cannot understand the unfairness of it. She says she is happy and has been happy and I wonder if that is because she is unhappy now. Her life has not been big or exciting but she says she is fulfilled. I cannot bear to see her pulled apart. People are sympathetic. It is my isolation from hope that is drowning me. She wrecked her life trying to keep her body whole. I did not ask her to be beautiful but to be there.

SALLY. The sun is warm on my thigh.

MAN. We sit together in silence and stillness.

SALLY. A lover.

Forty-two Lx 46

SALLY. Outpatients?

MAN. Gate 1.

WOMAN. Wait.

MAN. Block 2.

WOMAN. Wait.

MAN. Floor 4.

WOMAN. Wait.

MAN. Room 5.

WOMAN. Wait. Room change.

MAN. Room 6.

WOMAN. Patient?

MAN. Miss Bacon.

Forty-three

SALLY. I went into hospital to have a lump taken out of my breast. I woke up and the breast was gone. They'd cut it off. So I knew I had cancer.

WOMAN. And did they prepare you for the possibility of losing your breast?

SALLY. They told me I might.

WOMAN. And did they make it clear that you have a choice to be woken up after the biopsy? You have a legal right to know that the lump is malignant before they take the breast.

SALLY. What difference does that make?

WOMAN. It can make the waking less traumatic. You ought to see about getting a proper prosthesis. It needs to be weighted so you don't pull round to compensate. It's a lovely scar.

SALLY. Do you think so?

WOMAN. It's not going to stop you wearing a low-cut dress or bikini or anything.

SALLY. Going without a bra?

WOMAN. I don't see why you shouldn't have a breast implant done in the future.

SALLY. Sorry?

WOMAN. They insert a pad of silicone under the skin so you have a reshaped breast. They can't give you a life-like nipple yet but breast surgery techniques are improving all the time. Who knows.

SALLY. I could have it done?

WOMAN. I don't see why not. Unlike a prosthesis it will last you for life.

SALLY. How long's that going to be?

WOMAN. Your prognosis is good.

SALLY. Five years – ten – or am I completely cured?

WOMAN. We don't know yet. We haven't found an answer.

SALLY. The doctor goes to wash her hands.

WOMAN. Cancer is a cell run riot. An anarchist in the body. Cancer is the self-motivated, self-supporting growth of tissue.

SALLY. She washes her hands.

WOMAN. It starts from one single, malignant, mutant cell.

SALLY. She has washed her hands.

WOMAN. With cancer you never know if the war is over, or if it is just a long ceasefire.

SALLY. Cancer is.

Forty-four

SALLY. I don't want to be a victim without a struggle.

Help me! Help me! Help me! Hear! Hear! Hear!

MAN. Sally? — LX 47 (ON THIS LINE)

SALLY. Hear!

MAN. Wake up, wake up, Sally. It's only a dream.

SALLY. I'm sorry.

MAN. It's OK.

SALLY. I was running. But I was running after something and away from something else.

MAN. It's OK.

SALLY. Could you tell when you looked at me?

MAN. What?

SALLY. That I didn't have it.

MAN. I thought you did.

SALLY. Did you?

MAN. Of course I did. You expect women to.

SALLY. So you just thought I did?

MAN. Why should I have thought anything else?

SALLY. Because it shows.

MAN. You can't tell.

SALLY. It bulges at the side.

MAN. When I told my dad he said 'That's amazing. It looks better than the real thing. Which one is it, anyway?'

SALLY. Did he?

MAN. He couldn't tell. I could have taken money on it.

SALLY. Why did you tell him?

MAN. So he could get my mother to check.

SALLY. Did she?

MAN. I think so.

SALLY. I'll ring her in the morning and make sure.

MAN. You didn't mind me telling him?

SALLY. I don't suppose so — no.

MAN. So you needn't worry about it.

SALLY. What do you mean?

MAN. If he knows, what matter who else does?

SALLY. You beast.

MAN. I love you.

SALLY. Do you?

MAN. The Amazons were very sexy women. Hence their power. Their captives just swooned and fell at their feet. It was a walk-over.

SALLY. You make me laugh.

MAN. That's the sort of woman to get hold of, said my father. A woman who gets all her bras half-price. You'll be able to drink champagne on that.

Forty-five

MAN. Nice to see you.

WOMAN. Feeling better?

MAN. Are you well?

WOMAN. Glad you're back.

MAN. How you feeling?

WOMAN. We have missed you.

MAN. Where have you been?

WOMAN. How do you feel?

MAN. Thought you'd left.

WOMAN. Were you ill?

MAN. You're looking good.

WOMAN. What have they done?

SALLY. I realise that they are pleased to see me and that though I have told my boss he has respected me and not told them what has been done. I notice the cloakroom pegs are rearranged and a bottom one left empty for me.

Forty-six

SALLY. Suddenly I find I am standing naked in front of a mirror, watching the movements I can make with my body. And I notice that the marking I thought was livid and red is pale and tired and has sunk into the skin and that though there is no breast, there is no hole on me on the skin which is smooth and moves mysteriously. And I think it is fine and fun to stand in front of this mirror and to feel the air on my skin. I wonder what it would be like in a breeze. And in the mirror I touch myself.

MAN. She undresses for me for the first time. But does not turn out the light as I thought she would. Do I look or do I turn away? I am so frightened of being awkward about it. And if I look, should I say, and if I say will she take it the wrong way? I don't want to turn away from her. She takes off her jumper pulling on the sleeves, a butterfly struggling out of its cocoon. Her bra. For a second she pauses, intent on herself. I look at this woman and her body and it is sensuous.

Forty-seven LX 49

WOMAN. All this fuss about a pound of flesh.

MAN. God moves in mysterious ways.

WOMAN. It's not as if you're married.

MAN. It's only a bit of tissue.

SALLY. I watch myself.

Forty-eight LX 50

WOMAN. Sally!

SALLY. Fleur.

WOMAN. What are you doing?

SALLY. I've cleaned them twice this week. It's supposed to be good exercise for the muscles in my arm. They wrenched them when they clamped my arm back for the operation.

WOMAN. Sally, there's something – I have to say it.

SALLY. It's OK, Fleur.

WOMAN. When Simon rang me and said you'd had it done I thought – thank God it hasn't happened to me. Like that.

SALLY. I know.

WOMAN. I was so relieved. I even went to the hospital, not to see you but to get mine checked –

SALLY. They didn't find anything?

WOMAN. No, nothing there. Thank God. I'm sorry, Sal.

SALLY. I missed you.

WOMAN. Did you want me to come?

SALLY. Yes. When you didn't I guessed it was because it brought back memories of your cyst.

WOMAN. You came to see me.

SALLY. So what?

WOMAN. I wanted to see you and yet I couldn't come.

SALLY. You've come now.

WOMAN. But it doesn't make up for it.

SALLY. I'd have felt the same way. When I came to see you I didn't look at you once. Just trying to see if I could see where they'd done it. You had a horrid nightie.

WOMAN. Thanks.

SALLY. That's one thing I've got out of it, nighties. I had one when I first went in. I had five coming out. All the relatives sent me them.

WOMAN. You do look well.

SALLY. Roses in my cheeks and everything?

WOMAN. How do you feel?

SALLY. Like a woman without a breast, numb. They're being wonderful here. Mum's doing a great job, being practical and strict and encouraging and jollying me along. Well, you know Mum. Dad's more discreet about it. He's moved the bathroom mirror so I can't see myself in the bath any more. The funny thing is that the more careful they are – the more I know I'm being protected.

WOMAN. You can't be all the time.

SALLY. That's why it doesn't protect me at all. I can't see myself in the bath but everywhere there are whole women staring at me.

WOMAN. You're a whole woman.

SALLY. They're symmetrical women, Fleur, I'm not and I'm never going to be.

WOMAN. Come on, I'm taking you out for lunch.

SALLY. Fleur, I can't.

WOMAN. Who else is taking you?

SALLY. No one.

WOMAN. So you can.

SALLY. I can't go out. I can't.

WOMAN. Who's to know? I know you've had it done and I can't tell. The only clue I've got is the way you're cleaning windows and we aren't going window cleaning.

SALLY. I don't want to.

WOMAN. Of course you do. Pizza and ice cream?

SALLY. That's bribery.

WOMAN. Yes.

SALLY. No.

WOMAN. Sally, if you don't pull yourself together now it's going to be too late. The longer you put it off the worse it's going to get. OK, so there are people out there. Millions of them, and thousands of those are women without breasts. What makes you exceptional?

SALLY. They look at me.

WOMAN. So they don't bump into you, Sally. Come on.

Forty-nine $\angle x$ 51

SALLY. Can I have children?

MAN. We do advise against it.

SALLY. I can't have children.

MAN. I wouldn't put it like that. You're probably as fertile as the next woman.

SALLY. Then why not?

MAN. I'm not saying that you mustn't. Ultimately it's your decision.

SALLY. But you think it's better I don't?

MAN. Pregnancy produces a hormone reaction in the woman's body. We can't tell how it may affect any cancer cells you might have lying dormant. Maybe there would be no reaction, maybe there would be a reaction. We don't know yet. So you have to decide.

SALLY. So I could?

MAN. Yes.

SALLY. And I have to decide?

MAN. Yes. And I'll give you any facts you need to make that decision.

SALLY. When do you think they'll find an answer? Something definite.

MAN. We don't know. But we're finding things all the time and we've already given you more of that.

Fifty   *Lx 52*

SALLY. Always there are the dark moments, the bad ones when I wonder why they bothered. And why I didn't just waste away and what fate has allowed me to continue. I want to go out like a light, but to shine very brightly before the dark. It is the little moments when I think, if they hadn't done a mastectomy I might not be here, having these moments, that they might not have happened at all because I hadn't been there. Then I think what does it matter that a breast is not there, because I am alive.

Salonika

Salonika was first performed at the Royal Court Theatre Upstairs on 2 August 1982, with the following cast:

ENID	Sheila Burrell
LEONARD	Richard Butler
PETER	Garry Cooper
BEN	Christopher Fulford
CHARLOTTE	Gwen Nelson

Directed by Danny Boyle
Designed by Philippa Nash
Lighting by Jack Raby

PART ONE

A beach. Smooth. After a tide. Lying on the sand naked and the same colour as the sand, PETER. There are no footmarks to him. Enter CHARLOTTE. She is eighty-four. She is carrying an apple which she proceeds to peel with a penknife. She peels round the apple keeping the skin in one piece. She throws the peel over her left shoulder. She walks round it until she finds in it the shape she wants. She finds it and is pleased. She picks up the peel, brushes the sand off it, wraps it in her handkerchief and puts it in her pocket. She stands in the middle of the beach eating the apple off the knife in slivers. She looks at the horizon.

Enter ENID. She is CHARLOTTE's daughter. She believes in beige. She is carrying a deck chair and a bag. She thumps them down.

CHARLOTTE. I thought you were lost.

ENID. No. You might have brought your bag.

CHARLOTTE. I forgot.

ENID. I can't do it mother. Not all of it. Not any more. We'll have to stay at home if you can't do your share.

CHARLOTTE. I didn't want to come.

ENID. Of course you did. All this sun. It's lovely.

She struggles to put the deck chair up.

CHARLOTTE. We could have had a rug.

ENID. Where from?

CHARLOTTE. We could have taken one from the beds.

ENID. That would be stealing.

CHARLOTTE. It wouldn't have mattered, we'd have taken it back.

ENID. I can't, not with my joints.

CHARLOTTE. If you can manage that chair.

ENID. It's something to hold on to.

> ENID *goes off.*

> CHARLOTTE *sits in her chair. She gets her glasses out of her bag. She sees* PETER. *With difficulty she gets out of the chair and goes to look at him. She goes back and moves the chair so she can see him easily from where she sits.*

> *She goes on eating the apple.*

> *Enter* ENID *with deck chair and identical but different coloured bag.*

> *She waits.*

CHARLOTTE. Yes. As the day he was born.

> ENID *sets up the deck chair so its shadow falls on* PETER.

> It won't be all over.

ENID. What?

CHARLOTTE. His tan. It won't be even. You'll put him in the shade.

ENID. The wonder is he isn't burnt.

CHARLOTTE. It's a real baby's bottom. Yours was like a hare, skinned for jugging.

ENID. It's disgusting.

> CHARLOTTE *gets her knitting out. She measures a sleeve against* PETER.

CHARLOTTE. I was surprised that men were hairy where they were.

ENID. People will see you.

CHARLOTTE (*looking*). Who?

ENID. It isn't nice.

CHARLOTTE. He's got arms as long as Leonard's.

Pause.

She starts to unravel the sleeve.

I don't know if it's the pattern that's wrong or my eyesight.

ENID. At your age it's more sensible to buy a pullover ready done.

CHARLOTTE. It's a difficult pattern. You have to move the stitches and then work them again.

ENID. Think of the waste, all that wool – don't expect me to finish it after you've gone, my tension wouldn't be the same. You can always tell when two people have done sleeves.

CHARLOTTE. Do you think he should have oil or something on him?

ENID. It's none of our business.

CHARLOTTE *rummages in her bag.*

Pause.

Do you think he's a Greek?

ENID. I don't know.

CHARLOTTE. He's dark.

ENID. He's some sort of foreigner.

CHARLOTTE. I've never been on a beach bare, have you?

ENID. No.

CHARLOTTE. We could you know. There's no one to see us.

ENID. Don't be ridiculous. We'd catch our deaths.

CHARLOTTE. It's hot enough to take our things off.

ENID. A sun shining doesn't mean anything.

CHARLOTTE. The waiter –

ENID. Which waiter?

CHARLOTTE. Christos.

ENID. Is he the one with the beard or without?

CHARLOTTE. The one without the beard is Stephanos, he's married to Anna. She works in the reception when –

ENID. This is a holiday. I don't want their grubby little details.

CHARLOTTE. Christos is the one with the beard. He said it was going to be twenty-five. What's twenty-five in English weather?

ENID. Do you want to look in the guide book?

CHARLOTTE. No. I think it would be hot enough.

Pause.

Have you ever been with a man outside?

Pause.

Have you?

ENID. No.

CHARLOTTE. Your father and I once – in a barley field – stubble. I couldn't concentrate. They were burning the next field. We could hear it through the hedge. The birds were shot as they rose. I could smell singeing feathers. It made my eyes run. He thought I was crying. It was the smoke. He thought it was because he was coming back here. I didn't say. It didn't affect him. Perhaps because he was a smoker. That was the last time. Perhaps you weren't born late. Perhaps that's when you were conceived.

ENID. I didn't know father smoked.

CHARLOTTE. He did.

ENID. You never said.

CHARLOTTE. You didn't ask. I gave his pipes to the doctor who delivered me. If you hadn't been late enough for me to need a doctor I could have kept them.

ENID. Did you?

CHARLOTTE. What?

ENID. Smoke?

CHARLOTTE. Yes.

ENID. Why?

CHARLOTTE. Ben wanted me to. He liked women who smoked. He said it made them look independent.

Pause.

ENID. You should have kept his letters.

CHARLOTTE. They didn't say much.

ENID. You should still have kept them.

CHARLOTTE. What would you have done with them?

ENID. Read them.

CHARLOTTE. It's history what he wrote. Everybody's letter was the same. All the women's in the street. We'd go out whitening our doorsteps, those whose men were soldiers, so we could look out for the postman. Only it was a wee lass – but she were called a postman. And she'd come along and we'd take the letters in and read them. Then you went out and talked about them. And they were all the same. They wanted us, the food was dreadful, it would all be over by Christmas. That we were missed.

ENID. It's funny to think of him sitting here.

CHARLOTTE. He wouldn't have sat. Not in the army. Not with the creases they had to have in their trousers.

ENID. What did he say about here?

CHARLOTTE. I don't remember.

ENID. Mother, you were married to him.

CHARLOTTE. No reason to remember anything.

ENID. You've forgotten everything.

CHARLOTTE. I haven't forgotten. I don't remember.

ENID. A cup of tea would be nice.

CHARLOTTE. A cup of tea would be very nice. We should have packed a thermos.

ENID. Why didn't you?

CHARLOTTE. You were packing.

ENID. You can't expect me to remember everything.

CHARLOTTE. There was a shop with little burners. We could buy a little burner.

ENID. Here?

CHARLOTTE. We could make a nice cup of tea.

ENID. We'd have to boil the milk.

CHARLOTTE. What for?

ENID. We're abroad.

Pause.

CHARLOTTE. A cup of tea would be nice.

ENID. Yes.

Pause.

CHARLOTTE. In the end it would be cheaper than going to a cafe. In hot countries you need liquid. I thought I'd die of thirst in Athens.

ENID. In capital cities you have to be careful. They take advantage.

CHARLOTTE. If we'd had our own spending money I'd have had cups of tea with mine.

ENID. We might need money later on.

CHARLOTTE. For souvenirs? At our age! If I'd died of dehydration what would have been the point?

ENID. The prices are shocking.

CHARLOTTE. They didn't used to be. That's the future for you.

ENID. How do you know about the prices here?

CHARLOTTE. It's the Common Market isn't it?

ENID. Is it?

CHARLOTTE. Of course it is. It's why you can get tea here. So they can have Greek restaurants in England.

ENID. I didn't know.

Pause.

CHARLOTTE. Well?

ENID. What?

CHARLOTTE. Are we having that cup of tea or not? I'd go myself but
— when they see you're old they try to cheat you and it's a long way
in this heat. For someone of my age.

ENID. I'll go.

CHARLOTTE. A little burner would be a good idea if we're going to
be here for a week.

ENID. I've said I'll go mother. Will you be all right?

CHARLOTTE. I spent nineteen years of my life without you, another
half hour won't make such difference.

ENID. I shan't be long.

She looks at PETER.

What if he wakes up? You read such awful things.

CHARLOTTE. I'll see if he's got one of those little leaves like the
statues in Athens.

ENID. Mother.

CHARLOTTE. Looks as if he might need quite a big leaf.

CHARLOTTE *giggles.* ENID *remains impassive.*

He ought to turn over. He ought to be done on both sides.

She giggles again.

ENID *takes her bag and her umbrella and goes.*

Enid. Enid.

ENID *returns.*

ENID. What's the matter?

Pause.

What did you want?

CHARLOTTE. I've forgotten.

ENID *goes.*

Enid.

ENID *returns.*

ENID. What?

CHARLOTTE. Don't leave me. Not by myself. Not here.

ENID. Rubbish. I'm only going to be gone half an hour. Then we'll be able to have a nice cup of tea.

CHARLOTTE. Don't leave me by myself. I might have a heart attack from the sun.

ENID. Don't be so silly.

She puts up an umbrella.

A moment ago you wanted to take your clothes off.

ENID goes off.

CHARLOTTE looks at PETER.

She touches him to make him wake up. It is a caress. She gets the phrase book. She says in Greek to wake him:

CHARLOTTE. I should like to disinter the body and return home with it.

PETER does not move. BENJAMIN sits up out of the sand. He is dressed in a 1918 British Expedition to Salonika uniform.

I was waiting for you to wake up.

BEN. Were you?

CHARLOTTE. It's nice here, isn't it?

BEN. Very nice.

CHARLOTTE. Yes.

BEN. We could – you know.

CHARLOTTE. Could we?

BEN. If you wanted.

CHARLOTTE. Yes.

BEN. Do you remember that time in the field? That was a good time, wasn't it?

CHARLOTTE. Yes.

BEN. Nothing?

CHARLOTTE. No.

BEN. Not even a heartbeat?

CHARLOTTE. Not yet.

BEN. Well?

CHARLOTTE. I don't know.

Pause.

BEN. It's nice here, isn't it?

CHARLOTTE. Very nice.

Pause.

BEN. How are things at home?

CHARLOTTE. Fine.

BEN. Same as usual are they?

CHARLOTTE. Yes.

BEN. That's good isn't it.

CHARLOTTE. I sometimes wish something would happen.

BEN. Don't worry. Once the war's over it'll all be the same as ever.

CHARLOTTE. Will it?

BEN. Nothing changes.

CHARLOTTE. Doesn't it?

BEN. No. You wouldn't know where you were.

BEN *picks up the knitting.*

Is this for me?

CHARLOTTE. Yes.

BEN. I thought it might be for some other chap.

He laughs.

I thought you might find yourself a friend while I was gone.

CHARLOTTE. No.

BEN. Good. Of course if I was killed . . .

CHARLOTTE. What?

BEN. If I was killed – well –

CHARLOTTE. I wouldn't.

BEN. You'd lose your pension rights.

CHARLOTTE. Yes.

BEN. Besides, after a war there aren't many men left.

CHARLOTTE. I know.

> *Pause.*

> What's it like here?

BEN. Bit of a bore really. Nothing to do.

CHARLOTTE. What would you like to do?

BEN (*shrugs*). I don't know.

CHARLOTTE. Don't you have army duties?

BEN. I've got malaria. Tertiary.

CHARLOTTE. Isn't there anything else?

BEN. There's a group of us run a pack of beagles. The Bulgars are awfully good fellows. They always bring them back if they go over enemy lines. There's a band led by a chap called Vaughan Williams. I'd be in it but for the practising.

CHARLOTTE. It would give you something to do.

BEN. I don't have the time. Nice music. It helps you forget.

CHARLOTTE. Forget what?

BEN. I don't know.

CHARLOTTE. I'd like a cup of tea.

BEN. I could show you how to make a fire.

CHARLOTTE. Could you?

BEN. You need to collect dead sticks. Driftwood and sea weed. Things washed up.

CHARLOTTE goes off to collect driftwood and sea weed.

The tide comes in and in. They say that if you drown your life flashes before your eyes and you must watch. A drowned man was washed up once. A suicide. He had thrown himself in. To escape dullness. A body drowned is a horrible sight. Even kittens and puppies go in sacks with stones and tied with string. Not men. A man that's been in the sea a week has no eyes. You can tell how long he's been there, threshed around, by his face. Ten days and it's the lips and the nose. Any longer and they'll be picking out the brain. Greedy creatures, gulls. Scavengers. On the bones of the face they find cliffs and cling. Floating in the sea a body comes to them as a larder with an open door. Death by drowning is the most terrible. Not quick, not festering. But a filling up and a filling up with some other life going before your eyes and you seeing only the bad of it and how bad it was to lead you to be there in the water as you were in the womb. The body swells, like dough for good bread. But the skin sits tightly to the soles of the feet. There was a body washed up, where his eyes should have been there was an egg. He was buried with it. An egg that's bad will float.

Pause.

A body's always washed when it's dead. Even after a drowning. As though mortality dirties it.

BEN wanders off to find driftwood.

PETER gets up and lies down again facing the other direction.

Enter ENID with burner, brass saucepan, tea, bottled water, milk.

Enter CHARLOTTE with an armful of sticks and sea weed.

ENID and CHARLOTTE look at each other. CHARLOTTE drops the sticks.

ENID. You see, you were all right.

CHARLOTTE. He moved.

ENID. I don't think so.

CHARLOTTE. He has. He was pointing the other way before. We missed it.

ENID. I had to buy a saucepan. It can be our souvenir.

ENID *proceeds to make the tea.*

CHARLOTTE *tries to pick up her lost stitches.*

CHARLOTTE. You'll have to do it.

ENID. In a minute.

CHARLOTTE. I might have it finished when we get home.

ENID. Then what?

CHARLOTTE. I'll give it to Leonard of course.

ENID. Mother, you shame me.

CHARLOTTE. He'll like it.

ENID. Can you never stop throwing yourself at him?

CHARLOTTE. I never threw myself. Even your father, I didn't throw myself. I never have.

ENID. You run after him well enough.

CHARLOTTE. I haven't had a man since you were born.

ENID. You'd think you would have forgotten. Decent women would.

CHARLOTTE. It came about. Will you do this for me?

ENID *starts to pick up the stitches.*

ENID (*bitter*). You couldn't do this without me.

CHARLOTTE. Give it me back and I'll do it myself.

ENID. Your eyes aren't good enough. And you'd have him going round in a cardigan like a lettuce leaf after slugs.

CHARLOTTE. He doesn't have to wear it.

ENID. And have you go on and on at him?

CHARLOTTE. I wouldn't.

ENID. You would. You know you would. For his own health he shouldn't want to marry you.

Silence.

ENID *picks up the stitches.*

There.

CHARLOTTE. Thank you.

ENID. We should go and see the graves this afternoon.

CHARLOTTE. If that's what you want.

ENID. That's what we've come for.

CHARLOTTE. There's not much of a holiday to be had visiting graves.

ENID. We'll take some flowers.

CHARLOTTE. Your father didn't like flowers.

ENID. Everybody likes flowers.

CHARLOTTE. Ben didn't. He didn't like me to have a bouquet at the wedding.

ENID. Well I'd like to give him flowers.

CHARLOTTE. He won't thank you for it.

ENID. He's dead. It doesn't matter. It's a gesture.

CHARLOTTE. You have no respect in you. When I go I want my nightie on.

Pause.

Do you hear me?

ENID. Yes, mother.

CHARLOTTE. My nightie.

ENID. Your nightie, mother.

CHARLOTTE. And you're to take my rings off. I want none of them. They dig you up soon enough without giving them temptation.

ENID. Yes, mother.

ENID *has got the cups and saucers out. She has made tea.*

CHARLOTTE. Nice to have a saucer.

ENID. Yes.

They sit on the beach and watch the sea, drinking tea.

CHARLOTTE. I can still always taste the paper. I'll never get used to it. Not in a hundred years. When I'm a hundred you'll be my age now.

ENID. And who's going to do the fetching and carrying for me?

CHARLOTTE. You'll get your second wind.

ENID. Will I?

CHARLOTTE. If you're going to be tired all your life you might as well give up now.

ENID. I've worked all my life. That's why I'm tired. Looking after you. Selling people yards of elastic.

CHARLOTTE. Selling enough elastic to go round the world. That's something to be proud of.

ENID. Who's going to remember me for that?

CHARLOTTE. You'll have a nice headstone.

ENID. I'm being cremated.

CHARLOTTE. You can still have a headstone. If you want to be remembered.

ENID. What else have I got?

CHARLOTTE. I never knew how you didn't manage to get married in the war. Even somebody you didn't like. You'd probably have lost him. You'd have been married. You'd have got the pension for it.

ENID. I've got a pension. They've used me up just the same as a man would have done.

Pause.

ENID *gets out a packet of biscuits. She offers one to* CHARLOTTE.

CHARLOTTE. My heart is breaking.

ENID (*taking biscuit*). Rubbish. You die of hunger not heartbreak.

CHARLOTTE. How do you know?

ENID. It's quite obvious.

CHARLOTTE. I miss him.

ENID. You've spent enough of your life without him.

CHARLOTTE. Leonard.

ENID. Have a biscuit. You'll feel better.

CHARLOTTE. I want to go home.

ENID. Don't you want to see the graves and things?

CHARLOTTE. I never wanted to come.

ENID. You'll enjoy it once you settle down.

CHARLOTTE. I won't.

ENID. You liked Athens.

CHARLOTTE. I didn't.

ENID. You did. You wanted to see everything.

CHARLOTTE. No point just moping.

Pause.

ENID. Have you finished?

CHARLOTTE. I'll wash the cups.

CHARLOTTE *takes the cups and goes to the sea.* ENID *looks at* PETER.

ENID. Young boys in Athens, everywhere. Looking from the dark of doorways with brown eyes and white teeth. A young people's city with the past crumbling everywhere in it. The statues of gods and goddesses with their noses chipped and fingers missing. Boys with white, white teeth who smiled at me – wondering to pick pocket or not. Young men already older than my father was allowed to be.

Enter LEONARD. *He is in his middle seventies. He carries a rucksack, the old canvas sort. He carries a bunch of flowers.*

LEONARD. Where is she?

ENID. She's washing the cups. I hate the way she washes the cups without their saucers. Why are you here?

LEONARD. I missed her.

ENID. Did you?

LEONARD. I thought I'd come after you. Not in Athens, I thought you'd have left before I got there. I knew it would be easy to find you here.

ENID. But all the people. How did you know where we were?

LEONARD. I asked for two English ladies travelling together. They said you were on the beach.

ENID. Where did you get the money?

LEONARD. I had to hitch hike. They kept taking me to the police station. They thought I'd lost my mind. That held me up a bit. It's difficult explaining in a foreign language that you're trying to do it cheaply.

ENID. She isn't expecting you.

LEONARD. I wanted to be a surprise. How is she?

ENID. Very well.

LEONARD. Does she miss me?

ENID. My father was killed here. You can hardly expect her to miss you.

Pause.

LEONARD. I didn't think about that.

ENID. You should have done before you came.

LEONARD. I missed her.

ENID. Do your family know you're here?

LEONARD. No.

ENID. Well don't you think you should have told them?

LEONARD. They'd have stopped me.

ENID. Stopped you? Nothing stops you. Why do you pester us?

LEONARD. I haven't pestered her. We've got an understanding.

ENID. Where are you going to stay?

LEONARD. I was going in the youth hostel. I've brought a sleeping bag. Perhaps I could take a leaf out of his book. I didn't know they did that sort of thing here.

ENID. He ought to be arrested.

LEONARD puts down his rucksack.

LEONARD. I think I'll go and find her. Help her with the cups.

Pause.

He takes out his passport and money.

You can never be too careful. (*He indicates the flowers.*) For your mother.

LEONARD goes off with the flowers.

ENID looks at PETER.

Enter BEN.

BEN. The tea leaves.

ENID. Sorry?

BEN. The tea leaves.

ENID. What for?

BEN. They make cigarettes.

ENID hands BEN the plastic bag with the tea bags in it.

ENID. They come like that now. And we have paper handkerchiefs.

BEN takes the tea leaves out of the bag to dry them.

BEN. Do you smoke?

ENID. No. What was it like?

BEN. What like?

ENID. Here in the war.

BEN. You don't want to know.

ENID. I do.

BEN. If I tell you I won't be listened to.

ENID. I will listen.

BEN. It won't be the story you've got in your head.

ENID. Why not?

BEN. Wars never are. Did we win?

ENID. Yes.

BEN. What did we win?

ENID. I don't know.

BEN. No territory?

ENID. I don't think so.

BEN. Hardly worth it. If we didn't get anything to show for it.

ENID. We got peace.

BEN. Was it a better peace than the one we'd had before?

ENID. I wasn't alive before.

   Pause.

   My mother missed you.

BEN. Did she? Good.

ENID. Yes.

BEN. I wondered what sort of mother she'd be.

ENID. She's been a good mother.

BEN. I'm glad. Do you love her?

ENID. Of course. She's my mother.

BEN. Did she bring you here?

ENID. I brought her. She didn't want to come.

BEN. Perhaps it was too painful. What do you do?

ENID. I don't. I'm retired.

BEN. What did you do?

ENID. I ran a drapers.

BEN. You never married?

ENID. No.

BEN. Why not?

ENID. I never met anybody.

BEN. I didn't think you'd be a daughter.

ENID. Didn't you?

BEN. No. That's why I said to call a girl Enid. Because I thought you'd be a boy.

ENID. I'm sorry.

BEN. I wouldn't have known what to do with a girl.

ENID. You would have done if you'd been there.

BEN. Would I? I'd never have settled. None of it would have been comfortable.

ENID. Oh it would have been.

BEN. How do you know?

ENID. If you'd been there it would have been.

BEN. You can hardly have been the only child without a father.

ENID. You would have made a difference.

BEN. What difference?

ENID. I don't know.

Pause.

I wanted to be a dancer.

BEN. Did you?

ENID. Very much.

BEN. But you didn't?

ENID. I grew too tall. I could have been one but I grew too tall. That must have been your fault.

BEN. You can hardly blame me.

ENID. I thought you were a short man. Small, with a moustache.

BEN. I shaved it off. The heat. Flies. They used to get caught in it. Can you still dance?

ENID. Still?

BEN. Like you did when you were a girl. I'd like to see you.

ENID. I don't know.

BEN. Show me.

ENID. I can't.

BEN. Can't you do it?

ENID. I –

BEN. Can't you?

ENID. Not any more.

BEN. Show me.

ENID. I'll make a fool of myself.

BEN. Not in front of your father.

ENID. I will.

BEN. Just once. I never saw you.

ENID. Well –

> ENID *takes off her shoes.*
>
> *She dances à la Duncan on the sand.*
>
> BEN *watches. He goes.*
>
> PETER *sits up.*

PETER. I thought I was dreaming. I'm sorry.

ENID. I trained you know.

ENID *starts to put her shoes on.*

PETER *pulls on his shorts.*

PETER. I'm sorry – I wouldn't have. Only there's usually no one here. If I'd known I'd have put something on.

ENID. We didn't look.

PETER. No.

ENID. We thought you were a Greek.

PETER. We?

ENID. My mother and I.

PETER. Your mother?

ENID. Yes.

PETER. Aren't you too old to have a mother?

ENID. Mine isn't dead yet. She's down there washing cups.

PETER. Who's with her?

Pause.

Is the old man your husband?

ENID. No. He's –

Pause.

He – he's a friend of my mother's.

PETER. Friend?

ENID. He wants to marry her.

PETER. Is it worth it?

ENID. They seem to think so.

PETER. God.

ENID. Would you like a biscuit?

PETER. Thanks.

He takes a biscuit.

ENID. My name's Enid.

PETER. Peter.

They shake hands.

ENID. You are English?

PETER. Yes.

ENID. Not an American or anything?

PETER. No.

ENID. What do you do?

PETER. Sleep.

ENID. In the day?

PETER. Sleep mostly.

ENID. How can you sleep. You can't be tired at your age.

PETER. You shut your eyes. It's a habit. Like whistling.

ENID. You shut your eyes when you whistle?

PETER. No. The sleeping's a habit.

ENID. Do you dream?

PETER. What about?

Pause.

ENID. Do you swim?

PETER. No.

ENID. Why not?

PETER. I can't. There are sea urchins.

ENID. How do you survive? I mean where does your money come from?

PETER. I sell my blood.

ENID. Sell it?

PETER. Why not? It's a way to make a living.

ENID. But at home you could give it away.

PETER. I need the money.

ENID. Why do you stay here?

PETER. Why not?

ENID. Shouldn't you be working or something?

PETER. Why?

ENID. You can't go on and on selling your blood. It can't be good for you.

PETER. I haven't got the money to get home.

ENID. Do you want to go back to England?

PETER. Not much.

ENID. Aren't you homesick?

PETER. No.

ENID. What about your parents?

PETER. What about them?

ENID. Don't they miss you?

PETER. I don't know. I haven't seen them for two years.

ENID. I live with my mother. I've always lived with her.

PETER. That's stupid.

ENID. She's only got me.

PETER. They'd find somebody else if you weren't there. That's what the welfare state's for.

ENID. Nowhere will take her. There's not enough wrong with her. Everywhere I'd have to pay. Don't tell her I told you this. She doesn't know. She'll think I want to get rid of her. But I'm old myself. I've been retired for four years. I'd just like a little time, of my own. I thought she'd die before this or I would have gone long ago. I thought she didn't have very long. She'd hate it if she knew I wanted to put her in a home. That's why she mustn't marry. They won't take them if they're a couple. They'll be happy and I'll die first working for them.

PETER *has gone back to sleep.*

I mustn't go first because she'd have no one. I'd go and visit her. Every day probably. But if I go first she won't have that.

CHARLOTTE *and* LEONARD *come up the beach. She carries the flowers. He carries the cups.*

CHARLOTTE. Isn't he a darling?

ENID. Yes.

LEONARD. I'll take them to the hotel for you. They'll die on the beach.

CHARLOTTE. There are a lot of steps.

LEONARD. I can easily do it.

CHARLOTTE. You shouldn't in this heat. Not after coming all this way. Enid doesn't mind running inside, do you dear?

ENID. No.

PETER *coughs.*

CHARLOTTE. You should have brought a sun hat. You'll fry your brains.

LEONARD. At least you think old men still have brains.

He laughs.

CHARLOTTE. I've nearly finished your pullover. Only this sleeve.

LEONARD. It's beautiful. What love and care. What a kitten.

ENID. I'll take the flowers in. We're going to the cemetery this afternoon. To visit my father's grave.

ENID *goes off.*

CHARLOTTE. She doesn't like you being here.

LEONARD. She can't stop me.

CHARLOTTE. No.

LEONARD. Kitten, she may be your daughter but she was born a prune. Have you noticed there's always one in the pack not softened with soaking. You'd better put these away.

He gives her the cups.

CHARLOTTE. We've only got two.

LEONARD. I brought a mug. You have to have your own in the hostels. They're not provided.

He rummages for it.

Had that in the army.

CHARLOTTE. Enamel.

LEONARD. Of course. Been all over the world. Deserts, the Far East. Now across Europe.

CHARLOTTE. Can you remember your army number?

LEONARD. It's nearly forty years since.

CHARLOTTE. L919327. That were Ben. The number you looked for on all those lists. I've never forgotten.

Pause.

I missed you.

LEONARD. Did you angel?

CHARLOTTE. Yes I did.

She sits.

He's put his trunks on. She made him put his trunks on. He was getting such a lovely tan. Such a lovely colour.

LEONARD. Are you sure you don't mind him being there?

CHARLOTTE. Not at all. He's a nice looking boy. What did your children say about you coming away?

LEONARD. I didn't tell them.

CHARLOTTE. They could have the police looking and everything.

LEONARD. I sent a postcard from Dover. So Sophie didn't worry. She likes me to be out and about. It's being her father-in-law. Not being kin doesn't make her so tight about me.

CHARLOTTE. She's very good to you.

LEONARD. Yes, I'd have liked a daughter like that.

CHARLOTTE. Like Enid?

LEONARD. I've got the best sons a man could wish for. You can get your pension again when you get home. Did you know that? I think we could have got it sent out here. Probably wouldn't have had to queue. If we got them to send it us, we could stay here, for the rest of our lives. Would you like that?

CHARLOTTE. I don't know.

LEONARD. It's just a possibility. But worth considering. You live longer in the sunshine.

CHARLOTTE. Could Enid stay here too?

LEONARD. She wouldn't want to would she?

CHARLOTTE. I don't know. Perhaps. This is where Ben died you know. In the hills.

LEONARD. I'm sorry.

CHARLOTTE. I think it must have been in the hills. He spent a lot of time there. He used to cut down trees so they didn't get malaria. We're going to see his grave this afternoon.

LEONARD. Should I come?

CHARLOTTE. Do you want to?

LEONARD. I didn't know the chap. Seems the sort of right thing to do. See if he minds.

CHARLOTTE. Minds what?

LEONARD. If we get married. If you see what I mean.

CHARLOTTE. What do I do with his wedding ring?

LEONARD. You put it on your other hand don't you? I think that's what you do.

CHARLOTTE. A hand each!

LEONARD. Hardly his. Not after all these years.

CHARLOTTE. Sixty-four. That's how long. Sixty-four. Since before Enid was born. I've always thought she should have had a father.

LEONARD. She'll have one now.

CHARLOTTE. Yes. She'll like that. Can we have a church?

LEONARD. If that's what you'd like.

CHARLOTTE. I'd like it properly. I didn't have church the first time. Not white or anything.

LEONARD. I'm sure they'd let you have white after all this time.

CHARLOTTE. It wouldn't be proper. There's Enid. Grey. I'd thought grey. Made by a dressmaker perhaps.

LEONARD. You'll look lovely.

CHARLOTTE. Was your first one white?

LEONARD. Yes.

CHARLOTTE. Properly so?

LEONARD. Yes.

CHARLOTTE. He was a farmer's son. I'd never have had white.

LEONARD. Quite a goer eh?

CHARLOTTE. He explained to me what it was they were doing. The ewes and tups. But he never let me have a bouquet. It was funny that. With him coming from a farm.

LEONARD. It's the groom that pays the flowers. You'll have a bouquet however you want. You can have Enid as a bridesmaid. If you want that.

Enter ENID.

ENID. I've put them in water in the sink. They'll still die. It isn't humid enough here for flowers.

CHARLOTTE. Should we tell her?

ENID. Tell me what?

CHARLOTTE. Leonard and I are going to get married.

ENID. Oh.

LEONARD. We'd like you to be a bridesmaid.

ENID. What?

CHARLOTTE. Or a matron of honour.

ENID. Matrons of honour are married.

ENID starts to cry.

CHARLOTTE. Enid, don't dear.

ENID. Leave me alone.

LEONARD. There, there, no need for all these tears.

ENID. Go away.

CHARLOTTE. Perhaps you'd better.

LEONARD. Yes well – I ought to see if I can get a room in the hotel.

LEONARD goes off.

CHARLOTTE. There there.

ENID. What do you want to marry him for? Why? Why?

CHARLOTTE. I'm in love with him.

ENID. But you might wake up and find him dead next to you.

CHARLOTTE. I might wake up dead.

ENID. Then what's the point?

CHARLOTTE. I want to.

ENID. You know he's got false teeth?

CHARLOTTE. I don't mind. It's little things – like the way he irons his trousers.

ENID. What's going to happen to me?

CHARLOTTE. You can come and live with us.

ENID. What if I don't want to?

CHARLOTTE. Where else would you go?

ENID. Probably a home.

Pause.

CHARLOTTE. I don't think you want me to have any happiness 'til I'm dead.

ENID. I thought we were happy.

CHARLOTTE. You'd like me dead wouldn't you?

ENID. No, mother.

CHARLOTTE. You would. You won't be happy 'til then. I know the way your brain works. I might die of unhappiness here.

ENID. We can go home tomorrow if you want.

CHARLOTTE. I might go tonight, before that. I didn't bring my laying-out nightie. I'll have to be laid out in my clothes. You know I don't want that. That I've never wanted that.

ENID. Why don't you come and lie down?

CHARLOTTE. I knew I should have packed it. He'll have come all this way for nothing.

ENID. He shouldn't have come. It was very irresponsible. We can have the chairs all day. We'll leave them for when we come back later. He'll see to them.

They go.

PART TWO

PETER, *fully dressed, is making himself tea with the things* CHARLOTTE *and* ENID *left on the beach*.

Enter LEONARD.

LEONARD. Those things belong to the ladies.

PETER. I didn't think they'd mind.

LEONARD. Do you have their permission?

PETER. No.

LEONARD. Then it's stealing.

PETER. I know them.

LEONARD. How?

PETER. We met here. This morning. I met the daughter.

LEONARD. Ah.

PETER. She was dancing.

LEONARD. Enid dancing?

PETER. Yes.

LEONARD. The woman's mad.

PETER. Is she?

LEONARD. Dancing at her age.

PETER. What about yourself, sir?

LEONARD. What about me?

PETER. I thought—

LEONARD. There's nothing wrong with me. I'm not one of those mad old men. Not at all. I had a couple of varicose veins. But they've gone now. Had them out. Privately. I'll show you the scars. There, you see. You wouldn't get such a good sewing-up on the National Health. You can hardly see it's been done. No. You're looking in the wrong place. There. Can you see it?

PETER. Yes.

LEONARD. Neat isn't it?

PETER. Very.

LEONARD. You wouldn't know it had been done if I hadn't shown you, would you?

PETER. No.

LEONARD. That's what going privately does for you.

PETER. Yes.

LEONARD. Used my bonus on it when I retired. They wanted me to go on a cruise. Everyone else did. I wanted to be able to get around.

PETER. And you can.

LEONARD. Worth every penny. I couldn't get it done now. They'd rather replace your whole hip than do your veins.

PETER. Yes.

LEONARD. I've hitch-hiked from England. Remarkable at my age wouldn't you say?

PETER. Yes sir.

LEONARD. How old do you think I am?

PETER. I couldn't say.

LEONARD *struts about the beach like a pigeon.*

LEONARD. Well? Have a guess boy. How old do you think I am. I don't look it, mind you.

PETER. Eighty?

LEONARD. Have you been looking?

PETER. Give me a clue.

LEONARD. I'm seventy-five. Amazing don't you think?

PETER. Yes, sir.

LEONARD. Everyone I met wanted to talk. Not to me. Talk about themselves. No one was interested in me. I'm history.

PETER. You must be sir.

LEONARD. History.

Pause.

You know what's wrong. You dress too casual. You know that. When I was a boy you didn't dare sit down. You couldn't. Not if you wanted any shape in your suit. You didn't dare. You had to work because you couldn't sit down. Your trousers would have rubbed your arse off if you'd tried to. Did you know that?

PETER. No, sir.

LEONARD. Wool we wore then. British. None of your Australian stuff. We didn't dare sit down. How old are you? Eighteen, nineteen?

PETER. Twenty-seven sir.

LEONARD. One of those are you?

PETER. What do you mean?

LEONARD. If you were a man you'd have a job and a wife.

PETER. How do you know I haven't?

LEONARD. You wouldn't be here if you had. Not if you were a man.

Pause.

You don't even stand up for yourself.

PETER. It doesn't matter.

LEONARD. At your age I'd have fought. Fought like a monkey.

PETER. It doesn't matter.

LEONARD. Those are their biscuits.

PETER. Enid gave me one this morning.

LEONARD. How do you know she wants you to have one this afternoon?

PETER. She wouldn't mind.

LEONARD. You seem to be very friendly with her.

PETER. I woke up and she was dancing.

Pause.

Is it true you're going to marry her mother?

LEONARD. We have an understanding.

PETER. You're getting married.

LEONARD. We would like to.

PETER. Why don't you live together? You can't have much time.

LEONARD. We want to be married.

PETER. Enid doesn't want you to.

LEONARD. Enid's never wanted anybody to do anything.

PETER. Has she ever been married?

LEONARD. No.

PETER. Probably she's jealous.

LEONARD. Jealous. At her age?

PETER. Yes.

LEONARD. You aren't jealous at our age. You know life can't be fair. You learn that.

PETER. You could make life fair.

LEONARD. Of course you can't. Nothing you can do to make it fairer than it is.

PETER. How do you know?

LEONARD. I've lived a long time.

PETER. And yours hasn't been fair?

LEONARD. It's been all right.

PETER. What's all right?

LEONARD. I haven't watched many have better.

PETER. What would have been better?

LEONARD. More money.

PETER. That's all?

LEONARD. It would have been enough. It would have helped.

PETER. How?

LEONARD. I'd have felt I'd got something.

PETER. You'd show people your bank statements like you do your scars.

LEONARD. I've never been with a bank. I hold with the post office.

PETER. Were you married?

LEONARD. Of course.

PETER. Love her?

LEONARD. Hard to say.

PETER. In the beginning?

LEONARD. I suppose I did. You forget.

PETER. Wasn't it exciting at first?

LEONARD. She wasn't excited. She never was. She couldn't have cared. She wanted the children of course.

Pause.

She ran away. She's dead now. She was younger than me. She died first. You don't expect them to go before you.

PETER. I'm sorry.

LEONARD. I don't even know how she died. She ran away, not even leaving a note. Nothing at all. Just went. I wasn't worse than anyone else, not really. Not compared.

PETER. What made her go?

LEONARD. In the war. Well, I was away. When I came back. It was a different life. That's when she went. You expect them to look after you. You're like a baby when they've gone. I didn't know how long to cook things. Took me years to get a proper meal. Greens and everything, you know, on the plate at the same time. I used to have potatoes for my pudding. With a bit of sugar sprinkled on. I've got good now. I can do Yorkshire pudding. Except I can't afford the beef. I've a little oven thing in my room. Sophie got it for me. I make my own dinners. Independent you see.

Pause.

PETER. What was her name?

LEONARD. Who?

PETER. Your wife's?

LEONARD (*thinks*). Susan. I've tried to forget. All this time. Trying to wipe it all out but it won't go. Things happen and I think about things that haven't happened since I thought about them. They just come back again. The happy more than the unhappy. But she ran away. That makes them unhappy.

PETER. I'm sorry.

LEONARD. What?

PETER. I'm sorry that she ran away.

LEONARD. Yes.

PETER. Children?

LEONARD. She took the girl.

PETER. Haven't you seen her?

LEONARD. No. She wanted me to go to her wedding. Give her away. But she'd already been taken. Her mother took her. I didn't go. She sent me some cake in a box. It came while I was in the hospital. It was on the mat when I got home. That was when I was still on my own. It was all mould when I opened the box. She said she'd send me some photos. She never did. Perhaps it was for the best. You can't never say if things are for the good or the bad. I've got sons.

PETER. Good.

LEONARD. They were in the army when she went. They were their own men. I've got grandchildren of an age with you. And great grandchildren. They've all done something with their lives. I've even got grandchildren who are dead. In a car. Nothing left of them except in pieces. It should have been me. I've had my time. If I'd gone instead of them it wouldn't have happened. They'd have had their own lives.

PETER. But your life – Enid's mother?

LEONARD. Charlotte.

PETER. If you weren't here –

LEONARD. You mean if I was dead?

PETER. Yes.

LEONARD. We'd never have met. There's an end to it.

Pause.

PETER. What happened to Charlotte's husband?

LEONARD. He was killed years ago. In the Great War. That's where the ladies are. Looking at the graves. I should have gone with them. You owe a man something when you marry his widow. Especially a man like that, killed fighting.

PETER. It was a long time ago.

LEONARD. Time doesn't count for much, not when you have memories.

PETER. What was his name?

LEONARD. Charlotte's Mrs Swift. Ben – I don't know if he was a Benedict or a Benjamin. Never liked to ask.

PETER. They all had old fashioned names. Names you never hear now.

LEONARD. Killed a whole generation, that war did. There didn't seem to be as many gone after the second. When he fell he was younger than you are.

Enter BEN.

PETER. He died here?

BEN. Killed lad. It's killing in a war. You never knew 'til then how much blood made up a man's life.

LEONARD. Especially from wounds in the head. You can drown in the blood that comes out of your head. Did you want to stop for them? Help them?

BEN. Of course.

LEONARD. You could never have stood it.

BEN. No.

LEONARD. Counting was the fatal thing. Once you started to count – it became the most important number in your head. You can't imagine. Pity was the fatal thing.

PETER. Tell me.

BEN. You can't imagine.

PETER. Tell me.

BEN. We got peace.

PETER. Who for?

BEN. You.

PETER. There was another war after that one. Did you know that?

BEN. We won the peace.

PETER. For twenty years. Not even a life-time.

BEN. For some it was. Men who died here.

PETER. They were wasted. Lives not used up. It was a waste.

BEN. No.

Pause.

I'm promised the tea leaves.

LEONARD. You were up to that trick too?

BEN. Yes.

LEONARD. You could have one of mine, Ben.

BEN. I prefer my own.

LEONARD. Son?

BEN. Peter doesn't. I've watched you.

PETER. I haven't seen you.

BEN. That hasn't stopped me watching.

PETER. Watching what?

BEN. The way you spend your life.

LEONARD. He spends his life sleeping in the sun.

PETER. What's wrong with sun-bathing?

BEN. You do nothing.

LEONARD. At your age you ought to be out and about having a good time. Living your life.

PETER. I am living it.

LEONARD. What have you done today?

PETER. I woke up this morning.

BEN. So you woke up. Everybody does.

PETER. Most people. I woke up this morning. I couldn't remember the name of the woman I'd slept with. It was foreign – not important. I spent the night with her because it was raining. A warm bed rather than shivering on the sand. The first thing I thought was that I missed the dew. There was none. When you wake on the beach it's the first thing you feel. Damp on you. Dragging you to the ground. She was awake. Or perhaps I woke her. It didn't matter. I wanted to go out quickly but I wanted to eat first. I would have had to have woken her to ask for some food. She gave me scrambled eggs. She cooked them in a frying pan with a fork. She gave me the fork to eat them with. They don't have toast here. The fork was one of those ones in strange metal. Light when you don't expect it to be. There was a mess of water at the side of the plate. She hadn't cooked them long enough. I asked her for a piece of bread. She wanted to kiss me. I kissed her and she gave me some bread. When I had eaten the bread she asked me something about the night. I nodded and she looked pleased. She lived in an upstairs flat. A dog had crapped on the steps –

BEN. How many steps?

PETER. I don't know. I went down the steps and across the road. I had to wait to avoid the cars. I forget they go on the wrong side. I keep nearly getting myself killed. I don't look back. I can't remember what we did. It must have been ordinary. I don't remember her having pubic hairs. They don't shave them here. It isn't France. She must have done. I don't want to go back there tonight unless it's raining.

BEN. You don't look back.

PETER. I don't look back. I walk down to the sea as quickly as possible. I walk until I am out of sight. Until I don't think I can see myself. I take my clothes off and I lie down in the sand. When I wake up there is an old lady dancing.

BEN. Enid?

PETER. She was dancing. I saw her. I was there.

He gets up.

LEONARD. Where are you going?

PETER. To get a drink.

BEN. Are you coming back?

PETER. Perhaps.

PETER goes off.

BEN. Why does he waste his time?

LEONARD. Is he wasting it?

BEN. What else would you call it?

LEONARD. There's nothing else to do.

BEN. He could give it up.

Pause.

LEONARD. Have you seen the girl?

BEN. Must have done. There are lots like that.

LEONARD. Here?

BEN. Yes.

LEONARD. You expect it more in the Middle East don't you. And India. In India some of them would let you for a bar of chocolate.

BEN. Not for the old men. Not for the ugly ones.

LEONARD. I suppose not.

BEN. Have you tried?

LEONARD. Well . . .

BEN. Aren't you frightened that you mightn't be able to?

LEONARD. It doesn't matter any more.

BEN. Does it stop mattering?

LEONARD. It seems to have done.

Pause.

It doesn't. You expect everything in you to shrivel. All the hate and the longing. The lust. You don't expect to have them any more. But there isn't much else so you have them all the more. I could kill now. If I had the strength. I'd know why. You don't expect to survive long enough to break down slowly do you? You don't expect not to be able to taste much. To eat curry for the first time in your life because it's all you've got left to taste. That's not what you expect.

Pause.

BEN. I killed myself.

Pause.

Drowning. The ship on the way back here. I couldn't stand the strain. Watching and watching. Always expecting to be attacked. Watching for the enemy watching you. It was more than I could stand. I wasn't even doing it for myself.

LEONARD. They've gone to look at your grave.

BEN. Have they?

LEONARD. If Charlotte finds out —

BEN. No. She won't know.

LEONARD. But if you tell her.

BEN. Why should I tell her? She doesn't have the least suspicion. Think what it would do to her. Her heart will be broken.

LEONARD. But after all this time.

BEN. Time?

LEONARD. The time you've been dead.

BEN. I hadn't really noticed. My watch must have come off in the sea.

LEONARD. They've taken you wreaths.

BEN. I don't like flowers.

LEONARD. Couldn't you make an exception?

BEN. What do you mean?

LEONARD. Couldn't you like them this time? Just this time. They've come a long way.

BEN. What did they come for?

LEONARD. They wanted to find you. We wanted to tell you — Charlotte and I —

BEN. Yes?

LEONARD. We want to get married.

BEN. I asked her. She said there wasn't anybody else.

LEONARD. There is now.

BEN. But you're old enough to be her grandfather.

LEONARD. No.

BEN. I can see it with my own eyes.

LEONARD. No.

BEN. You won't have her.

LEONARD. I will.

BEN. I'll kill you first.

LEONARD. No.

BEN. I will.

LEONARD. I'll kill you.

BEN. You can't.

LEONARD. I'll tell her you drowned.

Pause.

There were no heroes here. We all knew that. It was all malaria and frostbite. I saw a turn at the music hall. She wore a skirt above her knees and she sang a song about if you wanted a holiday to go to Salonika. There were no heroes.

BEN *goes. Leaving, he meets* PETER.

He salutes.

PETER. You get crazy men like that here. Too much sun. Don't let it upset you. Have a drink.

He proffers LEONARD *the bottle.*

LEONARD. I don't think so.

PETER. Local plonk. A bit sharp, it's quite safe.

LEONARD. Almost a local aren't you? Speak any Greek?

PETER. A bit. Please and thank you.

PETER *offers him the wine again. This time he takes it.*

LEONARD. Thank you. It's all wine with young people now isn't it?

PETER. In England I used to drink beer. Well, lager. This is cheaper.

LEONARD. Ran away did you?

PETER. No.

LEONARD. A broken love affair eh?

PETER. Nothing like that.

LEONARD. I thought you were a keen one for the women.

PETER. I decided to go somewhere different. First I went to France, then I came on here.

LEONARD. Hitch did you?

PETER. Too much hassle. I flew from Paris.

LEONARD. You seem to be having fun though.

PETER. It's not bad.

LEONARD. Wouldn't mind being your age again. Free as air. Go where you pleased when you pleased.

PETER. You're not quite that free.

LEONARD. Had two sons and a wife by the time I was your age. 1934. The depression. Times were bad then. We didn't run away. We stayed to fight it out.

PETER. I haven't run away. I got a job here. Here are the ladies.

Enter CHARLOTTE *and* ENID. ENID *has a camera,* CHARLOTTE *a box of pastries.*

LEONARD (*getting up*). Charlotte, Enid.

They plonk themselves in the deck chairs.

CHARLOTTE. I'm exhausted. Rows and rows of them. You'd think they'd arrange them in alphabetical order. They might have all got killed at different times but they could have put the stones in alphabetical order. I thought we'd never find him.

ENID. Or even what's supposed to be him.

PETER. There's a catalogue at the entrance.

ENID. It wasn't open.

PETER. Because I'm down here.

ENID. You work there?

PETER. I'm supposed to.

ENID. Why weren't you there? Think of the distress it must cause people. People who don't find what they're looking for?

PETER. Who comes any more? For days and days. There's a man comes once a year and puts down grass seed. To try and make a lawn. Make it look like the graveyards in France but it never grows. There's nobody left who wants to remember.

ENID. I remember. I might want to report you.

PETER. Who to? They've even stopped paying me now.

LEONARD. You might have caused these ladies great distress.

PETER. Sorry.

CHARLOTTE. Were you the one with no clothes on?

PETER. Pardon?

CHARLOTTE. This morning there was a beautiful man here. With nothing on. Was he you?

PETER. Yes.

CHARLOTTE. Would you have recognised him Enid?

ENID. I don't know.

CHARLOTTE. I bought some cakes. I bought four. I know men like two. But Leonard will give you his, won't you dear?

LEONARD. I suppose so, yes.

CHARLOTTE. Good.

ENID. There isn't any water.

LEONARD. I found him making himself a cup of tea. And finishing off your biscuits.

CHARLOTTE. Did you dear?

PETER. I thought you wouldn't mind. It stopped anybody taking them. You shouldn't leave anything here. Things get stolen.

ENID. What are we supposed to drink?

PETER. I've got some retsina.

CHARLOTTE. What's that?

PETER. Wine.

ENID. Alcohol?

LEONARD. It's very good.

ENID. Have you been drinking?

LEONARD. Only a little.

CHARLOTTE. May I try some.

She drinks it from the bottle.

ENID. There are some tea cups.

ENID *rummages in her bag to find the tea cups.*

PETER. May I?

ENID. Thank you.

ENID *drinks wine from cup and saucer. The others drink from the bottle.*

CHARLOTTE. I got you ones with nuts in. I knew you like them.

LEONARD. Thank you. She doesn't forget a thing.

CHARLOTTE. Aren't you going to have one?

PETER. You don't mind?

CHARLOTTE. If Leonard doesn't.

ENID. He shouldn't eat two at his age. It's bad for him.

LEONARD. You can't believe that stuff you read. I've smoked all my life. Look at me now.

ENID. Think what you might have looked like.

Pause.

LEONARD. Did you ladies have a good afternoon?

ENID. You can hardly enjoy visiting a cemetery.

CHARLOTTE. I tried to think what it must have been like. What he must have seen when he was here.

ENID. He wouldn't have seen the same. The town was burnt down. It flamed for two days. There was nothing left except that church we saw the other day. It would have been quite different when he was here.

CHARLOTTE. It's a shame. I used to wonder what it was like. When we were at Blackpool. I used to wonder.

LEONARD. No point in getting depressed kitten. May I?

PETER. Of course.

CHARLOTTE *takes a large drink.*

ENID. Mother, you'll get squiffy.

LEONARD. Bet you haven't heard that one. Squiffy. Rather more graphic now aren't you?

PETER. Sorry?

LEONARD (*whispering*). Pissed.

PETER. Yes.

CHARLOTTE. I heard you.

ENID. Mother, I don't think wine is good for you with the sun.

CHARLOTTE. I should go on with my knitting.

ENID. You'll drop everything.

CHARLOTTE. You know you've got arms as long as each other. I measured. You were asleep. You didn't notice. You might have been boys together.

LEONARD. There must be fifty years between us.

CHARLOTTE. You might have been the same boy.

She looks at LEONARD.

What colour was your hair?

LEONARD. Dark.

CHARLOTTE. What colour?

LEONARD. Not as dark as his. A sort of brown.

CHARLOTTE. Oh.

LEONARD. What colour did you think it was?

CHARLOTTE. I thought it might have been fair. Your son is fair.

LEONARD. His mother.

CHARLOTTE. I suppose so. She was a red head. You wouldn't think it to look at her would you?

ENID. Mother!

CHARLOTTE. Well you wouldn't. Would you? The wonder of it is, where does all the colour go?

ENID. Your old hair drops out. Grey hair grows.

PETER. There are some women have beautiful hair. Even when they are old.

ENID. Those sort of women dye it.

PETER. My grandmother had.

ENID. Women who dye their hair can be very subtle.

PETER. After she had died and the skin on her scalp shrunk, there was no grey then. I looked particularly.

CHARLOTTE (to LEONARD). When did you start going bald?

LEONARD. I don't remember.

ENID. You must remember.

LEONARD. Why?

ENID. Didn't you look in the mirror and see?

LEONARD. One day. But by then I was really quite bald.

ENID. And you?

PETER. Not yet.

ENID. Not even thinning?

PETER. I don't think so.

ENID. Don't you comb it?

PETER. Not often.

ENID. Let me see.

PETER *goes to her. She runs her hands through his hair.*

It's thick.

PETER. Thank you.

She expects him to pull away from her.

I don't mind.

Pause.

LEONARD. What are we going to do tomorrow?

ENID. Are you staying?

CHARLOTTE. He is staying.

ENID. Where?

LEONARD. I'll find somewhere.

ENID. There's no room in our hotel. I checked at lunch time.

LEONARD. I know. I've got a sleeping bag.

PETER. If the worst comes to the worst he can stay out here with me.

ENID. You sleep out here?

PETER. Why not?

ENID. Isn't it illegal or something?

PETER. Not that I know of. No one comes.

ENID. Not robbers or anything?

PETER. What would they come for? I haven't got anything.

LEONARD. Would you mind?

PETER. I couldn't stop you.

LEONARD. No.

CHARLOTTE. A little more.

LEONARD. There isn't much more left.

ENID. Mother, we've already drunk all his wine.

PETER. It doesn't matter. I can get some more.

ENID. But you've no money.

PETER. It doesn't matter.

ENID. We should give you back what we owe you.

PETER. I can get some money.

CHARLOTTE. How?

PETER. I'll sell something.

ENID. Blood?

PETER. It doesn't have to be.

ENID. What else?

Pause.

LEONARD. Not your watch or anything. You shouldn't go selling anything important.

ENID. What have you got?

Pause.

Have you stolen something?

PETER. Semen.

CHARLOTTE. What did he say?

ENID. You heard, mother.

CHARLOTTE. What?

PETER. Semen. So women with infertile husbands can have children.

CHARLOTTE. Oh. Good heavens. Well you don't look that sort, not even with your clothes off.

PETER. I'm dark enough to count as a Greek.

LEONARD. Well, what are we going to do tomorrow?

ENID. There's a bus. Along the coast. We were going on that. The views are panoramic.

LEONARD. What are you going to do, kitten?

ENID. Why do you call her kitten? She's got a name hasn't she?

CHARLOTTE. He always calls me kitten.

ENID. Your name is Charlotte. You're eighty-four. He might at least call you cat.

Pause.

We're going on the bus along the coast road in the morning. My mother is frightened of the drivers. I shall sit next to her and hold her hand.

LEONARD. I'd like to come with you if I may.

CHARLOTTE. I want you to come. Hic. I'm squiffy.

ENID. We should go back to the hotel.

CHARLOTTE. Leonard will take me back. You've got to see to the chairs.

ENID. The chairs are rather difficult.

LEONARD. If you just take my arm.

ENID. You should have a bath. The heat makes you sweat. It blocks the pores.

LEONARD. I'll see to her. You leave it to me.

CHARLOTTE. Perhaps I should have a little nap.

LEONARD. A nice lie down will do you the world of good.

ENID. Mother, don't you want me —

CHARLOTTE. Leonard will look after me.

LEONARD. Come on, kitten.

CHARLOTTE. I usually only drink sherry.

CHARLOTTE *and* LEONARD *go.*

ENID. At Christmas. I only let her at Christmas.

ENID *starts to fold the deck chairs.*

PETER. I'll give you a hand with them.

ENID. I can manage.

PETER. Let me help.

ENID. I can do it.

PETER. It'll take you two journeys.

ENID. It doesn't matter. I'm used to it. This is a man's job. He should be doing it.

PETER. Let me.

He helps her.

If you let them get married, you could have a life of your own.

ENID. I've never had a life of my own. I wouldn't know what to do with it.

PETER. Don't you have ambitions?

ENID. Not to die first.

PETER. You're not an old woman.

ENID. But I am.

PETER. Where's the old man going to stay?

ENID. Out here with you.

PETER. He can't.

ENID. Why not?

PETER. It's cold in the morning. At dawn it gets very cold. It could kill him.

ENID. I see.

PETER. You wouldn't want that would you?

ENID is packing up the burner.

ENID. Would you like to use it? If you wanted a hot drink or something in the night. And if it's not going to be stolen.

PETER. I wouldn't mind.

ENID. I wanted to take a photograph of her. But not of him, not of both of them. Tomorrow it may not be sunny.

PETER. It always is here.

ENID. May I take one of you?

PETER *laughs*.

I'd like to take one of here. To remember it by. In the instructions for the film they say a figure makes landscapes more interesting.

PETER. Well if you like.

ENID (*fiddling the camera out of the case*). I'm not very good. Sometimes my hand – it's not very steady. If you just stand there.

PETER. The camera will be pointing into the sun. That's not very good for photographs.

ENID. Oh.

PETER. The pictures get over-exposed.

ENID. Well, you'd better be wherever you think best.

PETER. Which bit of landscape do you want?

ENID *looks round*.

ENID. It doesn't matter.

PETER *strikes a silly pose*.

You'll spoil it.

PETER. I'm sorry.

He becomes formal.

ENID. The other one seemed more lively.

She takes the picture and winds the film on.

PETER. Shall I take one of you?

ENID. What?

PETER. You ought to have one of yourself to show your friends.

ENID. They won't want to see.

PETER. It would remind you.

ENID. Yes.

ENID *positions herself where* PETER *stood.*

PETER. No.

> *He moves her.*

> That's better. Smile.

ENID. I can't.

PETER. Of course you can.

ENID. Not my teeth and everything.

PETER. Just smile naturally.

ENID. I feel silly.

PETER. Your eyes light up when you smile. You were smiling when you were dancing.

ENID. Was I?

PETER. A beautiful smile.

> ENID *of course smiles in response to this compliment.*

> PETER *snaps her.*

ENID. I wasn't.

PETER. You were.

> PETER *hands her the camera to put away. He picks up the knitting.*

> She'll want this won't she?

ENID. Yes. She always has it. She started knitting it for my father. You should have been at the cemetery. We wanted to see the roll of honour.

PETER. I could bring it down here if you liked.

ENID. Could you?

PETER. It would save you going all the way up in the heat.

ENID. Yes.

PETER. I'll bring it down.

ENID. Thank you.

ENID *smiles*.

PETER. You should smile more often.

PETER *and* ENID *go*.

PART THREE

The same. Evening. Almost dark.

Enter CHARLOTTE *and* LEONARD.

LEONARD. You shouldn't have had so much you know.

CHARLOTTE. I'm all right now.

LEONARD. Are you?

CHARLOTTE. Look, a straight line.

LEONARD. Shall we sit down?

They sit on the sand.

CHARLOTTE. Enid can't get this far. Her rheumatism.

LEONARD. Well?

CHARLOTTE. Not here.

LEONARD. No one to see. Just a kiss and a cuddle.

CHARLOTTE. Well – if it was anybody else.

They kiss.

LEONARD. I've got something to show you.

CHARLOTTE. Oh yes.

LEONARD *takes out a copy of some retirement magazine.*

LEONARD. Homes.

CHARLOTTE. What?

LEONARD. Lists of retirement homes. The ones that take married couples.

CHARLOTTE. Oh. Couldn't we have a little flat, a bungalow. Something without steps.

LEONARD. You have to think of the possibility.

CHARLOTTE. We could stay with Enid.

LEONARD. I can't live with her, kitten. Don't ask me to. I can't. Never in a million years. I wouldn't have a million years, she'd poison me.

CHARLOTTE. She wouldn't.

LEONARD. How do you know. They'd call it a mercy killing and nothing would be done.

CHARLOTTE. Enid wouldn't.

LEONARD. I think we should look into it. Go and visit a few. Some of them you can go for a few days. I thought for our honeymoon.

CHARLOTTE. I've never had a honeymoon. Two days at his sister's in the country and having to pick potatoes. She had us up the morning after the wedding at six o'clock. He didn't seem to mind.

LEONARD. We had a week in Skeggie.

CHARLOTTE. Skeggie used to be nice.

LEONARD. Yes.

CHARLOTTE. I haven't been for years, have you?

LEONARD. Not for years.

CHARLOTTE. I don't want to go to the sea. I couldn't stand it.

LEONARD. Everybody goes to the sea.

CHARLOTTE. I don't want to go with a load of old people. Do you?

LEONARD. Most of these are at the sea. The south coast.

CHARLOTTE. Well I'm not going.

LEONARD. I'd be coming with you.

CHARLOTTE. I'm not getting left at the sea-side. Nothing to do but watch it coming in and out all the time. What sort of life is that?

LEONARD. You'd get to like it.

CHARLOTTE. I might not have the time.

LEONARD. The air's good for you. You'd get a new lease of life.

CHARLOTTE. I shouldn't want one. I want to stay at home. With Enid. It wouldn't be fair to go off and leave her by herself. She isn't as young as she was.

LEONARD. You could come in with me.

CHARLOTTE. I want my independence.

LEONARD. I've got an oven. We could make our own dinners. Have our tea with the family.

CHARLOTTE. The same house as your family? They'd be forever interfering.

LEONARD. Sophie's very good.

CHARLOTTE. I've always had a house. Couldn't get used to being cooped up in your room. And right next to the front door. All those children in and out at night. They drive you mad.

LEONARD. They come in and say good night.

CHARLOTTE. I'd do that. They wouldn't want to if there were the two of us. How would you get a double bed in?

LEONARD. I hadn't thought.

CHARLOTTE. I've always had a double bed. I couldn't get used to a twin even if I had it to myself. There'd be no point anyway. I've had that double bed since I was wed, it might as well see me out.

LEONARD. Some of these places you can take your own furniture.

CHARLOTTE. I haven't got my reading glasses.

LEONARD. I'll read it to you.

CHARLOTTE. I know what those sort of advertisements are like. All lahdidah. I don't care for it. They're the workhouse. But people knew the workhouse was bad. Places like that, they think there's nothing to worry about. They rob you.

LEONARD. There's a nice place here at Mablethorpe.

CHARLOTTE. How much is it?

LEONARD. Ninety pounds a week each.

CHARLOTTE. Ninety pounds? They rob you.

LEONARD. Some of them are a hundred and fifty.

CHARLOTTE. Does that stop them robbing you at ninety?

LEONARD. I've got a little bit put by. I was saving it but I could go on the National Health.

CHARLOTTE. How much?

LEONARD. Nearly five hundred pounds. It's a lot of money.

CHARLOTTE. It would only keep you for five weeks. Then you'd have to go home again.

LEONARD. Haven't you got some?

CHARLOTTE. Where'd I have money from?

LEONARD. You've got a house. Things you could sell.

CHARLOTTE. Why should I? I'm sick of men at the door asking me for stuff and trying to come and see what I've got hidden. I don't care what happens to it once I'm gone. But not now. Why should I have to? I don't need things but I do. Some things I need to know I can put my hand out and touch. In the bombings when we all carried our emergency suitcases people had them stuffed with money. A woman was running and her case broke and the whole street was covered in gold. Money. She'd had nothing else in it. I had a suitcase and in it two china dolls and photographs of all the people I had ever known, and my lying-out nightie. Whenever there was danger I carried that case with me. It was a comfortable weight. I had to sell my dolls to come. The only things I can remember having all my life. I was saving them —

LEONARD. What will we do then?

CHARLOTTE. Perhaps we should stay as we are.

LEONARD. Separate?

CHARLOTTE. If there's nothing else to do.

LEONARD. You can't let me down.

CHARLOTTE. Let you down?

LEONARD. We were going to have a new life.

CHARLOTTE. There's you and me and Enid.

LEONARD. I should marry Enid.

CHARLOTTE. Marry Enid?

LEONARD. She'd look after me. Then I'd have someone.

CHARLOTTE. You have your family.

LEONARD. You know what I mean.

CHARLOTTE. Perhaps I could sell things. Things that were my own. Things that Enid doesn't want.

LEONARD. We wouldn't need very much.

CHARLOTTE. I suppose not.

LEONARD. Just four or five years at the most.

CHARLOTTE. You wouldn't even be eighty.

LEONARD. You have to face up to these things.

CHARLOTTE. I couldn't bear you to go first. Not again.

Enter BEN.

LEONARD. My wife went first before.

CHARLOTTE. She left you. That's different.

LEONARD. She still went first.

CHARLOTTE. It would be nice both of us together. In our sleep.

LEONARD. I've always wanted that.

CHARLOTTE. I always hoped that Ben – that he didn't know.

LEONARD. You don't hear the one that hits you.

CHARLOTTE. It would be terrible for Enid after. She'll have no one.

LEONARD. She's held onto your apron strings for too long, Charlotte.

CHARLOTTE. I'm used to her. She's comfortable.

LEONARD. We'll be comfortable together. Snug even. You could sell your table. You'd get a good price for your table.

BEN. That table came from my grandfather.

CHARLOTTE. It is too big.

BEN. It was his wedding present to us. It had been in the family for years.

CHARLOTTE. I've never sat ten down to eat. Not all together.

LEONARD. We'll have that many when we get married. At least that many.

CHARLOTTE. I've only got Enid to come.

LEONARD. You'll get grandchildren, great grandchildren when you marry me. Enid's never given you those.

CHARLOTTE. I'd have liked someone to pass things on to. A bit of future.

LEONARD. No point Enid having the table if there's no one to pass it to.

CHARLOTTE. She still might expect it.

LEONARD. What use has she got for it?

CHARLOTTE. I expected to be on that table in my coffin. There have been any number laid on it. Now they take you away and nobody sees you again.

LEONARD. You wouldn't miss it. Not after it was gone.

CHARLOTTE. Wouldn't I?

LEONARD. Think how cosy we could be.

He cuddles her.

CHARLOTTE. You're very warm.

LEONARD. Good circulation. The blood still flows. Right to the very tips of me.

CHARLOTTE. Leonard! We'll have sheets won't we? I don't like the things they have here. I like to feel the blankets on me when I'm sleeping.

LEONARD. We'll have sheets. Unless we find the continental things more convenient.

CHARLOTTE. They have snaps. I can't do those. Not any more.

LEONARD. I can.

CHARLOTTE. It's a hook and eye.

 LEONARD *is fumbling with* CHARLOTTE's *dress.*

It's a hook and eye and a zip. Enid has to do them for me.

LEONARD. You'll have me for that.

CHARLOTTE. Yes.

LEONARD (*about his fingers*). A bit stiff today.

CHARLOTTE. It's the dampness.

LEONARD. Shall we go in?

CHARLOTTE. I'd like to.

 LEONARD *helps* CHARLOTTE *up.*

LEONARD. Can you manage buttons?

CHARLOTTE. Yes.

LEONARD. Will you take my arm?

 They go in. BEN *watches them.*

 Enter PETER. *He has the book from the graveyard and another bottle of wine.*

PETER. You drowned.

BEN. Yes.

PETER. They don't know?

BEN. No.

PETER. I thought you were a hero. That's what Enid made you out to be.

BEN. I didn't send the letters home. 'Killed in action' was easier than making excuses. It stopped there being any questions. Will you tell them?

PETER. She wants to see the book. It says there.

BEN. You could tear out the page.

PETER. Yours isn't the only name on that page.

BEN. Who else is there?

PETER. Do you really want to know?

BEN. Yes.

PETER. Smiths, Snodgrass, Sparkes, Spenser, Spooner, Squire, Stephens with a Ph, Sterling, Stevens, with a V, Stock, Stroud, Stuart, Sturdy, Such, Sullivan, Sutton, Swift.

BEN. I don't remember any of them.

PETER. Shall I go on?

BEN. I don't want to know. Such a waste.

PETER. If you knew it was a waste why didn't you run away. Why did you kill yourself?

BEN. I didn't think I could survive.

PETER. Didn't you have anything to live for?

BEN. No.

PETER. Your wife.

BEN. Why should I have gone on for her and not for myself?

PETER. But their lives would have been different.

BEN. Is that a good enough reason?

PETER. All they went through. It must have been terrible for them.

BEN. But you can't say that anything else would have been any better.

PETER. It might have been.

BEN. You can never know. Never, however long you live.

PETER. But death's a disaster.

BEN. Who for?

PETER. The people left behind.

BEN. How do you know?

Enter ENID. *She carries a little brown case and a sleeping bag.*

ENID. He might as well stay with her. I'm not staying there and being ashamed of them.

PETER. I brought this down for you.

ENID. Thank you. This is what I sleep in isn't it?

PETER. You won't be very comfortable.

ENID. I don't mind.

PETER. I could find you somewhere in the town.

ENID. I should like to be out here. I didn't think there'd be stars.

PETER. Most nights in the summer.

ENID. Do you only stay here in the summer?

PETER. Yes. It's pretty cold here in the winter.

ENID. Where do you live then?

PETER. I've got friends.

ENID. Oh. Girlfriends?

PETER. Sometimes.

ENID. They must feel very lucky. You're attractive.

PETER. You should see some of the Greek boys.

ENID. Yes, I have. The girls are pretty too.

PETER. Did you really have red hair?

ENID. Auburn. The colour girls try to dye their hair.

PETER. You must have been considered quite dashing.

ENID. Not dashing, elegant perhaps because I was tall.

PETER. But too tall to be a dancer?

ENID. Yes. One day I was just too tall. They told me not to take any more lessons. I didn't go again.

PETER. You could have done. As a hobby.

ENID. I had responsibilities. I did ballroom dancing once. But there weren't enough men . . .

PETER. And you had to be the man because you were tall?

ENID. Yes.

PETER. You could go dancing again now.

ENID. We did. Mother and I went. They were starting up dancing in the afternoon and they sent free tickets for pensioners. That's where we met Leonard. After the free tickets it was a pound a time.

PETER. I'll dance with you now if you like.

ENID. I'm a bit tired.

She spreads out the sleeping bag.

Shall we sit down?

ENID *and* PETER *sit on the sleeping bag.*

PETER (*offering her wine*). Do you want a cup?

ENID. I don't mind. We're quite bohemian aren't we.

PETER. Yes.

ENID. I like it here. I didn't like Athens but this is different. My father must have liked being here very much. How long will you stay here?

PETER. Tonight?

ENID. In Greece?

PETER. A few more months. I don't know.

ENID. Do you know about the stars?

PETER. No.

ENID. I think I'd buy a book about them if I lived on a beach. Some of them have Greek names you know. After the old gods.

PETER. Yes.

ENID. I never thought people would land on the moon in my lifetime. Did you?

PETER. I've never thought of what I expected.

ENID. People might even go to the planets in your lifetime. It will be very exciting for you.

PETER. I don't see television or the newspapers. I wouldn't know.

ENID. People would tell you. You'd be bound to know.

She yawns.

PETER. You should go to bed.

ENID. Yes.

PETER. You should keep your clothes on.

ENID. Yes.

Pause.

My shoes and stockings?

PETER. No.

PETER turns away from her.

When you're ready.

BEN. Don't tell her.

PETER. If she wants to know.

BEN. Does she want to know?

PETER. She thinks you liked it here.

ENID. I'm ready.

She gets into the sleeping bag.

I've never slept like this before.

PETER. Did you brush your teeth?

ENID. No.

PETER. You should, you know. In the sea. The salt's good for you. I'll fetch you some.

PETER goes.

BEN. Fine young chap.

ENID. Were you like him?

BEN. Who can say? I never spent the night with an old lady on the beach.

ENID. Do you know what's going on in there?

BEN. I've something of an idea.

ENID. Can't you do something to stop them?

BEN. Are they happy?

ENID. I don't know. Don't you see? He should be mine.

BEN. Why?

ENID. I deserve him. After all this time. I ought to have a man of my own. I found him.

She picks up the book.

BEN. You could have him.

ENID. He's a boy.

BEN. If you gave him money he probably would. If you wanted.

ENID. I couldn't ask him.

BEN. He offered to dance with you.

ENID. Yes. He let me put my hands in his hair.

BEN. You should ask him.

Enter PETER.

PETER. Here.

ENID. Thank you.

She starts to brush her teeth.

I have trouble with them. My elbow.

PETER. Let me.

Pause.

Give me the brush.

She does.

Open wide.

ENID. They're all my own.

PETER. I can see.

    PETER *brushes her teeth for her*.

    Drink. Spit. Drink.

ENID. It's salty.

PETER. Sea water.

ENID. Isn't it poisonous?

PETER. Not with the salt. It stops it being.

ENID. Mother makes me gargle with salt when I've got a bad throat.

    Pause.

PETER. Leonard does love her, you know.

ENID. At their age?

PETER. Did you never love anybody?

ENID. Love?

PETER. You know.

ENID. Never.

PETER. No one?

ENID (*snaps*). I couldn't. I had responsibilities.

    Pause.

    Do you ever – you know – for money.

PETER. What?

ENID. With women.

PETER. You mean you?

ENID. I suppose so.

PETER. I haven't.

ENID. Would you?

    Pause.

I could pay you.

PETER. I —

ENID. My plane ticket back, I could give you that.

PETER. What would you do?

ENID. I could stay here. Sleep out.

PETER. You've already got rheumatism. It would kill you.

ENID. I'd rather that.

PETER. Because of the old man?

ENID. Yes.

Pause.

PETER. It must run in families.

ENID. Pardon?

PETER. Your father drowned himself you know.

ENID. Drowned?

PETER. You can see for yourself.

He shows her the book.

ENID. It must be a mistake.

PETER. Why?

ENID. He wouldn't do such a thing. Not him.

PETER. Perhaps in a moment —

ENID. He wouldn't. I know he wouldn't. I've got a sleeping bag. I'd be warm enough. You could go home. See your parents. I've got a little money. You could have that. Get some souvenirs. There are some nice little castanets. Your mother would like those. And your father. There are match boxes with paintings of Thesalonika on them. Have you got brothers and sisters?

PETER. A sister and a brother.

ENID. You could get her perfume on the plane and him a bottle of wine.

Pause.

PETER. I'm not ready to go.

ENID. You don't have to use the ticket for three months. As long as it's before then. Might I have a drink?

PETER. You ought to go in. You shouldn't be out here.

ENID. He's in there.

PETER. Would you like me to come up with you?

ENID. I like it here.

PETER. You should go in.

ENID. You aren't the only person in the world.

PETER. Haven't you got friends and things at home?

ENID. Some.

PETER. You should go back to them.

ENID. It doesn't bother me not seeing them.

PETER. It might worry them.

ENID. That wouldn't be my fault.

Pause.

I'll make myself hot milk. Would you like some?

PETER. You've cleaned your teeth.

ENID. It doesn't matter.

Pause.

ENID (*fiddling with stove*). You've broken it.

PETER. I don't think so.

ENID. What right have you got to break it?

PETER. Here like this.

ENID. What time does it get light?

PETER. Early, before five o'clock.

ENID. In England before we came away the birds started singing at four. You sleep less once you're my age. You'll find that. That you cannot sleep all day. And you'll dream too. Real dreams. So real that they exist. Sometimes so real you think they are memories. When you dream you aren't old. I'm forty-five. Always forty-five.

PETER. Why forty-five?

ENID. That's where I stopped.

PETER. Stopped?

ENID. I didn't have a future any more.

    PETER *slumps*.

ENID (*frightened*). Peter? Peter?

    She puts her hand in his hair.

    Peter don't. You frighten me. It's dark here. Don't.

    She realises something has happened.

    ENID *tries to revive* PETER.

BEN. Don't.

ENID. It's the kiss of life.

BEN. It's too late.

ENID. He's too young to die.

BEN. No.

    ENID *continues to try and revive* PETER.

    She bangs at his chest.

ENID. Peter!

BEN. It won't work.

    ENID *looks at* PETER.

ENID. What shall I do with him?

BEN. He ought to be washed.

ENID. Is that a heart attack?

BEN. Yes.

ENID. But he isn't old. He had all his life in front of him.

BEN. What life?

ENID. He could have gone home, got a job. Done something with himself. Made something of himself.

BEN. Him?

ENID. You never know.

BEN. We should wash him.

ENID. Yes.

BEN. I'll fetch some water. You should strip him.

ENID. Yes.

   BEN *goes for some water.*

   ENID *starts to undress* PETER.

   We used to have to in the war. You couldn't get ribbons then. Not one in the whole shop. Even all the green that they thought was unlucky for weddings was all used up. That's how I knew the peace was coming. When ribbons came again. Red, white and blue. For the victory. You should have gone home. Not here. You could have had my ticket.

   BEN *comes back with the water.*

   He's hurt himself.

   She shows BEN PETER's *arm—an elastoplast.*

BEN. Too much bleeding.

   ENID *has nearly got* PETER *naked.*

ENID. There's nothing to wash him with.

BEN. Don't you have something?

ENID. Oh, yes.

   She takes a sponge from her brown case.

BEN. I'll make a hole for him.

   BEN *starts to dig.* ENID *is washing the body.*

   Are you crying?

ENID. Yes.

BEN. It doesn't matter. Your mother used to weep about things I couldn't understand.

ENID. It's the waste.

BEN. He's one on his own. There were thousands here. Pointless deaths. Not even in a battle which would have made them heroes, but malaria. Rows and rows of men sweating like pigs but complaining they were cold. Mostly they were delirious. Those who had been in the trenches thought they were back there. And would rather have been. Sweat running down their faces like tears. You could wring the water from men's bodies out of their sheets and into a pail. In summer your teeth rattled from fever, in the winter you couldn't stop them chattering because of the cold.

ENID. How did they get malaria?

BEN. A parasite in the body of mosquitoes, that goes into the bodies of men and round them in their blood system. And you knew you would never be free of it and the delirium. That even in your old age it could creep up on you like a memory. After the delirium was gone you were yourself again. You would wake up looking at the stars. The world was still going on.

ENID. Did you know about the stars?

BEN. Not then. When we were lying there worn out with trauma they were the only things which moved.

ENID. Do you think there are other people up there?

BEN. I never knew.

ENID. Would you like there to be?

BEN. Not if it was like here.

ENID. You can only think of other places as being like here.

BEN. You can hope.

ENID *turns* PETER *onto his front.*

ENID. He'll still have the sand on him.

BEN. Sand doesn't matter.

ENID. His mother should do this for him.

BEN. Don't stay out here.

ENID. Someone ought to sit up with him.

BEN. He'll be all right.

ENID. Are you sure?

BEN. It's as good a place as any other.

ENID. Is this where you are?

BEN. Yes.

ENID. But you've got a stone up there. We thought you were up there.

BEN. Then it doesn't make any difference?

    Pause.

ENID. I suppose not. He could just be asleep.

    Enter CHARLOTTE.

CHARLOTTE. As the day he was born.

    CHARLOTTE *bends down to touch him.*

ENID. Don't touch him!

CHARLOTTE. What?

ENID. Don't touch him. Don't wake him up.

CHARLOTTE. Isn't it a pretty body?

ENID. Yes.

    They look at PETER.

I was making some hot milk. It will help us sleep. Would you like some?

CHARLOTTE. Yes.

ENID. You can sit on this. It's dry.

CHARLOTTE. If we both sit down we won't be able to get up.

ENID. We'll manage somehow.

Pause.

Where's Leonard?

CHARLOTTE. Asleep. He snores. I never asked him if he snored. I forgot men did.

She looks at PETER.

He doesn't.

ENID. You have to be lying on your back.

CHARLOTTE. I don't know what to do now.

BEN *goes.*

ENID *pours out the milk.*

It's nice to have hot milk again.

ENID. There were some biscuits.

CHARLOTTE. He ate them.

ENID. I forgot.

CHARLOTTE. Don't you remember?

ENID. Look at the stars.

Real Estate

Real Estate was first performed at the Tricycle Theatre, London on 3 May 1984, with the following cast:

GWEN   Brenda Bruce
JENNY   Charlotte Cornwell
DICK   Glyn Owen
ERIC   Tony Guilfoyle

Directed by Pip Broughton
Designed by Ellen Cairns
Lighting by Andy Phillips

ACT ONE

Scene One

The wood at the back of a house.

It is autumn – late dusk.

Dead leaves.

A ball crosses the stage.

GWEN (*off*). Cleo!

> *Enter GWEN. She carries a dog lead. She rattles the lead. She whistles.*
>
> Cleo! Cleo! You naughty girl!
>
> *She waits for the dog. She shouts off stage.*
>
> Thank you. She always goes back to the house when we get this far.
>
> *She waits. She picks up an acorn. The acorn has a small root and has leaves and mud round it.*
>
> *Enter JENNY. She is holding the ball. She is dressed almost identically to GWEN except that she is wearing silly shoes.*
>
> I never seem to go home without something in my pocket. The next time I find them they're withered.

JENNY. You should empty your pocket.

GWEN. Yes.

She throws the acorn away.

Cleo! Cleo! Samba died. Well put down. You don't expect dogs to last for ever do you? This one's called Cleo. Dick's choice. I couldn't do all the naming of them.

JENNY. No.

GWEN. Dick's dog more than mine really. Spends most of the day with him. It doesn't feel safe now to walk in these woods without some sort of companion.

JENNY. The same everywhere.

GWEN. Worse in towns I expect.

JENNY. I have a car.

GWEN. Oh.

JENNY. And a flat. Two bedrooms. Second floor.

GWEN. Where?

JENNY. London. Hammersmith.

GWEN. Oh.

JENNY. There's a view of the river from the balcony.

GWEN. I see.

JENNY *tries to get some leaves from her shoe.*

JENNY. Silly shoes for here.

GWEN. At least it's not wet.

JENNY. No.

GWEN. Did you drive in them?

JENNY. Yes.

GWEN. How long did it take?

JENNY. An hour and a half. Longer than it should. The traffic was choc-a-bloc coming out of London.

GWEN. I always go by train.

JENNY. I assumed the station would be closed by now.

GWEN. It is. Dick drives me to Didcot. You could have been collected.

JENNY. I didn't want to be a nuisance.

She holds out the ball.

GWEN. You still bite your nails.

JENNY. Yes.

GWEN. Most people grow out of it.

JENNY. I have tried. It was either this or smoking.

GWEN. I smoke.

JENNY. You shouldn't.

GWEN. You tell me that?

JENNY. Anybody would.

GWEN. It's my own life! I throw it away as I please.

Pause.

DICK *calls from the house.*

DICK. Gwen. Gwenny?

GWEN. Dick's waiting for me.

Pause.

Am I supposed to say something? Well?

What did you expect?

JENNY *shakes her head.*

DICK (*off*). Gwen!

GWEN. I'm here. (*To* JENNY.) I can't ask you to stay for supper because I don't know if there's enough. Are you expecting to be asked to stay? Dick's province not mine. He's the one who knows how long the mince has been in the freezer. How many sheets there are which haven't been turned edge to edge. Don't think we can't afford new sheets. We can, easily. It's just we prefer them to be linen and at our – that's what we prefer.

DICK (*off*). Gwen?

GWEN. It's not fair to keep him waiting—

GWEN starts to go.

JENNY. There are some questions—

GWEN. There had to be something.

JENNY. Why?

GWEN. Why else would you come?

They are very still.

It's not intuition. I'd assumed it would be money. It obviously isn't. I know how much Jaeger suits cost.

JENNY laughs.

This is my money. Not Dick's. Dick's as well as mine of course. I'm the one that works now.

JENNY. It suits you.

GWEN. Thank you.

Enter DICK.

JENNY. Hello Dick.

DICK. Jenny!

GWEN. It took her an hour and a half to drive from London.

JENNY. The traffic was bad.

GWEN. Did Cleo come in?

DICK. I thought she was with you.

GWEN. No.

GWEN starts to move offstage.

Cleo! You're a naughty girl. Cleo! Come back here this minute.

She has gone.

DICK. How are you?

JENNY. Fine.

DICK. Good.

JENNY. And you?

DICK. Bearing up.

JENNY. I hear you do the cooking.

DICK. Gwen's at work all day. She doesn't have the time. It's not how I thought my retirement would be. All rather piecemeal.

JENNY. Housework is.

DICK. She's an estate agent, a good estate agent. The clients like her. She sells houses very successfully. She found it very exciting at first. I don't know now. It's her name you see on the boards. She earns more than I was earning. Perhaps you expected to find us struggling?

JENNY. I don't know.

DICK. On your way here you must have thought.

JENNY. I thought you'd be old. Older. You are of course. And me?

Pause.

DICK *watches her.*

JENNY *bends down for an acorn. The gesture stops.*

Do I remind you of her?

DICK. Not particularly. No.

JENNY. Sometimes I think I am. It suddenly surprises me. Something I say. How I put my clothes in order in the drawers. The way I boil eggs.

DICK. It would be hard to better. Hers is a very reliable method.

JENNY. I've never compared it. The egg's just an example.

She throws the acorn away.

I can't explain.

DICK. You live in London?

JENNY. Yes. I have a flat. Two bedrooms. Second floor. Hammersmith. There's a view of the river from the balcony.

DICK. I see. You aren't married?

JENNY. No and I haven't been. Did you think there'd be step-grandchildren somewhere?

DICK. We've thought a lot of things. You couldn't have expected us not to. How do you earn your living?

JENNY. I work in a shop. Not behind the counter at Woolworth's as you promised me I would. More up market than that. You made the threat of working at Woolworth's sound terribly glamorous. Rather risqué. The sort of place it would be fun to work. I buy china. I've quite an eye for it. I can see if a teapot's likely to pour well. I've just got a big firm to reappraise their glaze. It cracked in dishwashers. That's quite a major victory. And of course there have been other things on the way.

DICK. I look forward to hearing about them. Will you stay for supper?

JENNY. She said she didn't know if there'd be enough.

DICK. It'll stretch.

JENNY. If you're sure.

DICK. It's not the fatted calf.

JENNY. I didn't expect it to be. I should lock the car.

Exit JENNY.

DICK *watches her.*

Enter GWEN. *She wears an apron which is obviously his.*

GWEN. I've turned the sprouts down.

DICK. Thank you.

GWEN. Do you think she's attractive? She is, isn't she? More than I thought she would be. I suppose I thought she'd come back in denim and with beads. It all looks as if it's real gold. She is attractive, isn't she?

DICK. Well –

GWEN. How did you think she'd be? Tell me. I've thought so many things I don't know.

DICK. Gwenny –

GWEN. I'm all right. You'd think Christmas or a birthday. Even over a weekend. But Thursday?

DICK. Perhaps she's on her way somewhere.

GWEN. Just dropping in. Is that all?

DICK. She's having supper with us.

GWEN. I wonder if she would like to stay the night.

DICK. She might want to drive back. It's only ninety minutes.

GWEN. The spare bed isn't aired. I could – put both hot water bottles in –

DICK. We might not want her to stay.

GWEN. Are sprouts a vegetable she liked? I don't remember. I know there's something she would never eat.

DICK. There are still runner beans. I'll do those.

Enter JENNY.

GWEN. Do you like brussel sprouts?

JENNY. Fine.

GWEN. What's the vegetable that you don't like?

JENNY. There isn't one I don't think.

GWEN. There was. You swore it made you sick. I thought it was a fad. I made soup with it and told you it was something different. You were sick.

JENNY. I'm not fond of turnip.

GWEN. No –

DICK. There are some beans from the garden in the freezer. I'll do those.

JENNY. I don't want to be any trouble.

GWEN. It'll come back to me.

DICK. Ten minutes.

Exit DICK.

JENNY. He looks very fit.

GWEN. He's not the sort of husband that has heart attacks. Not that you can ever say of course. It'll probably be me.

JENNY. Dick says you're a success.

GWEN. Just started as a hobby. It rather grew. We're not the biggest, not by any means. One branch that's all. We're not tied up to a building society either. The press is never good on estate agents but I like to think that I try. That I do care. Houses are about families aren't they? Will you stay the night?

JENNY *shrugs*.

It's just that beds need airing. That sort of thing.

JENNY. We might not like each other.

GWEN. I didn't mean it like that.

JENNY. But we mightn't.

GWEN. We can just talk. I'd like to hear about your life. You don't look as if things have gone badly for you.

JENNY. I suppose they haven't. Not if you treat them as a whole.

GWEN. I'm glad.

JENNY. This is all my own. I'm not married for it.

GWEN. You'd have a ring.

JENNY. And a diamond.

GWEN. Yes.

Pause.

JENNY *starts to move towards the house*.

JENNY. You've got a green house.

GWEN. Dick's domain not mine. He finally got aubergines to grow this year.

JENNY. Oh.

GWEN. You don't know for how long. They'd become an obsession.

There's always something he can't get to grow. Disaster with the celery this year. It was supposed to be self-blanche – it was celery you didn't like. I said the soup was onion and I made croutons.

JENNY. I was sick?

GWEN. Yes.

JENNY. News to me.

GWEN. There are probably a lot of things.

JENNY. Yes, there are some questions.

GWEN. Are you pregnant?

JENNY. How?

GWEN. There are some questions and you bite your nails instead of smoking.

JENNY. Yes.

GWEN. And not married?

JENNY. Not living with anybody either.

GWEN. So it's help?

JENNY *nods.*

I'd have thought abortions were easier to get in London. But here? Can you pay?

They look at each other.

Oh. I'm supposed to congratulate you?

JENNY. I think so.

GWEN. Jenny. How long?

JENNY. Only just. Six weeks.

GWEN. October, no September, October, November, December –

JENNY. May. Around the twelfth at a rough estimate.

GWEN. You're lucky. It's hell being pregnant in the summer. My own fault for putting on so much weight with you. Is it those sort of questions?

JENNY. Yes. I need to know if I've had German measles. My friend –

he had his daughter with him last weekend. Lottie had a
temperature and a rash and they called the doctor. There's an
epidemic at the moment.

GWEN. Your friend is married?

JENNY. Divorced. Not me. A long time before me. And we are
friends. We go to bed together. You'd probably call that lovers. We
aren't.

GWEN. You don't have to tell me about that side of things.

JENNY. I wanted to explain.

GWEN. And if you haven't had German measles?

JENNY. Then it'll have to be abortion. I need to know.

GWEN. And then you'll disappear again?

JENNY. Please mother.

GWEN. You have. And mumps and measles and chicken pox. All the
usual vaccinations.

JENNY. Thank you.

GWEN. You see I thought I was probably a grandmother by now. A
granny. In May.

JENNY. Probably. There are a lot of tests I have to have. I'm old for a
child. It's becoming a classic syndrome according to the doctor. A
woman who's worked and got somewhere and then panicked
because she's never used her womb. Wanting to see it's operational
before the guarantee runs out. It wasn't consciously like that. I've
never played Vatican Roulette. On the pill, I never missed a pill.
And I've never changed it even when I thought it was safe without a
diaphragm. It wasn't even anything special. Between the sheets
with the light off. Sleep afterwards and work in the morning. I
suppose there are a lot of beginnings like that.

GWEN. Does he know?

JENNY. Not yet. When I went to the doctor's this morning he was still
asleep. His arm was over the top of the duvet. He's got a ten year
old daughter and I thought he didn't look old enough to be a father.
He's younger than me. A couple of years that's all. You and Dick I
suppose.

GWEN. Five between us. But I never say it. In the beginning it was a joke. But as you get older. You will tell your friend?

JENNY. Eric. Of course. I haven't been sick yet. Were you sick?

GWEN. Not as much as some people. I put on weight and my ankles swole. That was the worst –

DICK (*off*). White or red?

JENNY. I'm not drinking.

GWEN. Not fussy.

DICK (*off*). One minute and counting.

GWEN. On our way.

JENNY. Will you tell him?

GWEN. Not if you don't want me to.

JENNY *goes towards the house;* GWEN *follows her.*

GWEN *stops to pick up the acorn she threw down before. She stands. The light goes out.*

Scene Two

The house; DICK *and* JENNY. JENNY *is looking at the contents of the room.* DICK *is doing a large tapestry.*

JENNY. Samba?

DICK. Yes. Already an old dog when that was taken.

JENNY. None of me?

DICK. No.

JENNY. Nowhere?

DICK. Not that I know of.

JENNY. Where's this?

DICK. The first house she sold.

JENNY. Oh. There used to be one of me as a baby in this frame.

DICK. I don't know what happened to them. There wasn't a great gesture of burning or tearing up. Nothing like that. One by one they just disappeared. You can't blame us. There have been a lot of tears. A lot of pain.

He sews.

JENNY. Forgiveness is rather overrated as a quality.

DICK. You don't have to like me even now.

JENNY. I know that.

DICK. What else could I have done? You promised to be home at eleven. You weren't. Are you surprised we were worried? Eleven o'clock you'd given your word. We didn't know what might have happened to you. It was nearly two. You could have telephoned. Asked if you could stay a little longer. If you'd asked us we would have come to some arrangement with you. I could have come and collected you.

JENNY. You didn't want me to go in the first place did you?

DICK. No we didn't.

JENNY. You didn't or she didn't?

DICK. Neither of us thought it was a very good idea.

JENNY. You were the one who came and got me. I've never been so embarrassed.

DICK. Because I cared?

JENNY. No one else's father stormed in and played the heavy.

DICK. I'm not your father.

JENNY. That made it worse.

DICK. Let's get this straight, I knocked at the door and asked for you and they let me in. There was no storming. You were the one who screamed and said that you weren't coming home. Do you know what it took me to walk into that party? Into the noise. A dark room filled with smoke and Beatles music. I was frightened. It wasn't my territory. I'd have left you to come home when you liked. But Gwen asked me to. A test. Bare feet on broken glass. The part of her that nothing else could convince.

JENNY. Don't!

DICK. Jenny —

She struggles with the photo frame.

JENNY. Some people put the new ones in on top of the old. Eric does that with Lottie's. All her school photos, one on top of the other.

This is not the case.

DICK. I had to encourage her to forget you. It would have torn us apart Jenny. I couldn't have faced that. I could have gone so you'd come back, but if you went once you could go again. Then where would she have been? We had friends who wanted to move from a big house to a smaller one. And another set who wanted to do the opposite. I encouraged Gwen to introduce them to each other and to run around with tape measures. A deal was done. They insisted on giving her something for her trouble. I think it was twenty pounds. With that she went out and ordered headed notepaper and foolscap envelopes. She stopped being your mother and went into business. I pushed her at first and now I can't stop her.

JENNY. You don't like her working?

DICK. I took early retirement so we could spend some time together. I still want her Jenny. I want her to look back when she goes out of the house in the morning.

He drops his needle. JENNY *returns it to him.*

Thank you.

JENNY. It's very beautiful. I'm hopeless at anything like that. I can't even knit.

DICK. Perhaps you'd like it when it's finished.

JENNY. Me?

DICK. I could send it to you. It would mean leaving your address.

JENNY. I'd like that. Thank you.

She watches DICK *sew. Enter* GWEN.

GWEN. I've taken the risk on two hot water bottles and the electric blanket. I know you shouldn't combine electricity and water but I've done the stoppers as tight as I could.

JENNY. Thank you.

GWEN. Cleo's scratching at the door to go out.

DICK. I forgot. She's a dog of very regular habits. How far did you take her this afternoon?

GWEN. Only to the stream and back. She ought to have a bit of a run.

DICK. Right. Into the night I go.

He whistles for the dog. The dog barks.

Walkies!

Exit DICK. *Mad barking from the dog.*

JENNY. Very much his dog.

GWEN. Yes. A drink?

JENNY. I'm not. The baby.

GWEN. Sorry. I forgot.

JENNY. If you want one.

GWEN. No. I just thought you might like one.

JENNY *yawns.*

Tired?

JENNY. I didn't sleep much. I knew it would be positive but until I saw the doctor.

GWEN. I know.

JENNY. I was trying to think things through. And the German measles. There was a moment when I wanted to ring you but it was the middle of the night.

GWEN. I wouldn't have minded.

JENNY. I thought you mightn't recognise my voice. That you'd think I was a hoax. Or that Dick would answer. I thought you wouldn't know me.

GWEN. It took me a second.

JENNY. The light was going.

GWEN. Yes. The bed won't take long to air. Your old bed in your old room.

JENNY. It doesn't look like my room any more. I was expecting everything to be the same. Wallpaper, furniture, my teddy and bunnies on the bed. Where did they go?

GWEN. Do you want them?

JENNY. The baby might like them.

GWEN. You want new things for a baby.

JENNY. Sometimes I wished I'd taken them. My teddy, at least.

GWEN. Where did you go that first night?

JENNY. I went.

GWEN. Where?

JENNY. Oxford.

GWEN. I'm sorry. I said to myself that if you came back I wouldn't ask any questions. I wouldn't pry. I'd be pleased to see you and it wouldn't matter. I've worried about you for twenty years. And not one phone call or postcard. As if I'd never been, Jenny. Those phone calls when no one spoke when I answered. Was any of those you?

JENNY. No.

GWEN. I once phoned someone just to hear his voice.

JENNY. No!

GWEN. We thought you'd gone to London.

JENNY. That's why I went to Oxford.

GWEN. Did you know we were looking for you?

JENNY. I knew you would. I changed my name for a while.

GWEN. Dick said you must have done. I thought you might go to your father.

JENNY. You'd have found me.

GWEN. You can imagine what it was like with him. The accusations of being a bad mother. What he said about Dick. He's dead. Did you know that?

JENNY. No.

GWEN. He got drunk one night and drove into a canal.

JENNY. I'm sorry.

GWEN. I couldn't tell you how many years ago. Six, seven. A sad man. I should have let him go in the first place after the war. Getting pregnant with you was a cheap trick to pull on him. I was desperate. I thought I'd die if he went back to the States. What time are you going in the morning?

JENNY. I'm not working. Whenever.

GWEN. I try to leave by eight-thirty. Gives me an hour to see to the post. I like to start the mornings with my desk clear. You don't have to go when I go. You could sleep in. Have breakfast in bed.

JENNY. I could see your office. We could have lunch.

GWEN. I never have lunch – no – that would be lovely. There's a Boots across the road. They do teddies and rattles and things.

JENNY. Not yet. Please not yet.

GWEN. No, of course. When you're sure you could let me know and I could send something.

JENNY. We could have a look tomorrow. I could choose what I wanted and then you'd know.

GWEN. Yes. You could stay the weekend if you wanted.

JENNY. There's someone I have to see.

GWEN. Eric?

JENNY. Yes. Usually he has his daughter but not this weekend.

GWEN. You could invite him down.

JENNY. He's always talking about weekends in the country. Rugged. Not my sort of thing at all.

GWEN. There'd be no problems. I wouldn't try and push you.

JENNY. Divorce must be a good money spinner for estate agents.

GWEN. Yes. Hard though sometimes. There was a couple I showed round a house when they were engaged. I sold it them as a love nest and no doubt he carried her over the doorstep.

Enter DICK.

He went back there one night after it was put on the market. Chopped up the floors with an axe. I know it's not professional but my heart bled. Have you locked?

DICK. Yes.

JENNY. It's very quiet here after London.

GWEN. Yes.

JENNY. I've got double glazing but the noise still comes in, and of course in the summer with the windows open – (*She yawns.*)

GWEN. You should go to bed.

JENNY. Um.

GWEN. I've put a towel on your bed and a nightie.

JENNY. Thank you.

DICK. Do you want to be woken in the morning?

JENNY *shakes her head.*

Anything special for breakfast?

JENNY. Just tea not coffee. I'm not that fussy.

GWEN. I may not see you in the morning.

JENNY. Lunch?

GWEN. Yes.

JENNY. I'll find you. Goodnight.

GWEN. Sleep well.

JENNY. Thank you for the supper.

DICK. Goodnight Jenny.

JENNY *goes.*

GWEN. She went to Oxford.

DICK. When?

GWEN. The first night.

DICK. It's one of the places we thought.

GWEN. Was it?

DICK. Where didn't we think?

GWEN. You didn't go there.

DICK. I couldn't look everywhere.

Pause.

I spent a week at Paddington watching every train. Every person who got off. Every dubious man that approached girls who were uncertain where to go. If you wanted Oxford scouring you could have done it from here.

GWEN. What if I'd been out and she'd come home?

DICK. She had her own keys.

GWEN. I wanted to be there.

Pause.

DICK. She asked if there were any photos left of her as a baby. I said I didn't know. Are there?

GWEN. Yes.

DICK. Oh.

GWEN. Did you think I'd thrown them away?

DICK. Yes.

GWEN. My own daughter?

DICK. I thought so.

GWEN. They're in the office. Photos, her baby teeth, cards she made me at school. Her teddy and the bunnies. She has a file. Locked. I didn't want to keep stumbling on them. Do you like her?

DICK. Difficult to say so quickly. You?

GWEN. I'm her mother. It needs time.

DICK. She might go as suddenly as she came Gwen.

GWEN. She's staying tomorrow. And perhaps the weekend. The longer she stays . . .

DICK. I have things to do tomorrow.

GWEN. She can look after herself. She's not a child.

DICK. Come to bed.

GWEN. I've got some work.

DICK. Please Gwen.

GWEN. She and I are having lunch tomorrow. I have to. Or I'll never catch myself up.

DICK. You'll kill yourself.

GWEN. There's a contract I must push through tomorrow. Go to bed. I won't be long.

DICK. Wake me.

GWEN. Perhaps.

Pause.

Go to bed.

She kisses him.

Go.

DICK *goes.*

GWEN *finds the acorn in her pocket. She looks for something to grow the acorn in.*

GWEN *tries to suspend the acorn above water.*

She unthreads three needles from the tapestry.

She stabs them in the acorn so it will balance over the water.

Enter JENNY wearing GWEN's nightdress.

JENNY. You are sure about the German measles?

GWEN. Certain.

JENNY *goes*.

Scene Three

The wood.

    Enter ERIC.

ERIC. Lottie would love it here.

    He stamps on chestnuts to get them from their cases.

    These are empty as well. The woods are dying out. Any luck?

JENNY (*off*). None.

ERIC. I promised Lottie we'd roast chestnuts together when I got back.

JENNY (*off*). Buy some.

ERIC. Not the same.

JENNY (*off*). She'll never know.

    He hides.

ERIC. Chestnuts from the woods Jen. It was a promise.

    Enter JENNY.

JENNY. Eric! Look don't. Please don't. With Lottie. Not me. I hate it. Eric?

    He jumps on her.

    Don't.

ERIC. Jen?

JENNY. You nearly scared the bloody life out of me.

ERIC. Nature red in tooth and claw.

JENNY. Don't!

ERIC. Sorry.

JENNY. They can see from the house.

ERIC. No one to see. Your mother's working, your father's shopping.

JENNY. I don't –

ERIC. Should I change my toothpaste or something?

JENNY. My mother's house.

ERIC. What do they think goes on between us?

JENNY. Not them. Me.

ERIC. Why?

JENNY. It doesn't feel – I can't. Could you at your parents?

ERIC. Depend on you, wouldn't it?

JENNY. Have you?

ERIC. With Linda of course. Let's not discuss Linda.

JENNY. Sorry.

ERIC. If we'd spent the weekend in London?

JENNY. Yes probably. A bottle of wine and we usually do.

ERIC. But you're not drinking at the moment.

JENNY. No.

ERIC. If you want me to go I'll go. I'll spend the weekend at Linda's playing snakes and ladders with Lottie.

JENNY. Don't go.

ERIC. What's happened?

JENNY. Nothing.

ERIC. There has to be something Jenny. You come back here after how long? Demand I come too, then you treat me like a stranger.

JENNY. It's not to do with you.

ERIC. You were up and out like someone had shouted fire on Thursday morning. You didn't even say goodbye.

JENNY. I tried not to wake you.

ERIC. That's not what I'm complaining about.

He stamps on chestnuts.

He discovers a ball and throws it to JENNY.

Catch.

She does.

JENNY. It must be Cleo's.

ERIC. Surely you should throw a dog sticks in a wood.

JENNY *throws the ball back.*

You don't think I could keep it. Something to take back for Lottie?

JENNY. I won't say anything.

He throws the ball back to her.

ERIC. This time last year Lottie couldn't catch. This year she can. Linda's taught her I suppose.

JENNY. I've caught.

ERIC. What?

JENNY. Caught. It's the expression the little girls that come down from the North use. Pregnant.

ERIC. Fuck.

JENNY. Exactly.

ERIC. You can't be.

JENNY. But I am.

Pause.

ERIC. I'll pay for the abortion of course.

JENNY. I don't want you to.

ERIC. We'll go Dutch then.

JENNY. I don't want any money.

ERIC. You might let me play some part.

JENNY. You'll be a father.

ERIC. What?

JENNY. Its father. Is that so very difficult to understand?

ERIC. You're having it?

JENNY. Is that so very unusual?

ERIC. But when we talked about – accidents.

JENNY. We were talking.

ERIC. It is an accident?

JENNY. My mother had me to keep my father. You think I'd make the same mistake?

ERIC. You don't have to make a mistake. You know that.

JENNY. I didn't think that offer was open at the moment.

ERIC. It's always open.

JENNY. Sometimes more than others though?

ERIC. It's open. I've said I'll marry you. I won't unsay it because of this. Only this time you ask.

JENNY. I'm not asking.

ERIC. You never will.

JENNY. No, probably not.

ERIC. But us? Your job? Everything, your age. You're nearly forty.

JENNY. Thirty-eight. That's why.

ERIC. A baby's hard work Jen. I've done it.

JENNY. I haven't.

ERIC. You haven't been to the moon.

JENNY. I haven't had the chance.

ERIC. It's not that I don't want you to have it.

JENNY. It's mine. In me. There. Mine.

ERIC. How long?

JENNY. About six weeks.

ERIC. This big Jen.

JENNY. Yes.

ERIC. Jenny it's nappies, broken nights, total responsibility.

JENNY. So.

ERIC. Nothing will be the same again. Never.

JENNY. It's hardly how I'd planned the rest of my life. It used to be that when I was a day late I assumed I was pregnant. This time I assumed it was the menopause come early. It's not. I am. The proper tests. The scrubbed out jar and urine sample at dawn. I have conceived.

ERIC. An egg and a sperm Jen. Hardly a miracle.

JENNY. Better news than chestnuts.

 Pause.

ERIC. Better news than the chestnuts. I can't wait to tell Lottie.

JENNY. Not yet.

ERIC. But you're certain.

JENNY. Not that there'll be a child at the end of it.

ERIC. That's what Linda – what every woman thinks when she first gets pregnant.

JENNY. Lottie's got Rubella. Spotty Lottie. The list of what it can do to a foetus is pretty impressive, blind it, deafen it, maim it –

ERIC. Not Lottie's fault.

JENNY. I know.

ERIC. A child of ten to have that hung round her neck –

JENNY. A virus, not Lottie.

ERIC. Don't blame her.

JENNY. No –

ERIC. Any of those things she'd blame herself.

JENNY. What about me?

ERIC. You're a grown-up. You understand.

JENNY. That there are risks. Yes, yes I do. I got a full list of them on Thursday morning. No congratulations. No smiles and handshakes. When the doctor looked at her notes she was positively apologetic. The suit and the briefcase. I suppose I hardly looked the maternal role. She started on the fact that I was more likely to have twins and ended on the increased risks of mongolism. She asked me if I'd had German measles and I said I didn't know, but that I'd seen Lottie and she had it. The doctor told me to ask my mother.

ERIC. There had to be some reason –

JENNY. I don't like sleepless nights.

ERIC. You haven't started yet.

JENNY. My mother put me out of my misery. The list of my childhood ailments is quite comprehensive. It includes Rubella. I'm in the clear.

ERIC. For certain?

JENNY. So far so good. More snakes than ladders at my age. I'll have to have an amniocentesis. That shows up mongolism and spina bifida and a host of other disasters and the baby's sex. But not until the sixteenth week. After that it's decision time. If I don't get rid of the child I have to get rid of the flat. My stairs would be impossible with a pram.

ERIC. Live with me.

JENNY. I don't love you.

ERIC. You don't have to.

JENNY. I do.

ERIC. Then how can I be its father?

JENNY. You'll always be welcome.

ERIC. I already have a child for weekends.

JENNY. It doesn't have to be weekends.

ERIC. Two nights a week like playing squash? Like Lottie? Never seeing her learn, just the results of what Linda taught her. I can't bear that again Jenny. I'd rather go now and know nothing more.

JENNY. Eric!

ERIC. I'd rather go now Jen.

Pause.

Please.

JENNY. I don't know.

ERIC. I'd rather be sent away Jen.

Pause.

JENNY. I need you.

ERIC. What for?

JENNY. I do.

When ERIC *turns to walk away he meets* DICK.

DICK. Great thing about the autumn, makes it difficult for people to get lost here. I could see you from the bathroom. Not much luck?

ERIC. No.

DICK. A bit late perhaps.

JENNY. I don't think so. The cases are still green.

DICK. They're all about this size. Not worth the effort.

JENNY. The way you stamp on them anything decent would be smashed.

ERIC. I haven't got gloves.

DICK. Shouldn't need to get your fingers pricked. They should burst of their own accord once they're ripe. Still better luck next year. You'll have to come down again. I usually pop down to the local for lunch. I thought you might care to come. I'm a cider man myself but there's a lot of praise for the beer.

ERIC. Jenny?

JENNY. It sounds nice.

DICK. Their steak and kidney pudding is certainly to be recommended over mine.

ERIC. I'll take these off. Put some proper shoes on.

DICK. Probably be as well.

JENNY. Can you get my purse?

ERIC. Whole bag?

JENNY. Just my money.

DICK. My treat.

JENNY. A working woman Dick. I pay my own way.

DICK. We'll see. The door's on the latch. Just pull it behind you.

He goes.

I like him.

JENNY. Thank you.

DICK. The outdoor type?

JENNY. Yes.

DICK. A walker?

JENNY. When he has the time.

DICK. You're not.

JENNY. Never have been.

DICK. Your mother neither. A stroll through the woods at the end of the day, that's all. Perhaps he might care to come with me tomorrow. Weather permitting. Take Cleo up to the downs, give her her head off the lead.

JENNY. He'd probably like that.

DICK. Be nice for me. A companion. You wouldn't mind?

JENNY. As long as I don't have to go.

DICK. You should come with us. A lot of people enjoy it once they get going. Put roses in your cheeks.

JENNY. Am I pale?

DICK. Well – you had such good colour.

JENNY. Used to. Did Gwen tell you I was pregnant?

DICK. Should she have done?

JENNY. I am.

DICK. Really?

JENNY. Yes.

DICK. Congratulations.

JENNY. Only just –

DICK. But still. (*He moves towards her*.) You must be delighted.
    Congratulations!

JENNY. You know there's not going to be a wedding?

DICK. Hardly matters nowadays does it? You must be thrilled?

JENNY. Sort of. Yes.

DICK. A grandchild. Gwen's grandchild.

JENNY. And you.

DICK. Not my own flesh and blood.

JENNY. Dick –

DICK. Eric's baby?

JENNY. Yes.

DICK. He's got a daughter by his first wife already hasn't he?

JENNY. Her mother has custody.

DICK. Best thing. Mothers are the ones who are good at all that sort of
    thing. I can do food and washing but nappies and bottles would
    have foxed me. Gwenny!

    Enter GWEN.

GWEN. Hello!

DICK. To what do we owe this?

GWEN. We have guests. I wondered where you all were. The house all
    unlocked. Eric says you're off to the pub.

DICK. What about the office?

GWEN. The girls would have to cope if I was ill. Have you had a good morning Jenny?

JENNY. Thank you.

DICK. They had breakfast and washed it all up.

GWEN. Good.

ERIC *enters. He gives* JENNY *her purse.*

JENNY. Thank you.

DICK. All on me. Seeing it's a celebration. I believe you're to be congratulated?

ERIC. Oh – er – Jen not me.

JENNY. Eric.

DICK. Both of you.

ERIC. Thanks. The door's locked. You have got keys.

DICK. I have mine.

DICK *starts to lead* ERIC *across the stage.*

I was thinking of going up on the Downs tomorrow. Ten miles or so. Jenny says you might care to come.

They are out of earshot.

GWEN. Now we all know.

JENNY. Yes, you didn't tell him.

GWEN. You asked me not to. A secret between us. Pillow talk's not all it's cracked up to be.

JENNY. No.

GWEN. I like Eric. I thought he'd be – one doesn't really think of the private lives of accountants. He's nice.

JENNY. Mother.

GWEN. That's all. Honestly Jenny. I've never imagined I'd see you radiant in white.

JENNY. Once upon a time?

GWEN. That's what everyone expected. White, flowers, churches, true love.

JENNY. Babies?

GWEN. Of course. I'm glad you've stayed.

DICK (*off*). Come on.

GWEN. We don't usually have lunch together on Saturdays. The day most people look at houses. A deciding day. No buying and selling. You can't get anything moving, banks, building societies, anything like that.

JENNY. I moved in on a Saturday.

GWEN. All the finances will have gone through on the Friday at the latest.

JENNY. It's funny to hear you being a business woman.

GWEN. Is it?

JENNY. Of course.

GWEN. I'm sorry.

JENNY. Your work.

GWEN. More like life sometimes.

   DICK *comes back*.

   Yes, yes we're coming. I'll just shut the gate!

ERIC. It'll be closing time.

JENNY. Rounding us up?

DICK. It gets very full. We won't get a table for four.

ERIC. Race you Jenny. First one there buys the drinks!

JENNY. A game we play with his daughter. He always likes to win. He buys us ice creams.

ERIC. Come on.

   JENNY *runs*.

DICK. Should she run like that?

GWEN. Now you know why she's come back.

DICK. Yes.

GWEN. Another thing we were wrong about.

DICK. Nicer than a grandchild suddenly turning up fully grown. A baby.

GWEN. I'm not keen on small babies.

DICK. Jenny.

GWEN. Not even Jenny. Not at the very beginning. Moments of course when my heart melted. Times when she was quite defenceless. But other moments when I loathed her. I had a black angora cardigan. Very precious after the war. She was sick on it. Ruined it.

DICK. A silly thing to wear with a little baby.

GWEN. She was pretty and cooed over. I wanted to feel special. I never dared afford another.

DICK. You could now.

GWEN. They have to go to the dry cleaners.

DICK. We can afford dry cleaners.

GWEN. Not if I went bankrupt tomorrow.

DICK. Are you likely to?

GWEN. Of course not. But I couldn't bear to have one and not afford to have it cleaned. Jenny has all that to find out.

They stop.

I held a pillow over her face once. Not very hard, not very tight – not even very long. She wouldn't even have whimpered.

DICK. Why didn't you?

GWEN. I didn't.

DICK. What stopped you?

GWEN. The effort I'd put in. You want to hang on.

Pause.

We're not taking Cleo?

DICK. She'd only have to stay outside.

GWEN. Seems mean to leave her on her own.

They go.

Scene Four

The wood.

After lunch. ERIC and JENNY. ERIC has bought a pound of chestnuts for Lottie.

ERIC. Far too many. You don't mind if I go with him tomorrow?

JENNY. Rather you than me that's all.

ERIC. I like him.

JENNY. I meant the walking.

ERIC. He's hardly your description of him.

JENNY. People change. He's mellowed. And my mother?

ERIC. Mothers are mothers.

He looks in the bag.

Far too many.

JENNY. Half of them are probably bad.

ERIC. Do you think so?

JENNY. The risk you take.

They have crossed the stage.

Scene Five

The house.

ERIC *and* DICK *are making a swiss roll for* GWEN's *birthday.*

JENNY *is cracking eggs into a bowl.*

DICK is lining a swiss roll tin with greaseproof paper.

JENNY. Oh God.

ERIC. It doesn't mean it's fertilized.

JENNY. It turns my stomach.

DICK. Why don't you go next door? The fire's lit.

JENNY. I think I might.

She stops.

You have remembered to put the oven on?

ERIC. Yes.

She goes.

DICK. Gwen always says that. Is the oven on? The obvious thing to do is to put that at the beginning of the recipe but they never do.

ERIC. I whisk this lot together over hot water?

DICK consults the recipe.

DICK. Yes.

ERIC does so.

And four ounces of plain flour.

DICK weighs it.

Ought to be sieved I suppose. Don't want any disasters.

ERIC. There aren't going to be any.

DICK (*sifting flour*). I can't see how it's going to rise without baking powder or something.

ERIC. The eggs.

Enter JENNY.

JENNY. Bowl.

She takes the washing up bowl.

Thank you.

She goes.

ERIC. Poor Jen.

DICK. The doctor recommended Gwen had champagne. I pointed out we couldn't afford it, he said lemonade would do just as well.

ERIC (*mixing on the cooker*). Sorry?

DICK. For morning sickness. He told Gwen to have champagne. Didn't realise it went on for so long, I suppose, because she lost the baby.

ERIC. I'm sorry.

DICK. Yes.

ERIC. Your baby?

DICK. Yes. Mine –

ERIC. Sorry.

DICK. Long time ago –

   Pause.

ERIC. Next?

DICK. Remove from heat. Fold in flour and water with metal spoon.

ERIC. Metal spoon?

DICK. In the drawer.

   ERIC *finds it.*

   Careful, you'll burn it.

   ERIC *takes the pan off the heat.*

ERIC. Sorry.

   ERIC *begins to stir in the flour.*

DICK. Touch and go from the first. I never thought Gwen's heart was really in it. She had this notion. She ought to give me a child. She had Jenny. And Jenny was almost grown-up. Shaped before I met her. Spoilt. What she wanted she got. Gwen stinted herself to give Jenny things. Still you can see why it happened, just her and Gwen together.

ERIC. I sometimes think Linda's too strict with Lottie. A lot of mustn'ts, not allowed. You will make sure she cleans her teeth whenever she's eaten.

ERIC *tastes.* DICK *looks at him.*

Cook's prerogative.

DICK. I did want a child. I never pressed her but she felt she owed it me. When Jenny went, her womb let go –

ERIC *has begun to scrape the mixture into the tin.*

Bleeding and bleeding and bleeding. Everything in it. No torrent just an oozing, like the sap from a tree. Day after day. A slipping away. In clots. It could have been any of them. She said there was no pain, nothing, that it was Jenny she was crying for. Soak the sheets she said. First cold water and then boiling. I buried them in the wood, it might at least have done some good. I didn't want to see the froth on the top of the pan like boiling bones. They scraped Gwen out, though what there was to scrape. No question of children after that.

He picks up the tin.

In?

ERIC. Might as well.

DICK *puts the cake in the oven.*

DICK. How long?

ERIC. Seven to nine minutes.

DICK *sets the timer.*

Want to scrape?

DICK. Seems a shame to waste it.

ERIC. Yes.

They sit down to scrape the bowl.

This is the bit Lottie likes best.

DICK. My mother always used to leave some on the spoon. Not very much but she never pushed it off with her finger. My treat.

ERIC. Lottie's treat too. With me.

DICK. Must be nice watching her grow up.

ERIC. Yes.

DICK. You should bring her down. Fresh air. The woods to run in.

ERIC. Lottie'd love that.

DICK. Bring her.

ERIC. Perhaps.

DICK. Better wash all this up before Gwen gets back.

ERIC. What about candles?

DICK. Too old for candles.

ERIC. Special birthday. She ought to have them.

DICK. You can't put candles on a swiss roll.

ERIC. You've got some?

DICK. For power cuts. In the drawer. Gwen doesn't like the dark.

ERIC *gets out the candles.*

Not birthday candles.

ERIC. Better than nothing.

DICK. She'll think we're making a fuss of her.

ERIC. Aren't we? Lottie's like the queen. She has two birthdays, one with me and one with her mother. Cake and candles at each.

DICK. Never made Gwen a cake before. We usually go out for dinner.

ERIC. No point going out for dinner with Jenny in her condition.

DICK. No.

ERIC. A notch for every decade.

Enter JENNY.

JENNY. All over?

ERIC. Yes. A notch for every decade. Ten, twenty, thirty, forty, fifty, sixty. Is she going to retire?

DICK. She says she won't. No one to take over.

ERIC. She could sell.

DICK. Not yet she says.

JENNY. She'll have to eventually.

DICK. Try telling her that.

JENNY. She might as well do it while she can still spend the money.

DICK. My point entirely.

ERIC. She ought to get a partner. Someone who could take over from her gradually.

JENNY. The ideal sort of job to do part-time I'd have thought. You have set the timer?

ERIC. Yes.

JENNY. Sometimes people forget.

DICK. Don't worry. There we are, all ship-shape. Gwen'll have no idea of what we've been cooking up. I think I'll just take Cleo down to the stream. You coming?

JENNY. Go if you want. I can be left.

ERIC. I'll look after the cake.

DICK. Right.

DICK goes.

ERIC. You okay?

JENNY. It was just that egg. Silly really. Was Linda like this?

ERIC. Not as bad as you've been.

JENNY. Do you think I'm making a fuss?

ERIC. My experience is limited.

JENNY. Mother said she was sick but an easy labour. I seem to be on course for a pretty similar experience to hers.

ERIC. You know she had a miscarriage?

JENNY. Linda?

ERIC. Gwen.

JENNY. No.

ERIC. She did Jenny.

JENNY. I don't want to hear.

Pause.

They say you have contractions when you miscarry. Do you think that's true?

ERIC. I don't know.

JENNY. When?

ERIC. When you left. You didn't know?

JENNY. I had no idea. It's my fault I suppose?

ERIC. Dick didn't say that.

JENNY. Is that what they think? There could have been a hundred reasons. She must have been older than me, there could have been all sorts of things wrong. Better that than a – don't you think?

ERIC. She didn't tell you?

JENNY. I didn't ask. She knew I was pregnant. She stood there and she looked at me and she knew I was. She could tell . . . Twenty years.

ERIC. Intuition. Linda had that about Lottie. When Lottie was a baby she could tell what the cries meant. If it was nappy or food or colic.

JENNY. Do you think I will?

ERIC. Depends doesn't it.

JENNY. It could all be so perfect. But it won't be will it? When they put that needle in through my navel.

ERIC. It could be Jenny.

JENNY. Don't say it. You know how things go wrong if you say them. Did Dick tell you?

ERIC. Yes.

JENNY. You get on very well with them.

ERIC. Nice people.

JENNY. Really?

ERIC. Really.

JENNY. I find it hard to tell. Whether they're being nice to me or whether they aren't.

ERIC. Twenty years. You can't expect it to sort itself out in a few visits. Not even friends in that time.

JENNY. They're parents, not friends.

ERIC. It's a lovely place to live.

JENNY. Could you live here. In the country I mean?

ERIC. Love to if it wasn't for work and Lottie.

JENNY. It's a lovely place for children. I used to play such games in the woods. And so safe. It's safe here. You could have a child here and not be worried about it every minute.

ERIC. Trees to fall from. Streams to drown in.

JENNY. It's a different sort of danger.

ERIC. You thinking of moving here?

JENNY. Not for myself but for the baby.

ERIC. Don't talk about it you said.

JENNY. It's very hard to have no plans at all. No thought. I can't have it inside me and not in my head.

ERIC. It's a dream, Jenny. What would you do here? What is there?

JENNY. But if I was here with a baby would you come?

ERIC. On what conditions?

JENNY. Like we are now. You could commute from Didcot.

ERIC. I'm not the commuting sort. Neither are you a housewife. And anyway Lottie's in London.

JENNY. Do you have to be where Lottie is?

ERIC. What do you want?

JENNY. I don't believe in happy endings.

The buzzer on the oven goes.

ERIC. Could you put a damp tea towel under there please.

She does so. ERIC *turns the swiss roll out.*

JENNY. Perfect.

ERIC. It isn't rolled yet.

Scene Six

The wood.

Christmas Eve. Enter JENNY *in nightdress.*

JENNY. Child? Child? Can you hear me? Your mother. Me. Are you there? Child? Please. Move. Quicken. Just once. Something. It's Christmas. Do you know that? Christmas Eve. After midnight so Christmas really. Do you know when it's light or night? Can you tell when I'm asleep? If I'm happy? Or I'm sad? Do you know? Anything. Please. Your mother. Child.

She waits.

Enter ERIC.

Who's there?

ERIC. Father Christmas.

JENNY. Have you got your reindeer?

ERIC. Having a rest.

JENNY. Oh.

ERIC. Have you hung your stockings up, little girl?

JENNY. I'm too old for stockings.

ERIC. You could still make an old man very happy.

Pause.

Come in. You'll get cold.

JENNY. Can't sleep.

ERIC. Not likely to sleep much out here.

JENNY. I'm so frightened.

He holds her.

ERIC. Don't be.

JENNY. I am.

They stand in the wood.

They are caught in a car headlight.

They hide their eyes.

The light goes.

They're back from church.

ERIC. Yes.

JENNY. Happy Christmas.

ERIC. Happy Christmas.

JENNY. I wonder what tomorrow will be like? What the rituals are?

ERIC. The same as when you left presumably.

JENNY. Think so?

ERIC. Christmases tend to be.

JENNY. Like being a child again.

ERIC. I wonder what Lottie's doing.

JENNY. Be asleep by now.

ERIC. Yes.

JENNY. She have a stocking?

ERIC. Pillowcases. In Linda's family they have pillowcases.

JENNY. Oh.

ERIC. And beef for Christmas dinner. My turn for Lottie next year.

JENNY. What will you do?

ERIC. Depends on Lottie.

JENNY. And me?

ERIC. Goes without saying.

JENNY. Do you think it knew when the needle went in?

ERIC. They're supposed to be able to hear music. Some people play them Mozart.

JENNY. If there's any blood I have to ring the hospital immediately. One of the things the amniocentesis can do. There are risks and risks and risks. It would be easier not to have the chance in the first place.

ERIC. There won't be any bleeding. It'll be okay. The results will all be positive. All systems go.

JENNY. No.

ERIC. Come in.

JENNY. I can't sleep.

ERIC. Tell you a story. Lottie's favourite. Once upon a time there was a king's daughter who lived in a palace on the top of a hill. And because she was a king's daughter she was a princess. One day the princess said to the king I want to find a handsome prince to marry –

He has walked her offstage.

Enter GWEN.

She whistles for Cleo.

She sings to herself.

GWEN. The angel Gabriel from heaven came
His wings as drifted snow
His eyes as flame
All hail said he
Thou lowly maiden Mary
Most highly favoured lady
Gloria.

She has gone.

ACT TWO

Scene One

GWEN's *office.*

GWEN *is working. Enter* JENNY.

GWEN. Hello.

JENNY. I saw her. All her bones like a feather. Like a fossil in a rock. I had to come down and tell you.

GWEN. And everything's all right?

JENNY. Perfect. Her heart beats.

GWEN. I'm glad.

JENNY. A little girl. They asked if I wanted to know that. I wanted to know everything. She's even got a name. I had thought Anna but suddenly Jessica just came into my head. A name I'd never thought of before. Jessica.

GWEN. I thought of calling you Anna. Ann. After your grandmother. But your father thought differently. He registered your birth. Made you a Jennifer. Shouldn't you ask Eric?

JENNY. My daughter. Jessica.

GWEN. How can you name a child before it's born?

JENNY. I've seen her. My baby, Jessica.

GWEN *goes to the filing cabinet. She unlocks it. From a drawer she takes* JENNY's *teddy etc.*

GWEN. I didn't want to keep stumbling across them. I didn't want Dick to know how I longed.

There is a long moment. JENNY *picks up the teddy.*

Twenty years. Twenty Christmases and twenty birthdays. Not one letter. Not one phone call. Not one postcard. You might at least have bestowed hate on me. You might have had the grace to hurt me face to face.

JENNY. It wasn't you. It was Dick.

GWEN. Then me through Dick. We could have sorted something out. We could have talked about it.

JENNY. You wouldn't have talked.

GWEN. But to run away. I told myself an hour, a day, a week, a month, a year. Then she'll be back. When we were burgled I didn't let Dick change the lock. Because you had a key.

JENNY. I threw it in the river at Oxford. The day I changed my name.

Pause.

GWEN. What did you call yourself?

JENNY. Katherine.

GWEN. Katherine.

JENNY. Katherine. With a K.

GWEN. Why?

JENNY. It could be Kate, Kath, Kathy, any number of things.

GWEN. Which did you prefer?

JENNY. There are still people who call me Kate.

GWEN. From a long time ago?

JENNY. Quite a long time. There was someone who called me Kitty. I liked that.

GWEN. Someone you were fond of?

JENNY. More than that.

GWEN. It didn't work?

JENNY. He went away. His job. It was important for him.

GWEN. He didn't ask you to go with him?

JENNY. He asked.

GWEN. You should have gone.

JENNY. I'd just bought my own flat. How could I? What would I have done on my own abroad if anything went wrong? He never wrote. Different to Eric. A million miles apart.

GWEN. Don't go. Not completely. Not again. I couldn't bear it.

JENNY. The thing I won't be able to do with a child is travel. I know there'll be other satisfactions of course. But that's been the joy of the job I do. Being able to come and go.

GWEN. You can't come and go in this job. I don't even take holidays.

JENNY. Wouldn't you like to? You and Dick? Go somewhere nice together? Somewhere warm?

GWEN. I don't want to come and go.

JENNY. Not at all?

GWEN. No, I have no feelings of discontent. Oh, that a deal would happen faster, that a structural survey was better. Not for myself.

JENNY. But you should do.

GWEN. Why?

JENNY. Do you have no ambition?

GWEN. Is that so very hard to understand?

JENNY. Yes.

GWEN. For years what I wanted was for you to come back. You've come . . . There's nothing now.

JENNY. Jessica?

Pause.

She's real now mother. A real child.

She looks at the teddy.

Was he always like this – his nose squashed?

GWEN. You loved him too much.

JENNY. Heaven knows why. Revolting old thing. Fancy saving him all this time.

She throws the teddy away.

You were right. You want new things for a baby. The very best of everything.

Enter DICK.

DICK. Well?

JENNY. Perfect.

DICK. We have lift off?

JENNY. Yes. A little girl.

GWEN *rescues the teddy.*

DICK. A girl.

JENNY. She's even got a name.

DICK. What a perfect start to the New Year.

JENNY. I saw her. Like a fossil in a rock. All her bones like a feather.

GWEN. Her name's Jessica.

DICK *sees the teddy in* GWEN's *arm.*

Pause.

Have you taken Cleo out today?

DICK. I'll give her a proper run tomorrow. They're predicting a thaw.

GWEN. She should go out today.

DICK. She gets balls of ice in her fur. The floor will have to be mopped.

GWEN. I'll do it when I get back.

DICK. Eric must be pleased.

JENNY. I expect so. He'll be able to tell Lottie.

DICK. She'll be thrilled. A little sister.

JENNY. Yes.

DICK. We'll have to see about cots and things for when you come and stay.

GWEN. She'll have one of those carry cot ones. Won't you? That you can bring with you.

JENNY. I hadn't thought.

DICK. I'll cook something special. A celebration. Do you think you should get Eric to come down?

JENNY. He'd only have to go straight back and the roads are lethal. Especially in the dark.

GWEN. There are some duck portions in the freezer that need eating. If you take them out as soon as you get back they'll thaw for tonight.

DICK. Good.

Pause.

I should get back then. I'll see you both later.

JENNY. If I want to come back earlier will you be in?

DICK. If I've not taken Cleo out. We ought to give you keys. Then you can come and go as you please.

GWEN. She can always borrow mine.

JENNY. Be nice to have my own.

DICK. I'll get you one cut on my way home.

JENNY. You're an angel. Thanks.

DICK. It's a pleasure. And I'm delighted for you.

Exit DICK.

JENNY. I've bought some fabric. I thought you could make her dresses like you made me.

JENNY *gets the fabric out.*

GWEN *fingers it. It is sensual for her.*

GWEN. Tana lawn. You had gingham.

JENNY. And this pattern.

GWEN. I can afford to buy things for my grandchild.

JENNY. Not the same thing.

GWEN. By the time you've cut out, pinned, tacked and sewn. Time is money.

JENNY. You could teach me.

GWEN. If I had time —

JENNY. If I helped you out here whenever I could. You could show me what to do. I'm used to buying and selling. Striking a hard bargain.

GWEN. Help me here?

JENNY. I'm a much better typist than you.

GWEN. You have a job.

JENNY. They have to give me maternity leave. I'll hate sitting around with time on my hands.

GWEN. You don't have time on your hands with a baby.

JENNY. When they're asleep. If I have a carry cot I'll be able to bring her with me. I could get on with things and still be there whenever she needed me. And you'll help won't you Mother? Your grand-daughter.

GWEN. You should ring Eric. Tell him the good news.

JENNY. I wanted you to know first.

GWEN. The phone's there.

JENNY. I'll wait.

GWEN. I can go outside. You can be private.

JENNY. It can wait.

GWEN. Doesn't being certain make a difference?

JENNY. Why should it?

GWEN. A child'll be hard on your own Jenny. Hard.

Pause.

And lonely. So lonely you wouldn't believe it.

JENNY. I don't love him.

GWEN. You're fond of each other.

JENNY. Fond!

GWEN. I married Dick because I was fond of him. It wasn't anything like it was with your father.

JENNY. Not at the beginning though. Not in the very beginning?

GWEN. You were an onlooker.

JENNY. You were obsessed by him.

GWEN. Never.

JENNY. You were.

GWEN. Never Jenny.

JENNY. Cuddles, giggles, pulling your skirt down on the sofa.

GWEN. No.

JENNY. Dick this, Dick that. Always. He likes eggs for his breakfast. We must all have eggs.

GWEN. Cooking one breakfast instead of three.

JENNY. But his choice.

GWEN. He was paying the grocery bills.

JENNY. You married him for that?

GWEN. No.

JENNY. Then what?

GWEN. I was on my own.

JENNY. You had me.

GWEN. I was lonely. I don't mean to sound harsh but you were hardly a companion. He wanted me. You no longer had any need of me. Not really Jenny. Not a need. I'd passed on everything I could.

JENNY. I need you now.

GWEN. You have Eric.

JENNY. Fond was the word.

GWEN. There's no room for great passion with a baby, Jenny. You don't have the energy. The nights are broken.

JENNY. I'll have Jessica.

GWEN. She won't be able to hold you when you feel like weeping.

JENNY. Then I won't weep.

GWEN. Can you be that strong?

JENNY. If I set my mind to it.

Pause.

GWEN. You frighten me.

JENNY. My own mother.

GWEN. Yes.

JENNY. Why don't you have a look at the pattern while I finish this.

Scene Two

Winter.

   Early morning in the wood.

   ERIC *crosses the stage. He is going back to London.*

JENNY (*off*). Eric. Darling.

   He stops. Enter JENNY *for the first time very visibly pregnant.*

   Please. I feel so ugly. I'm supposed to be radiant and I feel so ugly.

ERIC. I have to go.

JENNY. Ring.

ERIC. No.

JENNY. Am I so very hideous?

ERIC. No.

JENNY. Then stay.

ERIC. I promised Lottie.

JENNY. Can't Linda take her?

ERIC. Linda can't swim.

JENNY. Why not?

ERIC. She never learnt. I have to take Lottie.

JENNY. I could ring her. Lottie would understand.

ERIC. Jenny, Lottie doesn't understand. That is why I have to go.

JENNY. I feel so ugly.

ERIC. I'm sorry.

Pause.

I can't not go. I gave my word.

JENNY. Please.

ERIC. You sound like Lottie.

JENNY. Please.

ERIC. No.

JENNY. Just today.

ERIC. Today is the day we go swimming together. Lottie and me. Then we have a hamburger and she has a strawberry milkshake. Then we go to a film or the zoo or something fun. And she has an ice cream. Strawberry. And we do her homework and she stays the night with me.

JENNY. You could explain.

ERIC. I can't.

JENNY. It's very simple.

ERIC. She doesn't understand.

JENNY. She has sex education.

ERIC. The human biology of it. Yes. Match A to B and do C. She feels she's being left out. That I won't have enough time for her. That it'll be you and me and a baby —

JENNY. Jessica.

ERIC. She isn't born.

JENNY. She will be.

ERIC. That it'll be you and me and whatever you want to call it — her. And that Lottie will be left out.

JENNY. She won't be left out.

ERIC. She feels she will.

JENNY. That's ridiculous.

ERIC. Is it?

JENNY. Lottie's half-sister.

ERIC. Jenny I feel left out. And if I feel left out where does that leave her?

JENNY. I'm asking you to stay.

ERIC. Why?

JENNY. You know why.

ERIC. *Why?*

JENNY. I want you to make love to me.

ERIC. A fuck because you feel so ugly.

JENNY. Yes. I want you.

   Pause.

   I need you.

ERIC. It's not that I don't want you. I love you. I have to go.

   Pause.

   I love Lottie you see.

JENNY. You love her most?

ERIC. My daughter.

JENNY. Your daughter here.

ERIC. I can't understand that.

JENNY. Didn't you with Lottie?

ERIC. Not till I saw her born. No. I used to lie with my head on Linda's belly and feel her kicking. Like a kitten in a sack.

GWEN *whistles for Cleo offstage.*

Gwen's up.

JENNY. Even I'm getting used to getting up early when I'm here.

ERIC. Morning.

Enter GWEN.

GWEN. Did you let Cleo out?

JENNY. Oh God, I left the door. I'm sorry.

GWEN. Why don't you think sometimes.

JENNY. I'm sorry.

GWEN. You have a key. You can let yourself out, you can let yourself in.

JENNY. I'm sorry.

ERIC. She won't have gone far will she?

GWEN. How should I know?

Enter DICK.

Cleo's done a bolt.

JENNY. I'm sorry.

GWEN. It's so irresponsible Jenny. Two seconds' thought.

DICK. She's said she's sorry.

GWEN. There are early lambs you know that?

DICK. Cleo doesn't chase sheep.

GWEN. There's always the first time. They're allowed to shoot on sight. You know that?

JENNY. I'm sorry.

GWEN. Shoot to kill. Not to maim or warn off but to kill.

JENNY. I've said I'm sorry.

GWEN. The call of the wild. How's she supposed to resist?

DICK. Gwen this is silly.

GWEN. Your dog too.

DICK. She won't have gone far.

GWEN. She's out of ear shot. I've called her.

DICK. She comes much better on the whistle.

DICK *whistles.*

JENNY. I'm sorry.

DICK. You weren't to know.

GWEN. Don't treat her as if she's a child. I'd told her.

JENNY. I didn't realise.

DICK. Everybody round here knows her. No one will shoot her.

ERIC. More likely to get hit by a car.

JENNY. Oh shut up!

DICK. This happens time and time again when we're out walking. I walk on. Let her have her sniff of rabbit or whatever and when she's had a taste of freedom she comes back. Just when you don't expect it: there she is.

JENNY. Cleo! Cleo!

DICK. She comes much better on the whistle.

JENNY *attempts to whistle – it is hopeless.*

DICK *whistles expertly. They wait.*

JENNY. Oh what's the point in standing here? Let's go and look for her.

ERIC. Which way is she likely to go?

GWEN. Depends on the temptation.

DICK. I'll go up to the farm.

JENNY. I'll come with you Dick.

GWEN. Thank God she's not on heat. That's all we need, a bitch in whelp.

They go. GWEN and ERIC remain.

ERIC. I'm sorry.

GWEN. Not your fault.

ERIC. In a way. She wanted to say goodbye to me. I thought she was asleep.

GWEN. Your weekend for Lottie?

ERIC. Um.

GWEN. I'd like to meet her.

ERIC. Perhaps one day.

GWEN. You'd be very welcome to bring her here.

ERIC. Thank you. It's kind of you.

GWEN. I mean it.

ERIC. Things are very difficult at the moment. Jealousy I think. Lottie won't have anything to do with me. I'm supposed to take her swimming. The past couple of times she's refused to come with me. I don't like to force the issue.

GWEN. Sounds like Jenny and Dick. She wouldn't speak to him. She developed a system of grunts that could mean either yes or no. I —

Cleo! Cleo!

We don't have many chances to talk you and I.

ERIC. No.

GWEN. It's only natural that I should worry about her.

ERIC. Yes.

GWEN. You have behaved very decently. I do think that. But what will happen?

ERIC. I don't know.

GWEN. Do you love her?

ERIC. I – I'm –

GWEN. I'm finding it very difficult. I do want to. Her mother. I should. But – there are times I don't know what to say. Twenty years of silence. Her past. I don't belong to it. It makes questions between us. Does she talk about me?

ERIC. Of course.

GWEN. Not now. When you first knew her? What did she say about me then? Was I castigated?

ERIC. She's never been a rememberer.

GWEN. She must have said things. You must have asked.

ERIC. She didn't talk about you.

GWEN. Nothing?

ERIC. Nothing. I'm sorry.

GWEN. Not even that she hated me?

ERIC. Nothing.

GWEN. You do love her, don't you?

ERIC. Yes.

GWEN. Does she know?

ERIC. Yes.

GWEN. I suppose you blame me.

ERIC. No.

GWEN. You must do sometimes.

ERIC. I just think one day she'll change.

GWEN. Or you might.

ERIC. We've broken up three or four times. It's always me who comes back.

GWEN. Why?

ERIC. I do.

Pause.

GWEN. I am trying Eric. I am trying. I've started to say to myself, perhaps when Jessica is born. Through Jessica. She'll have to think with a baby. Doesn't she realise that? Her life won't be her own ever again. She's made no preparations at all so far as I can see.

ERIC. She's put her flat on the market. Didn't you know?

GWEN. No. She's going to live with you?

ERIC. I have asked her Gwen. The answer's always no.

Pause.

Isn't she coming here?

GWEN. Here?

ERIC. I thought that was the plan.

GWEN. She can't come here.

ERIC. You'll have to ask her.

GWEN. She can stay – you can both stay as often as you like of course. Did Dick ask her? Did he say she could?

ERIC. I don't want her to come here. It would make things impossible. Lottie is in London. I have to be where Lottie is. If Jenny comes here then it has to be over between us. It has to be.

GWEN. But she's coming?

ERIC. That's what she says. I have to go, Gwen.

He kisses GWEN.

GWEN. You'll look for Cleo?

ERIC. Of course.

GWEN. Are you coming back?

ERIC. Only one car. I'll come back for her tomorrow.

GWEN. I could take her to the station.

ERIC. I'll come.

He goes.

GWEN *whistles for Cleo.*

Scene Three

The wood.

   A bit later. GWEN *is whistling for Cleo.*

DICK. Gwen, come and have breakfast. She'll be back when she's ready.

GWEN. It's not as if I haven't told Jenny.

DICK. You've said your piece for today.

GWEN. Well really.

DICK. Come and have breakfast.

GWEN. I don't want any.

DICK. Jenny's cooked it.

GWEN. No thank you.

DICK. You know you reduced her to tears.

GWEN. Don't be silly.

DICK. You did.

GWEN. I didn't mean to.

DICK. She's in a highly emotional state Gwen.

GWEN. I do know. I have been through pregnancy.

   Enter JENNY.

JENNY. Your eggs'll be hard.

DICK. Right.

   DICK *goes into the house.*

JENNY. She moved.

GWEN. He says I made you cry?

JENNY. A kick. A real kick.

GWEN. Did I?

Pause.

JENNY. I wish Eric hadn't gone. Am I coming into the office?

GWEN. Up to you.

JENNY. Do you need me?

GWEN. You know what Saturday mornings are like. We've got eleven accompanied viewings on the books at the moment.

JENNY. I'll do those shall I?

GWEN. It would help.

JENNY. Fine.

GWEN. Why are you so willing?

JENNY. Helping out.

GWEN. Why?

JENNY. You need help.

GWEN. Only because it's offered.

JENNY. So let me help.

GWEN. Do you want something?

JENNY. No.

GWEN. You're here every weekend.

JENNY. I've missed you.

GWEN. You could have come before.

JENNY. I'd left it too long. I needed an excuse.

GWEN. Because you wanted something.

JENNY. A few questions.

GWEN. You could have gone once they'd been answered.

JENNY. I didn't want to.

GWEN. Do you like it here with us? Two old people.

JENNY. It's home.

GWEN. Is it?

JENNY. I was brought up here. The place I've always remembered. I had my first kiss here. My first true kiss. It has memories for me.

GWEN. The cottage where I was born's five miles away. I didn't go there.

JENNY. I thought you were glad to grow up. Get away.

GWEN. Weren't you?

JENNY. It's quite safe here. Safe. I sleep at night.

GWEN. I hear you're selling your flat.

JENNY. Yes.

GWEN. Oh.

JENNY. A second floor flat without a lift will be impossible with a pram.

GWEN. Yes.

JENNY. I'm hoping to get around fifty thousand – of course there's my mortgage but – selling myself.

GWEN. I see.

JENNY. I'll do it Mother, I will.

GWEN. Yes, you will.

JENNY. Of course you'll be the first person I'll come to if there are any problems. But aren't you proud of me? How much you've taught me? I wouldn't have had the first idea of what to do without you. We do work well together, don't we?

GWEN. I do loathe typing.

JENNY. Perhaps you should employ me as your secretary.

GWEN. I thought you'd done all that?

JENNY. Yes. I couldn't do it again. Not even for you. I'm used to being top dog now. There'll be money from the flat. I could put that

into the agency. Twenty thousand, that would pay for more
secretarial help. A duplicator, bigger premises. You'd be able to
expand.

GWEN. I'm already run off my feet.

JENNY. I'd help. Together we could be so much bigger.

GWEN. Buy me?

JENNY. No. Put capital in. Favell and daughter on the boards. You
don't see that do you? It would be good publicity. A little gimmick,
the papers would pick up on it.

GWEN. Favell and mother. More interesting still.

JENNY. You see so many possibilities. And with the profits we could
open another branch, a chain.

GWEN. I haven't said yes.

JENNY. It's a wonderful idea.

GWEN. Your idea.

JENNY. We'll be able to take turns with Jessica. Share her. All the
cuddles you could want.

GWEN. And dirty nappies and broken nights?

JENNY. She's not going to be that sort of baby.

GWEN. All babies shit and puke. It's the one factor they have in
common.

DICK (*off, shouting*). More toast going in now.

JENNY. I must eat before I go. You ought to have something.

GWEN. Not hungry.

JENNY. That's silly.

Pause.

I must have something. All those accompanieds. I'll wear my
support tights.

GWEN. Do they help?

JENNY. Supposed to.

   Enter DICK.

DICK. The food is going to be ruined.

JENNY. She doesn't want anything.

DICK. It's Cleo. You can always get another dog.

JENNY. I'll buy you one Mother. The best. One with a pedigree.

DICK. You'll be late for work.

JENNY. I can't seem to start the day on an empty stomach.

   She goes in.

GWEN. Did you invite her here? Tell her she could live here?

DICK. Plenty of space.

GWEN. It isn't that. Don't you see? I have tried Dick. I have tried.

DICK. I said it would take time.

GWEN. The more time there is the more gaps. I don't want her to live here. Please make her go. I don't want her here.

DICK. Your own daughter.

GWEN. Not mine. Someone else's. Not mine.

DICK. We get on swimmingly.

GWEN. You get on. I work my way from one day to another. Get rid of her.

DICK. How?

GWEN. It doesn't matter.

DICK. Play the heavy stepfather?

GWEN. If that's what you have to do.

DICK. No.

GWEN. Please. For me. Please.

DICK. I like her. I'm looking forward to there being a baby in the house.

GWEN. You know nothing about it.

DICK. I fetched her from that party for you. And wished a thousand times I never had.

GWEN. One o'clock in the morning. I was worried sick.

DICK. Your daughter. You could have got her.

GWEN. I was pregnant.

DICK. That didn't stop Jenny coming here from London. I've never held a baby. All my life. Never.

GWEN. You'll get enough practice with Jenny's. Well who else do you think is going to look after it? That's why she's come.

Enter JENNY *with bit of toast.*

JENNY. Mother, you'll be late. Shall I keep your coffee?

GWEN. I'll have one in the office.

JENNY. What do you think about getting a proper coffee machine for the office? Be so much nicer for people than instant. I'll see you in a minute.

She goes to the car.

DICK. You see. She's a great help.

GWEN. Watching me. Criticising me because I give people instant coffee.

DICK. They do things differently in London.

GWEN. Then let her stay there. She's worming herself in Dick. Can't you see that?

DICK. But you wanted her?

GWEN. Not like this.

DICK. Then how?

GWEN. Not all the time. I don't want the responsibility for her life. Not any more.

Enter ERIC.

ERIC. I've found Cleo. About five miles down the road. She's okay.

DICK. I said it was a fuss about nothing.

ERIC. Tied up my tow rope. She's – um – and not in dirt either by the smell of her. I didn't feel I could put her in my car. Not my car. Someone ought to get her.

GWEN. Thank you.

ERIC. Best thing would be for someone to walk her back. Chuck a few sticks in the stream to give her a swim. Shall I give you a lift?

GWEN. I'll get her. I'll get the lead.

ERIC. I'd like to go straight away.

DICK. You coming tomorrow?

ERIC. To pick Jenny up.

DICK. The forecast's good. I thought we could have a walk.

ERIC. Not tomorrow. Maybe next weekend.

DICK. Look forward to it.

GWEN. Shall we go?

ERIC. Heaven knows where she's been. She's not a pretty sight.

They go. As they go JENNY comes out ready to go to work.

DICK. Eric's found her.

JENNY. Eric! Eric! Please stay. She moved. She moved. Please stay.

We hear a car drive off.

Scene Four

The kitchen.

The acorn still in the bottle is an established plant. DICK enters with ERIC.

DICK. We could have had our walk –

ERIC. Yes –

DICK. You'll have lunch?

ERIC. Yes.

DICK. I've come back to do the veg. The girls are in the pub –

ERIC. I passed the car. Cleo okay?

DICK. Right as rain. Mind you Gwen spent half the morning throwing sticks in the river for her. Don't think she's ever been so clean. Mind if I get on?

ERIC. Go ahead.

DICK *puts his apron on.*

Anything I can do?

DICK. Sprouts to peel.

ERIC. Fine. Little crosses in the bottom?

DICK. For some reason it does actually make them cook better. Trick Gwen taught me. Sprouts. Colander. And a knife.

ERIC *starts to peel sprouts.* DICK *makes a pudding.*

ERIC. Sometimes you wonder if there's any sprout.

DICK. End of season.

Pause.

A problem?

ERIC. Yes.

DICK. Want to talk about it?

ERIC. It'll come out anyway.

DICK. Lottie?

ERIC. Yes. I was two hours late to pick her up and this week she wanted to go. She got hysterical as soon as she saw me. I tried to explain that I'd been looking for Cleo so she didn't get run over. It was no good. Nothing I could say was. She told me she never wanted to see me again. She and Linda are going to learn to swim together. There was nothing I could say. Linda had tried her best but two hours! Lottie's furious with Jenny for being pregnant. Me for letting her down. I came away because I didn't know what to say.

DICK. Our fault for expecting you to look.

ERIC. I wasn't looking. I was driving home. There was Cleo in the middle of the road. The last thing I wanted. I was late as it was. I have to spend more time with Lottie. It's all I can do. Stop going away at the weekend so if she wants me to take her swimming I'll be there.

DICK. You can't let a child dictate your life.

ERIC. They do.

DICK. Can't you talk to her?

ERIC. A ten year old? I have to be there for her. It's the only way.

DICK. Bring her with you.

ERIC. It doesn't work between Lottie and Jenny. Up till now it has always been a sort of uneasy truce but since the baby. Lottie wanted to choose the name.

DICK. She's not named yet.

ERIC. For Jenny she is. What Lottie wants is me and Lottie.

DICK. Jealousy. I went through all this with Jenny. Hardly ever in and when she was in wanting all Gwen's time. Wanted to snap her fingers at Gwen. There were times when *I* felt like a stranger. I wanted to leave.

ERIC. Didn't you realise before you married Gwen?

DICK. I thought I could sort it out. Through Gwen to get at Jenny. But Gwen would always say 'She expects it'. And she did. I don't know how she coped when she left. I thought it wasn't serious. That she'd be back with her dirty washing. Did she tell you?

ERIC. A little. Not a time she talks about much.

DICK. And?

ERIC. She moved in with a boy who was at the university.

DICK. We thought at the time she would probably come back pregnant. If she had done I would have thrown her out.

ERIC. Not now?

DICK. Times have changed. I like you. I enjoy your company. I'd prefer you to be married.

ERIC. Stop her staying here Dick. Please. Stop her staying.

DICK. Much better for a child here than in London.

ERIC. I can't come here.

DICK. Commuter belt.

ERIC. Hardly.

DICK. Spend the week in London. Weekends –

ERIC. Lottie. It's impossible.

DICK. You have to talk to Jenny.

ERIC. Find an excuse. A reason why she can't stay. Don't make it easy for her.

DICK. Throw her out?

ERIC. Discourage her. The idea of broken nights. Anything – it's too easy for her you see. So easy. Sell her flat and move in here. What could be safer?

DICK. You are as welcome as she is.

ERIC. I have Lottie.

DICK. Build a whole relationship with Jessica.

ERIC. I did with Lottie and look at it.

DICK. Time. Twenty years it's taken me with Jenny. And we're friends now. It's as if we'd never quarrelled. Of course if Lottie means more to you than Jenny.

ERIC. She does that. Half an hour longer with me. Half an hour less with Lottie. Don't let Jenny live here.

DICK. Bring Lottie.

ERIC. The countryside is not a panacea. Linda has custody. Where Lottie is concerned our relationship is good, there's no argument that I should see Lottie more than the two weekends a month I am supposed to be allowed. When she's older she'll get the chance to decide if she wants to live with me. At that stage she'll probably want neither of us.

DICK. Do you think there'll be enough?

ERIC. Yes.

DICK. You could start to lay the table.

ERIC does so. He now knows his way around the kitchen.

I'd like to have you here too Eric. Both of you. However you wanted. It's so empty in this house. Gwen always working. Always waiting for her. There soon wouldn't be a footpath we hadn't done. Cleo would love it. Two masters.

The phone rings.

Yes. Yes. He is.

He hands the phone to ERIC.

Your daughter.

ERIC. Lottie? Lottie? It's Daddy.

Scene Five

ERIC *and* JENNY.

JENNY. Don't you want to feel her kicking?

ERIC. No.

JENNY. She moves a lot now. A little acrobat.

ERIC. I don't want to hear.

JENNY. Your child.

ERIC. I don't want any rights.

JENNY. I suppose Gwen'll come with me for the birth.

ERIC. I suppose so.

JENNY. Not even for that?

ERIC. No. That's when I fell in love with Lottie. The sheer perversity to be born. There was a moment when she slithered out and then inflated. The life going into her. Of course financially. A standing order would be best — you could be sure of getting it —

JENNY. She's not a rates demand.

They walk a little.

If I said I'd marry you.

ERIC. No.

JENNY. You asked.

ERIC. I've un-asked.

JENNY. You spoil her.

ERIC. You'll spoil Jessica.

They walk.

There are some of your things at my place. A few records. Clothes.

JENNY. I haven't missed the records. Or the clothes.

ERIC. What would you like me to do with them?

JENNY. Oxfam or a jumble sale I suppose. You won't throw them out in the street or burn them?

ERIC. No. I threw out all Linda's things. You don't do it again. It's not the sort of contingency insurance is designed to cover.

JENNY. Give the clothes to Lottie. She can dress up in them. All the bits of make-up. You should give her all the other bits of eye-shadow and lipstick that have collected under your basin.

ERIC. No one since you.

JENNY. Never?

ERIC. No.

JENNY. Not all the times you left?

ERIC. Why, I come back. Not this time Jenny.

JENNY. No.

DICK *comes out of the house. He carries* ERIC's *wellingtons.*

DICK. You forgot these.

ERIC. Thank you.

DICK. Yes. Well.

ERIC. Wonder when I'll wear them next.

DICK. You'll be welcome here, any time.

ERIC. I know.

DICK. Miss you up on the Downs.

ERIC. Miss walking them.

   Pause.

   And Cleo. If you're in London.

DICK. Yes.

ERIC. Jenny has my number.

DICK. Good. Give you a ring. Have a drink.

ERIC. All fake log fires around me I'm afraid.

DICK. Well —

ERIC. Thanks.

DICK. Been a nuisance if you'd had to come back for them.

ERIC. All this mud. Have to go in the boot.

DICK. We'll meet in London then?

ERIC. Yes.

DICK. Or here. You don't have to ring. I'm usually about. I'm sorry.

ERIC. I'd better go. You know how quickly the traffic builds up into town.

   Pause.

   Well — of course in an emergency —

JENNY. Of course.

DICK. I'll hold your hand.

JENNY. I know you will.

ERIC. If there's anything else –

DICK. We'll send a parcel.

ERIC. I did think I'd checked. I'm usually pretty methodical.

JENNY. Give Lottie my love.

ERIC. I'm sure she sends hers.

JENNY. Yes.

> ERIC *goes.*

I'm cold.

DICK. Stupid to be out here without a coat.

JENNY. It looked warm.

DICK. Still only April. Best time of year up on the Downs. Things beginning.

> *He starts to go.*

Come in. You won't see him wave from here.

Scene Six

The office. A coffee machine has appeared; JENNY is working at GWEN's desk.

> *Enter GWEN.*

GWEN. I do hate going round houses, left with their furniture and fittings and no one there. I don't know how people can bear to leave their lives like that.

JENNY. Aren't they dead?

GWEN. Not always. Pack their bags and go. Send instructions to sell.

JENNY. News for you.

GWEN. Yes?

JENNY. Briar Cottage.

GWEN. What?

JENNY. Fifteen hundred on the offer. Cash. No strings.

GWEN. Have they had a survey?

JENNY. Seeing is believing.

GWEN. Not with a house.

JENNY. Fifteen hundred more. Aren't you impressed?

GWEN. But the Garrads?

JENNY. If they want the property they'll have to match it.

GWEN. They can't.

JENNY. There we are then.

GWEN. Jenny no one should have looked at it. It's under offer.

JENNY. Exactly what these people wanted. And no strings. Money
on the table.

GWEN. It was under offer.

JENNY. Do be realistic.

GWEN. The Garrads' offer had been accepted.

JENNY. It's been unaccepted.

GWEN. You shouldn't have sent anyone to see it.

JENNY. Fifteen hundred pounds.

GWEN. It's not the way I do business.

JENNY. It's no wonder you're stuck with one office is it? Throwing
away commission.

GWEN. As far as I'm concerned that house is the Garrads'.

JENNY. The new offer has been accepted.

GWEN. It shouldn't have been offered.

JENNY. Well it has been and in fairness to our clients.

GWEN. Have you asked the Garrads if they can match it?

JENNY. We know they can't. Look at the scrabble they've had for a
    mortgage.

GWEN. But they've been offered one.

JENNY. The principle's established. If the building society can
    commit to one house for them they can commit to another.

GWEN. They don't want anywhere else.

JENNY. Then they'll have to change their minds. You're silly to fall in
    love with a house.

GWEN. You can't do it.

JENNY. I have done. The sellers have accepted. Needless to say
    they're delighted. It means they'll be able to afford upstairs carpets.

GWEN. You can't do it.

JENNY. The new deposit is in the safe.

GWEN. Get it out and give it them back.

JENNY. Look this happens all the time.

GWEN. Not here.

JENNY. Oh come on mother. The real world.

GWEN. It's Dutch auction.

JENNY. A better offer was received and has been accepted.

GWEN. On whose authority?

JENNY. My own.

GWEN. You have no rights here.

JENNY. Our partnership.

GWEN. What partnership?

JENNY. We agreed.

GWEN. I have never agreed.

JENNY. Jenny you can take this client and show them round. Can you
    go to Woolworths and get keys cut?

GWEN. You offered.

JENNY. You knew on what terms.

GWEN. They weren't accepted.

JENNY. Of course they were. Why go on using me?

GWEN. I haven't used you.

JENNY. Dogsbody.

GWEN. I thought you wanted to learn?

JENNY. I have learnt.

GWEN. Nothing.

JENNY. I got a thousand pounds more for my flat than I dreamed I would. Now this.

GWEN. I don't do business that way.

JENNY. Then what are you doing here?

GWEN. I'm successful.

JENNY. In whose terms?

GWEN. My own.

JENNY. Then aim higher. Push.

GWEN. I don't need to.

JENNY. You've never thought of it.

GWEN. My word. People trust my word. Buyers come here because they know they won't be gazumped.

JENNY. Then it's the sellers who are fools.

GWEN. A lot of people wanting to buy means a lot of sales.

JENNY. I know you started this business as a game but it's real now.

GWEN. It's always been real since I ordered the notepaper and envelopes.

JENNY. There's more to business than stationery.

GWEN. Yes and I've given it.

JENNY. You might have got a better return on your investment.

GWEN. We are quite comfortable. We have two cars. In my childhood I thought people with bicycles were the aristocracy. I didn't dare dream of a bicycle.

JENNY. Then dream now.

GWEN. What of?

JENNY. Whatever you want. Why settle for comfort?

GWEN. What is there after that?

JENNY. The icing on the cake. A little luxury. Why do I have to sleep on sheets that have joins down the centre?

GWEN. My wedding sheets.

JENNY. You divorced him.

   Pause.

GWEN. Briar Cottage belongs to the Garrads.

JENNY. They can't afford it.

GWEN. They can.

JENNY. How?

GWEN. I'll find them the money.

JENNY. Where?

GWEN. My bank account if necessary.

JENNY. St. Joan?

GWEN. I gave my word the house was theirs. I promised.

JENNY. A final offer has been made and accepted.

GWEN. The Garrads' was the final offer.

JENNY. A better final offer.

GWEN. I'll give you a better final final offer. An extra two thousand.

   Pause.

   It's good business Jenny. I'll match you all the way.

JENNY. What if the Garrads don't want your beneficence?

GWEN. Buy it myself. Sell it them at a price they can afford.

JENNY. Cash?

GWEN. Pound notes on the table if you like.

JENNY. What would you do with a cottage?

GWEN. Live in it. Or perhaps you could go there with your baby. The one that isn't going to cry in the night. I'd forgotten. You've thrown up your job, you'll have all day to catch up on your sleep.

JENNY. You promised. A deal. I've sold my flat.

GWEN. It was voices St. Joan heard wasn't it?

JENNY. I've come back.

GWEN. You've gone once. You can go again.

JENNY. Where?

GWEN. Oxford. Throw your keys in the river. No – one thing you might have learned is keys are expensive. I'd rather you gave them back.

Scene Seven

The kitchen.

> *Early morning.*

> GWEN *looking at the tapestry on the frame. It is all but finished.*

> *Enter* DICK.

DICK. You making tea?

GWEN. If you like.

> *She plugs in the kettle.*

DICK. Up early.

GWEN. Couldn't sleep.

DICK. You should stop worrying.

GWEN. How?

DICK. Relax more. Once Jessica's born and Jenny's back at work –

GWEN. Come home and change nappies.

DICK. I'll do that.

GWEN. Six or seven times a day for two and a half years?

DICK. It will be fun.

GWEN. For how long?

About the tapestry.

Nearly finished.

DICK. Yes. Promised it to Jenny.

GWEN. Jenny?

DICK. When she first came she liked it. I said I'd give it to her.

GWEN. It's for the dining chair.

DICK. I can do another. I have the time.

GWEN. Can't she wait?

DICK. I said she could have it.

GWEN. It's one of a set. Doesn't she realise?

DICK. Another one. It's easy enough.

GWEN. Let her wait her turn.

DICK. I told her she could have it. Makes a change. Your making tea for me.

GWEN. Do you hate it so much?

DICK. I do it for you.

GWEN. Do you hate it?

DICK. I do it gladly.

GWEN. Then why do you want me back here?

DICK. You're not so young as you were. You work crazy hours. I want us to spend time together.

GWEN. With Jenny here?

DICK. She'll make her own friends. Be out all the time.

GWEN. And we babysit.

DICK. It's what grandmothers are for.

GWEN. Not this one.

DICK. You can't throw her out.

GWEN. It's going to be her or me Dick. In the end.

DICK. You haven't slept. Come back to bed.

GWEN. No. I mean it.

DICK. Yes. Yes.

GWEN. Yes.

DICK. She'll get sick of us soon enough. Find a place of her own.

GWEN. We're too convenient.

DICK. Wait until after the baby.

GWEN. And throw a mother and child out on the streets.

DICK. Oxfordshire is hardly the streets.

GWEN. As soon as I saw her I knew she wanted something.

DICK. You've always given in to her before.

GWEN. Not this time.

DICK. Any digestives?

GWEN. Did you buy any?

DICK. No.

GWEN. Then there aren't.

DICK. Jenny sometimes gets some. She likes one with her tea.

> GWEN *looks in the tin.* There are digestive biscuits in it. DICK *lays a tray for* JENNY.

GWEN. A cup of tea with a biscuit in the saucer.

DICK. I like to do it properly for her.

GWEN. She's hardly a guest.

DICK (*goes back to the table and pours*). Have this argument with her. Not with me.

GWEN. The two of you thick as thieves.

DICK. You can't expect us not to talk.

GWEN. You didn't used to.

DICK. We have a lot in common.

GWEN. What?

DICK. You.

GWEN. Her or me Dick.

DICK. You make it sound like an ultimatum.

GWEN. It is.

DICK. We'll sit down all of us and talk.

GWEN. With her there?

DICK. Something has to be sorted out. It can't go on like this.

GWEN. Send her away.

DICK. Your daughter. You do it.

　Pause.

GWEN. How?

DICK. However you do.

GWEN. But she might go for good.

DICK. The risk you'll take –

GWEN. That I couldn't bear but this –

DICK. Tea –

GWEN. No.

DICK. Biscuit —

GWEN. No. I'm going to sell the business.

DICK. Pardon?

GWEN. Sell it. Unencumber myself.

DICK. Jenny's job.

GWEN. What job? I've never given her one.

DICK. She works for you.

GWEN. For herself. The pound signs ticking up behind her eyeballs.

DICK. You don't have to sell it if you want to retire.

GWEN. I don't want to retire. I won't work with her.

DICK. Find her a job somewhere else.

GWEN. Pull strings.

DICK. Your own child, it's natural.

GWEN. At her age? What would they think of me? Or her? Her own mother can't work with her?

DICK. Wait until after the baby.

GWEN. Wait? What for?

DICK. You'll love the baby when you see her. You'll love her.

GWEN. It isn't like that. It doesn't happen in that way. They're dependent. That's what's attractive about babies. The power you have over them.

DICK. Maternal instinct.

GWEN. Aching breasts and passion poured down an empty hole.

DICK. Bonding.

GWEN. A gamble. The stock exchange.

DICK. You have no rights.

GWEN. Does she?

DICK. You chose to have her.

GWEN. I wanted him not her. I didn't think about her. Him doing his duty. Me in a white dress. Look what I've ended up with.

DICK. Me and Jenny.

GWEN. Do you think this is your child to make up?

DICK. In a way. I've never held a baby Gwen. Just a pile of bloody sheets. She's asked me to go with her to the hospital. Nowadays a loving partner is all they specify.

GWEN. Will you go? Screaming. All that blood?

DICK. I can hold her hand.

GWEN. She didn't even ask me.

DICK. We thought you'd be working.

He picks up the tray.

GWEN. I'll take Cleo out. Let her sniff at the primroses.

DICK. Good.

GWEN. Dick –

DICK. Yes?

GWEN. I tried for you.

DICK. You didn't have to.

GWEN. But I did.

DICK goes.

GWEN cuts the tapestry from the frame and puts it in her briefcase.

She takes the oak tree from the glass.

She takes Cleo's lead and dog bowl.

She takes her key from the key ring and leaves it on the table.

She goes.

Scene Eight

The wood.

 The moments before dawn.

 Enter GWEN.

 She is dressed as in the first scene, smart with her briefcase.

 She carries the oak tree.

 She plants it, using her hands to dig.

 She crosses the stage and looks back at the house.

 She crosses the stage and goes.

 She whistles for Cleo.

 Dawn breaks.

Golden Girls

This version of *Golden Girls* was first performed at the Royal Shakespeare Company at the Other Place, Stratford-upon-Avon, on 20 June, 1984, with the following cast:

DORCAS ABLEMAN, *black athlete*	Josette Simon
MURIEL FARR, *black athlete*	Alphonsia Emmanuel
PAULINE PETERSON, *white athlete*	Katherine Rogers
SUE KINDER, *blonde white athlete*	Kate Buffery
JANET MORRIS, *black athlete*	Cathy Tyson
MIKE BASSETT, *white athlete*	Kenneth Branagh
LACES MACKENZIE, *coach*	Jimmy Yuill
VIVIEN BLACKWOOD, *doctor*	Jennifer Piercey
NOËL KINDER, *Sue Kinder's father*	George Raistrick
HILARY DAVENPORT, *sponsor*	Polly James
TOM BILLBOW, *journalist*	Derek Crewe
HOTEL PORTER, *white*	Norman Henry
THE GOLDEN GIRL, *everything the name suggests*	Jan Revere

Directed by Barry Kyle
Designed by Kit Surrey
Music by Ilona Sekacz
Lighting by Wayne Dowdeswell

Acknowledgement
Special thanks to Ron Pickering for the sports commentary on page 277.

ACT ONE

Scene One

A pile of luggage in a hotel lobby. Enter TOM. *He looks at the luggage. Enter the* PORTER *with more luggage.*

PORTER. You think they'd have the energy to do their own fetching and carrying. Bloody athletes. When Sheffield Wednesday were here they were gentlemen. (*He goes.*)

TOM *looks at the luggage. He turns over the tags on the bags.*

TOM *goes.*

Enter MURIEL. *She limps to the bags and sits down. She begins to unbandage her foot. Enter the* PORTER.

PORTER. Gentlemen! (*He goes.*)

MURIEL *begins to flex her foot. Enter* VIVIEN.

VIVIEN. Right, let's have a look. How's that feel?

MURIEL. O.K.

VIVIEN *moves the foot.* MURIEL *winces.*

VIVIEN. I'll strap it up as tightly as I can now and have another look in the morning.

MURIEL. Should I have an X-ray?

VIVIEN. It's a ligament.

MURIEL. I pass casualty.

VIVIEN. If I thought you needed an X-ray you'd have had one by now. (VIVIEN *bangs on her chest indicating where* MURIEL *is to put her foot.*)

No need to kick me in the teeth. (*She starts to strap.*) Doesn't seem too bad.

MURIEL. No?

VIVIEN. A sprained ligament. Hardly the end of the world. It could have been your Achilles tendon.

MURIEL. I've only been out twice before.

VIVIEN. You've been unusually lucky.

MURIEL. Age is catching up on me, isn't it?

VIVIEN. If your times are good enough, keep on running. You ought to be pleased with your own event.

MURIEL (*shrugs*). When did you give up?

VIVIEN. When I couldn't go to Helsinki. The longest women's race there was the 200. Not my event. It was Finland for the Olympics or Charing Cross Hospital. Can you flex that?

MURIEL *tries but can't.*

Good. Medicine was tough for a woman then. They still had the quota system. I knew I wouldn't get a medal and I wanted a degree. I had to take myself seriously. It was a different world. Terrific fun. Then the four minute mile was cracked and it all seemed to get serious. Perhaps we were just younger then.

Enter LACES.

LACES. I've given them the hurry up. Is it the problem she's pretending it is?

VIVIEN. There's a lot of flexibility. I'll have another look at it in the morning. (*To* MURIEL.) There's no point pushing yourself for a situation you can't save.

LACES. Dorcas is pretty mad about it. She's gone off somewhere.

MURIEL. What she's mad about is Sue's time in the 200. To be beaten in that and have Sue blow it in the relay.

VIVIEN. You can't blame it all on Sue. The German girls have really got it together.

MURIEL. We can get it together.

LACES. Then why didn't you?

MURIEL *shrugs.*

Vivien?

VIVIEN. I deal with bodies not minds.

LACES. Some ideas must have gone through your head.

VIVIEN. They believed absolutely they could do it.

LACES. And that gave them the upper hand?

VIVIEN. Amongst other things.

LACES. Oh! You think they are?

VIVIEN. If they are it's nothing that's shown up yet.

MURIEL. Common gossip in the changing-rooms.

LACES. Hazzard a guess.

VIVIEN. A hundred and one things. All sorts of drugs they could be taking and flushing out of their system before the tests.

LACES. Name them.

VIVIEN. There have been some interesting reports on a drug called di — the shorthand name for it is hydromel. After the stuff the Romans used to dope their horses but this is new. Derived from the embryos of rats.

MURIEL. Yuk!

VIVIEN. It speeds up the motor processes. It's already on the black market here. But I can't see us ever being allowed to prescribe it. Then again it could all be weights.

MURIEL. We use weights.

VIVIEN. It's not a couple of nights a week sort of muscle.

MURIEL. Thank goodness.

VIVIEN. You have to decide if you want to be a winner or a star.

Pause.

You can't have East German times without the East German system. And they've got the lot, from the kudos of the sports personality to the chemistry. We haven't got it together here —

there's no money.

LACES. Ortolan?

VIVIEN. A drop in the ocean. All it buys is tracksuits for the girls and a bit of your time. If I were to charge for this you couldn't afford it.

MURIEL. I'm sorry.

VIVIEN. That's the system. Why should you apologise?

Pause.

LACES. If I could get the money would you come in — full time?

VIVIEN. It doesn't happen in this country.

LACES. If I made it?

MURIEL. You sound like the fairy godmother in Adidas.

LACES. If the money was there, Vivien?

VIVIEN. Ortolan isn't going to pay for a team doctor.

LACES. Why not?

VIVIEN. O.K. Find me the pay cheque.

LACES. How much?

VIVIEN. A lot.

LACES. The love of the game?

VIVIEN. Times have changed. Mine is the leather suitcase. It's a business now.

MURIEL. Is it O.K. for me to phone George?

VIVIEN. As long as you don't put your full weight on it.

MURIEL *goes to the phone.* LACES *watches her go.*

LACES. Technically she's the best we've got. If she could just understand that. She needs Dorcas's killer instinct. She can break records in training. She could do in competition if she'd just believe in herself.

VIVIEN. Perhaps she doesn't want to.

LACES. Why not?

VIVIEN. Frightened.

LACES. How can you be frightened of winning?

VIVIEN. It sets you apart.

It's also called being a woman.

LACES. Don't! Don't! Don't!

VIVIEN. I am trying to explain. You could at least listen.

LACES. Sue wants to win. Pauline wants to win. Dorcas wants it more than the whole world. So being a woman is hardly a hypothesis. You're hardly a shrinking violet.

VIVIEN. I'm a doctor. People have to believe in me. People like Ortolan.

MURIEL. Have you got a dialling code booklet?

PORTER. Bulawayo is it?

MURIEL. Buxton.

The PORTER *grudgingly finds her the code book.*

Enter MIKE.

LACES. Found her?

MIKE. No.

LACES. Any ideas?

MIKE. No.

LACES. Your time wasn't bad.

MIKE. Hers was.

LACES. All her stuff here?

MIKE. Think so.

LACES. I'm not waiting once we're all here. It's up to you if you come with us or hang on for her.

MIKE. I've a tutorial at ten.

LACES. On?

MIKE. Community access to educational sports facilities.

VIVIEN *looks at her watch and yawns.*

VIVIEN. I've got a surgery.

MIKE. I'll go and give them a shout.

LACES. I've tried that. Progress!

   Enter NOËL.

LACES. Where's Sue?

NOËL. Taking her Qwells.

LACES. You know they stay in the system.

NOËL. Didn't take them on the way down.

LACES. She managed.

NOËL. Empty stomach. No point in tempting fate.

MIKE. I'll get the others. (*He goes.*)

LACES. You haven't seen Dorcas?

NOËL. No.

LACES. This time I really am going without her.

VIVIEN. Laces, you can't.

LACES. She's been warned.

VIVIEN. You can't leave her here in the middle of the night.

LACES. Can't I?

NOËL. Teach her her lesson.

   Enter SUE.

MURIEL. You look as if you should be going out on the town.

SUE. Thanks.

LACES. You've checked your room?

SUE. Pauline's having a last look.

LACES. Good, then we can go.

NOËL. I'm ready.

SUE. Please Dad.

LACES. It's been a lousy day. Let's just get home. (NOËL *and* LACES *look at the map.*)

NOËL. The sooner I get to my bed the better.

LACES. That goes for all of us.

VIVIEN. Are you always travel sick?

SUE. Better safe than sorry.

VIVIEN. Have you ever tried ginger for it.

SUE. Ginger?

VIVIEN. It might help.

MURIEL. Sounds old wives to me.

VIVIEN. Placebo effect. You'd be surprised how often something patients belive in will work.

SUE. Not now you've told me.

VIVIEN. It might be worth trying.

NOËL. What might?

VIVIEN. Ginger.

MURIEL. To stop her feeling sick on the bus.

NOËL. Sounds like mumbo jumbo to me.

(*Enter* PAULINE.)

PAULINE. I've lost Split Second.

NOËL. That bloody bear.

LACES. You've looked in your room?

PAULINE. Of course.

VIVIEN. Your bag.

(PAULINE *looks in it*.)

PAULINE. No. He's been stolen. Some bloody fan.

SUE. Who'd steal Split Second. He's got mange.

PAULINE. He hasn't.

LACES. If they find him they can send him on.

PAULINE. I'm not going without him. I can't run without him.

NOËL. In my day luck depended on how you tied your shoelaces.

PAULINE. I can't.

NOËL. Sure he wasn't lost before the relay?

SUE. Dad!

NOËL. Sorry. Silly joke. Late at night.

VIVIEN. Where did you have him last?

PAULINE. He came down to the track. Then we came back here. I had a bath, dinner, then the bar.

MURIEL. You had him at dinner.

LACES. You looked in the bar?

PAULINE. I'm not going till we find him.

LACES. You want to spend another night in this place?

PAULINE. I know you don't care.

VIVIEN crosses to desk.

VIVIEN. Excuse me —

PORTER. Half past ten it was you were supposed to be going.

VIVIEN. They've lost something.

PORTER. Every race they've run.

VIVIEN. Have you had anything handed in. A toy. A children's toy?

Enter MIKE.

PORTER. That Mike Bassett?

VIVIEN. Yes.

PORTER. He do autographs?

VIVIEN. Yes.

PORTER. Might be worth getting I suppose.

VIVIEN. It's a sort of bear — with a ribbon.

The PORTER begins to throw up lost property with bad grace. All watch. He holds up Split Second. PAULINE rushes for him jumping over cases as she goes.

PORTER. You should try going in for the hurdles.

LACES. Yippee. Right. Let's go.

Variously they claim their baggage and go — MIKE last.

PORTER. Your autograph worth anything?

MIKE. Sorry?

PORTER. You know, your name?

MIKE shrugs.

Might as well — eh — just in case. Never know what might happen in the future.

MIKE writes in the book. As he's about to go, enter DORCAS with a laundry bag.

MIKE. Where the hell have you been?

DORCAS drops the washing.

I was worried.

Enter NOËL.

NOËL. Will you get your bum on this bus. (*He glares at DORCAS.*) Go walkabout did we? (*He goes.*)

MIKE. Well?

DORCAS. The drier wouldn't work.

Enter TOM BILLBOW.

MIKE. Let's get home.

PORTER (*to DORCAS*). Can you write? (*She looks at him.*) You know. Writing? (*He mimes. She puts out her hand for the pen. She writes her name.*) You have to put more than that. Don't suppose they have autographs were you come from. You have to put 'to Denis and Diana' — (*She does.*) Then they usually put best wishes or good luck or something.

(*She does.*)

You'll get the hang of it. And the date. (*She does.*) Ta. (*The PORTER looks at the autograph.*)

How come you don't run for Jamaica?

DORCAS. I don't need the tan.

Pause.

MIKE. Let's get home. (*He goes.*)

TOM. The name Dorcas — means gazelle doesn't it?

DORCAS. Yes. (*She picks up the washing. She goes.*)

Blackout.

Scene Two

Darkness. Out of the darkness the sound of a runner running. Lights up to pre-dawn. The runner is SUE.

SUE. You know which direction you're going in at home. The north slopes and the south. The south slopes have posh houses. The ones that get the sunlight. There's a saying there about downhill being uphill but it's all running on the flat here. No hills. No view out over it all. You could go on and on. The time was when I thought there must be something would make me stop before the horizon. A tree, mountain, mole hill. Some obstacle. Nothing. Just further and further to go. On and on towards the sun. (*She continues to run.*)

Enter NOËL *with a stopwatch.*

NOËL. Bugger!

The floodlights come on. NOËL *times the stopwatch to his own watch, counting. Enter* LACES.

LACES. Morning.

NOËL *nods. The stopwatch is obviously broken.*

NOËL. Can you lend us a stopwatch? This is buggered. Forty-two seconds and then stops dead.

LACES. Give it to the East Germans.

NOËL. Glad somebody can laugh.

LACES. They'd make no bones about it being a record attempt. The psyching was brilliant.

NOËL. Sue knows not to let a thing like that throw her.

LACES. If you're psyched for long enough, well enough, you've got no chance of winning.

NOËL. She knows she's got twenty-one seconds in her legs.

LACES. If she doesn't over do it.

NOËL. I know what her legs can do.

LACES. I think you should watch it. Lay up a bit. Do you think she should be out this morning?

NOËL. Why's today different?

MIKE *runs across the stage.*

LACES. She's run four races in two days.

NOËL. Sue knows how much effort you have to put in before you dare hope for a bit of magic.

LACES. And if there's no magic?

NOËL. You do without.

MIKE. Morning.

LACES. Morning.

NOËL. It's wasting her to use her at less than 200.

LACES. Do you want me to drop her from the squad?

NOËL. You've got us over a barrel. She needs the facilities.

LACES. I'd like it back. (*He gives* NOËL *the stopwatch.*)

NOËL. Ta.

LACES. Tell her not to push it too much. (LACES *jogs off.*)

NOËL. One minute recovery.

SUE. I hate running tired. Running with your mind, not your body. Waiting for the moment when the two fuse. Knowing that some days they won't. That all it will have been is putting on your tee-shirt, your tracksuit. Tying your laces. The routine. Other days the most perfect, perfect thing. No thoughts at all. Absolute symmetry in your head. Like the perfect races when you know just what to do. Not yesterday, a ragbag of tactics and strategy. I could feel the clock in my head. Time running out. And knowing every fraction of a

second that there wasn't going to be a moment which lasted
for ever.

NOËL *shows her the time on the stopwatch.*

NOËL. Again.

SUE. No.

NOËL. I said again.

SUE. No.

NOËL. Don't take that tone with me, miss.

SUE. I can't better that.

NOËL. You can and you will.

Pause.

You're a winner, love. You just have to get it together. Then it
won't be living in a camper for decent facilities. You'll have
everything you deserve. A pretty girl like you, Sue. Think
about it.

SUE. It's impossible.

NOËL. It's not, love. I've shown you it's not. You're a winner,
love. From the day you were born.

SUE. Don't throw that at me.

NOËL. You were a winner then.

SUE. Don't tell me that.

NOËL. She'd be proud.

SUE. Not listening.

NOËL. Me proud then. Crack it and you can stay in bed for ever.

SUE. Who wants to stay in bed in a camper?

NOËL. If you want everything they've got here.

Pause.

What do you want?

She shakes her head.

We'll go home. I'll drive you twenty miles there and back

everyday. But you still won't get the half of what they've got
here.

SUE. I can't run any faster for you, Dad —

NOËL. Then run it for yourself. Come on. Again.

She runs off. He watches her. LACES *jogs back on.*

She could have gold, couldn't she? Real gold.

LACES. There won't be anything if she over-does it.

NOËL. She wasn't allowed to run her own event without
running the relay.

LACES. It's the same for all four of them.

NOËL. It's hardly the same amount of glory.

LACES. Muriel, Pauline, Dorcas, Sue — I'm not saying that they're
the most perfect team — yet.

NOËL. Certainly weren't yesterday —

LACES. But they could get so near. So exciting. Certainly be
the best there's been in this country for a very long time. I
know it's not peace and light between the four of them but
when they're on that track with the baton — they could be —

NOËL. I don't like the word perfect.

LACES. But nearly that. I don't want Sue to let it slip through her
her fingers. Not now they've come this far together.

NOËL. You don't think she's any good on her own?

LACES. She's superb.

NOËL *is pleased.*

That's why I need her in the relay. She's got that power for
that first leg.
I know it's been hardest for her. That she's giving up a bed and
bathroom back home. But if she can run the way she does
living in a camper, with the money that's coming for the team
from Ortolan, it could be a different world for her.

NOËL. Tea?

LACES. No, haven't finished.

NOËL *pours some tea.*

Wish I'd got it together the way you have. (LACES *runs off.*)

Enter MURIEL *and* PAULINE.

MURIEL. It wasn't your fault.

PAULINE. It was.

MURIEL. The stupid idiot was in the wrong lane.

LACES (*shouting to them*). Don't you dare try anything on that ankle until Dr Blackwood's seen it.

MURIEL (*shouting*). I know.
The thing you mustn't do is panic. Slowing down's a fatal mistake. If you stall, switch off the engine and start again.

PAULINE. I'll never get the hang of it.

MURIEL. You will.

NOËL *comes past them with* SUE'S *things and some tea.*

Morning.

NOËL. Morning.

PAULINE. You should park your camper up here. You could make a fortune from bacon sandwiches.

NOËL. Might end up doing that yet. (*He gestures to* SUE.) Come on, get your things, have a shower. (*He goes with* SUE')

PAULINE *and* MURIEL *start to stretch and warm up.*

LACES *is doing press-ups. Enter* TOM.

TOM (*to* NOËL). Morning.

PAULINE.⎫
MURIEL. ⎬ Morning.

TOM. Keep thinking I should get fit. Lose a bit of this. Had a girlfriend once, bought me a tracksuit. Think it was a hint. I find the mornings difficult.

LACES. Can I help, Tom?

TOM *gets down to look at* LACES.

TOM. Laces Mackenzie?

LACES. Yes.

TOM. Used to be a great fan.

LACES. Thanks.

TOM. They say you have a lot of trouble with your knee.

LACES. Some days.

MURIEL *is trying out her ankle.*

TOM. Saw you run in Munich. One of the great moments of my life. Made one proud. Tears behind the eyes. Must help having something like that to remember.

LACES. Yes.

He shouts:

Farr, it'll be your own funeral.

MURIEL (*shouting back*). Spoil sport!

TOM. Her injury bad?

LACES. She's seeing the physio this morning.

TOM. I could have wept. Thinking what those girls must feel. Seeing robots taking women's medals. (*Pause.*) What was it like? Standing up there? Seeing the flag go up? Hearing your national anthem!

LACES. I'm a Scot. (*Pause.*) A lot of noise. An awful lot of noise. And I felt very tiny in the middle of it and huge at the same time.

TOM. Two years is a long time to keep a steeple chase record.

LACES. There to be broken.

TOM. The name Laces? Always wondered.

LACES. Trade secret.

Enter VIVIEN.

VIVIEN. Do you never listen to a word?

MURIEL. A few stretches. That's all. Just to see how it feels.

VIVIEN. Well?

MURIEL. It's a bit tight.

PAULINE. The bandages. I told you.

VIVIEN. My strapping?

MURIEL. Yes.

VIVIEN. I've seen it done before now. Whip off the bandage. Do a few strides. Put it back on again and think I won't notice.

MURIEL. I'm not stupid.

VIVIEN. Twenty-four hours without any pressure on it.

MURIEL. I've got a day's teaching to do.

VIVIEN. That's up to you.

MURIEL. I can't not show up.

PAULINE. Stand on the sideline and blow your whistle. Take the pressure off them as well.

MURIEL. You try it.

PAULINE. No thanks. (*She yawns.*) Can I have a word, Dr Blackwood.

VIVIEN. Is it urgent?

PAULINE. I'll probably live.

VIVIEN. If she's insisting on going to school I'd better have a look at her first. You can catch me after that. But had better be snappy. I've got to be at the hospital by 9.30.

PAULINE. Will do. Thanks. (*She runs off.*)

TOM. Those four girls have got a wealth of talent but it needs polishing.

LACES. Any suggestions?

TOM. I'd drop Muriel Farr.

LACES. Why?

TOM. She's not consistent. (*He watches* VIVIEN *and* MURIEL *leave.*) There's a young girl up and coming. Very promising. Janet Morris. People are saying great things.

Enter MIKE. *He starts his recovery.*

Mike Bassett's the sort of lad you should take on. Girls are all very well but — second division stuff. No hope of promotion to the big time. I mean all this Ortolan stuff. How much are you getting from them?

Silence from LACES. MIKE *pants.*

Silence one of the conditions?

LACES. Not the sort of thing you discuss.

TOM. I'm Tom Billbow. I'm not a spy from the three As.

PAULINE *comes on.*

MIKE. O.K?

PAULINE. Fine. No Dorcas?

MIKE. No.

PAULINE. Drove all the way in this morning. Nearly stalled at a roundabout. Muriel thinks I'll pass next time.

MIKE. Then what?

PAULINE. I'll get one, one day. You'll see. Not a Porsche but something.

Enter HILARY. *Very smart in fur. She looks round.*

I'd kill for a coat like that.

TOM *watches* HILARY. *Pause.* LACES *starts to get ready to go in.*

TOM. You know anything about this film that's supposed to be going on?

LACES. Sorry?

TOM. Film?

LACES. Bottom track.

TOM. Thanks. (TOM *goes.*)

MIKE. One more. (*He runs.*)

LACES. You must have been up with the lark this morning.

HILARY. The early bird catches the worm. I'd like you to make some introductions.

LACES. I've got to take a shower.

HILARY. On your way in. And I want a word.

LACES. Urgent?

HILARY. I think Saturday deserves some explanation. (*They have reached* PAULINE.)

LACES. Pauline, have you met Hilary Davenport?

PAULINE. Hi.

HILARY. Hello, I represent Ortolan.

LACES. I'll be in the changing-room.

HILARY. Right.

> LACES *goes.* HILARY *smiles at* PAULINE.
>
> *Pause.*

HILARY. Are you always out this early?

PAULINE. When we can get the lights.

HILARY. Lights?

PAULINE. Floods. Laces has to be here. They don't call it a proper training session without him.

HILARY. And he's here every morning?

PAULINE. Most.

> *A pause which is fortunately filled by the entrance of* SUE *and* NOËL *going home.*

PAULINE. Have you finished?

SUE. Yes, for this morning.

HILARY. Hello, I'm Hilary Davenport.

PAULINE. From Ortolan.

SUE. Pleased to meet you.

NOËL (*shaking hands*). I'm Sue's Dad.

> *Pause.*

HILARY. All this. You must all be very fit.

The lights go out.

PAULINE. Shit!

SUE. Pauline!

HILARY looks at her.

HILARY. It's all right — I don't mind. As long as it's not in public. We do have an image to think of.

NOËL. She understands all that. Don't you love? Not that she does swear, Miss Davenport.

HILARY. I have to find the changing-rooms.

NOËL. I'll show you. (*They go.*)

PAULINE. Well?

SUE. I thought they'd be like the clothing companies. Just send you a list to tick.

They watch her.

PAULINE. What you doing today?

SUE. Not much. You?

PAULINE. Not much.

SUE. Four-thirty tonight?

PAULINE. Yes.

NOËL *comes back.*

NOËL. They're called after the bird. Ortolan. The garden bunting. A migrant. I think it's brown and gold. Never seen one.

You coming?

SUE. Yes. (*They go.*)

PAULINE *continues.* MIKE *runs across the stage.*

Scene Three

The men's changing-room.

> *Enter* HILARY. *She reads* TOM BILLBOW's *column while she waits for* LACES *to come out of the shower. Enter* LACES *in a towel.*

HILARY. I thought it would smell. Jock straps and all that. Men's feet are notorious.

LACES. I'm a fresh-socks-every-morning man.

HILARY. I'd guessed that. I'd noticed that next morning women smell their knickers and men smell their socks. I bet you're the sort that takes a clean pair with you.

LACES. I've been known to go barefoot. (*He throws his soap and shampoo beside her.*)

HILARY. I hope the commercial will finally convince you about the value of our shampoo.

LACES. You don't do a dandruff version.

HILARY. Any problem you don't have.

LACES. I'm sure you'll come up with it for me.

HILARY. I want to know what went wrong yesterday.

LACES. They were outclassed.

HILARY. Why?

LACES. Let's not mull.

HILARY. In my world if a product flops you look for a reason.

> *Pause.*

LACES. The whole of the sporting press is throwing reasons at us.

HILARY. Yes and most of them are words like third-rate and amateur.

LACES. They *are* amateurs. That's why they need Ortolan to sponsor them.

HILARY. If they don't win Ortolan doesn't sell.

LACES. You can't buy results in athletics.

HILARY. The weekend we announce the whole sponsorship deal is hardly the weekend to flop. Our rivals must have been thrilled. I can hear them laughing. (*Pause*.) We were led to expect a certain amount of competence.

LACES. They were competent.

HILARY. Only to the degree that no one dropped the baton. Newton's law of gravitation when applied to a baton not passed properly I could have explained. But it was the tortoise and the hare.

LACES. I didn't say anything was certain.

HILARY. Almost. Do you know how much is tied up in that commercial?

LACES. More than our pittance.

HILARY. You've hardly proved you deserve that.

LACES. You can't expect results overnight.

HILARY. When *can* we expect them? (LACES *shrugs*.) All right. You and I are in this until Athens. Let's try and get something out of it. Why don't you sit down and tell me — realistically — what I can expect?

LACES. I'd like you to see a doctor?

HILARY. I beg your pardon?

LACES. Doctor Vivien Blackwood. Used to be an athlete. In the early fifties.

HILARY. You trying to pass the buck?

LACES. No. (*He starts to dress.*)

HILARY. Have you ever tried using a sunlamp?

Enter MIKE.

MIKE. Ah —

LACES. Do you know our sponsor?

HILARY. Hello, Hilary Davenport.

MIKE. More post-mortems?

HILARY. In a manner of speaking.

LACES. She's just going.

MIKE. It's O.K. I'll shower at home.

LACES. How's Dorcas?

MIKE. Had the video on all night. Thirty, forty times. Not even the whole two hundred. Just the moment when Sue moves in front.

LACES. Record your own?

MIKE. My start's a bit slow. I was quite pleased with the rest of it.

HILARY. What's the relay like on the video?

MIKE. Sue started very slowly and Muriel went flat out and pulled something coming out of the bend. It was lost before Dorcas got the baton. She runs bloody well when she gets it.

LACES. She coming in?

MIKE *shrugs.*

HILARY. Have you any ideas how we could improve things?

MIKE. You know how it is. They could run the same race today and be terrific.

HILARY. What I ask is a little consistency.

MIKE. They don't get enough time together to be consistent. Ask him.

HILARY. Is that always going to be a problem?

LACES. Not now we've got some money behind us. Before it was a case of taking what we could get. Running whoever was around at the time. No matter if they'd practised together or not. If we couldn't afford to bring Sue down we had to put in a hurdler or someone who was available, but not a sprinter.

MIKE. Dorcas thinks you should pull Sue. Bring in Janet Morris.

HILARY. Who?

LACES. 200 meters runner. Trains with the Cheetahs.

HILARY. She good?

LACES. Very young.

MIKE. She is good.

HILARY. Perhaps you should try her out.

LACES. I am. Lunchtime.

HILARY. I beg your pardon.

LACES. It's called teaching your grandmother to suck eggs.

HILARY. She's got potential?

LACES. I'll tell you when I've seen her. It's a pretty mature team here. She's seventeen, eighteen; there could be all sorts of problems.

HILARY. I'm sure you'll be able to sort them out.

LACES (to MIKE). I was going to ask you if you'd like to come down. I could give you half an hour on your start before I see her.

MIKE. Be great.

LACES. Bottom track. 12.30-ish?

MIKE. I'll be there. I've got to get the milk for the muesli.

HILARY. What shampoo do you use?

MIKE. Washing-up liquid. It's cheaper.

HILARY. If you don't mind a product aimed at women, I'll get you a box of Golden Girls.

MIKE. Great. (He goes.)

HILARY. I can't have them bringing out Squeezy bottles in front of cameras. How good is this Janet Morris girl?

LACES. There's a lot she could improve.

   HILARY paces.

HILARY. Enough to add her to the team?

LACES. First you have the attitude, then the physique and the rest you make up on training.

HILARY. How much can she improve?

LACES. They say the most anyone can do is 15%.

HILARY. 15?

LACES. By conventional means. You can push it a bit further with drugs of course. But a woman who looks like a man is hardly going to sell shampoo.

HILARY. We want girls. Real girls. Wholesome.

Legally and decently how are you going to improve them?

LACES. I want a team doctor. Not just running repairs but some-one who could really work things out. What they should be eating, when. Just how much more they could improve their oxygen take up. It wouldn't be everyday stuff. But graphs and charts. And their minds. Vivien ran herself. She understands the psychology.

HILARY. I can't see any objection.

LACES. It means more money.

HILARY. More? I know the myth about big organisations is that they can throw money about as they please. But we have shareholders. We are accountable.

Pause.

LACES. You want results. Not results. Records. Medals. To win gold medals you have to come first. That means beating other countries. Behind the iron curtain they test them for athletic potential at five. Then it's special schools, indoor tracks, monitoring. Doctors. Vivien would give us a chance against that. I'm asking you to add her to the list.

HILARY. This woman's good?

LACES. She's ambitious. She knows her stuff.

HILARY. Is she a close friend?

LACES. Vivien's fifteen years older than me.

HILARY. I'm not making any promises.

LACES. She could convince you.

HILARY. We should meet.

LACES. You'll like her. You've got a lot in common. (*Their eyes meet.*)

Scene Four

MIKE *and* DORCAS's *house. Early morning.*

DORCAS *sits on the floor watching the video. She sits in the middle of a shaft of light through the curtains, in front of her on the floor a bowl of muesli. She watches the moment when* SUE *overtakes her several times.*

DORCAS. I know not to say anything before a race. Never speak, not even if they want to shake your hand and wish you luck. Don't let them be there. My head opened in the midde of the race. Cracked. Noise, everything came in. I could feel my spikes going into the track. My feet on the ground. I found myself running wide on the bend. I knew it. Knowing as I did it that I did it. White arms and legs in front of me coming out of the bend.
Scrub it.

Silence. She wipes the tape.

Enter MIKE *with milk and morning paper.*

MIKE. I'm home.

He picks up the bowl of muesli from in front of DORCAS. *He puts milk on it but she won't take it from him.*

MIKE. Paper? (*Silence.*) Tom Billbow isn't pleasant. I thought you could do without me bringing that back. (*Silence.*) At least admit it's today and open the curtains. (*Silence.*) Sometimes I wish I lived with a bus conductress. (*She looks at him.*) I didn't mean it. I'm sorry. (*Pause.*) Sorry. (*Pause.*) Is there nothing I can say? (*Silence.*) I know what it's like. But you have to snap out of it. Forget it. It's over and done. (*Her silence is frightening. Pause.*) You've said that to me enough times. Why can't you do it? Dorcas? (*He tries to give her the bowl.*) The shampoo woman was at the centre. Talking to Laces. He wants to change the squad. He's going to try out Janet Morris. Thought you'd be pleased. (*She remains silent.*) You can't win every time, Dorcas. Even you. The world's not like that. The relay was lost before the baton even got to you. You know that. You can see it on there. When Pauline comes up to you. I can see you know. It's all over your face. Why didn't you just drop the baton? At least it would have been cut and dried. (*Silence*.) I've not got time to talk you out of it. I've got a tutorial at ten. Have you got choir practice tonight?

DORCAS. Yes.

MIKE. You going?

DORCAS. No point. The performance is the same day as the Gateshead meet. Won't be here. Why?

MIKE. We can afford a drink each this evening or the Totem on Friday night?

DORCAS. Totem, on Friday night.

Enter SUE *with two buckets. Silence.*

SUE. Someone's bust the hose to the camper. We can't wash the pots.

MIKE. It's free. Help yourself.

SUE *goes through to the kitchen.*

DORCAS. Why did you tell her she could?

MIKE. It's stupid them trekking back and forth to the centre.

DORCAS. She'll be wanting baths here next. Leaving talcum powder all over our floor.

MIKE. It's pretty rough on Sue.

DORCAS. It's creepy. Living like tramps. Why don't they get a flat.

MIKE. Lots of students live in caravans.

DORCAS. They don't live with their Dads. All that stuff on the way back last night, about how many things he could cook at the same time on one gas ring.

MIKE. Perhaps we ought to ask them for a meal or something.

DORCAS. He'd really love sweet potato!

MIKE. I could do chips or something.

DORCAS. If they want chips there are chip shops.

MIKE. It's tough on Sue.

DORCAS. They don't have to live like that. They could go back up north where they belong.

MIKE. Who'd she have to coach her?

DORCAS. She isn't doing that badly with Noël.

MIKE. He's not that hot.

DORCAS. Yesterday?

MIKE. Fluke and you know it. Laces reckons if he could get her off Noël —

DORCAS. 200.

MIKE. Yes. (DORCAS *goes silent*.) It would make a lot of sense. (DORCAS *is silent*.) All four of you with the same trainer. That's what Ortolan wants.

Enter SUE *with buckets of water*.

SUE. I had to move your things to get the bucket under the tap.

MIKE. That's okay. Would you like a hand?

SUE. I wondered if I could have a look at the video. If it's not a nuisance.

MIKE. We're not watching anything. Dorcas?

SUE. Not if it's any trouble. Just while it was fresh in my mind.

MIKE. I'll just set it up for you.

SUE. Thanks. Have you seen it?

DORCAS is silent.

MIKE. Doesn't Noël want to see it?

SUE. Twenty minutes without him talking tactics in my ear. It's called peace and quiet. O.K?

MIKE. Do you want a cup of tea or anything?

SUE. I'll just have a quick look then go.

MIKE is puzzled by the fact that the tape seems empty.

MIKE. Have you changed the tapes?

DORCAS. No.

MIKE. This is empty.

SUE. Dorcas, I'll set it if you can't make out how the timer works.

DORCAS. It's wiped.

SUE. You what?

DORCAS. Wiped. O.K. All gone.

SUE. Why?

DORCAS. I'd seen what I wanted.

SUE. My tape.

DORCAS. Half your tape.

SUE. You couldn't have a video if we didn't put in half.

DORCAS. Who says?

SUE. You were the one who asked us to.

DORCAS. Then don't. We'll be O.K.

SUE. All right.

MIKE. That was a pretty stupid thing to do.

SUE. No one wins all the time Dorcas. It's not like that.

> DORCAS *throws a bucket of water at* SUE. SUE *tries to dry herself.*

> You ought to be reported.

DORCAS. Who to?

SUE. To the W three As.

DORCAS. For what?

MIKE. Do you want a towel?

SUE. It's O.K. I'm sorry about the carpet.

MIKE. I'll fill it up for you.

SUE. It doesn't matter. (*Pause.*) Can i have my bucket. Please? (DORCAS *gives it to her.* SUE *goes.*)

MIKE. You're impossible. Do you know that? (*Pause.*) It'll get round, you know.

DORCAS. I don't care.

MIKE. Don't you want friends?

DORCAS. No.

MIKE. I'll get a cloth

> DORCAS *stands.* MIKE *comes back with a cloth.*

> If you feel so angry, vent it out there. Run it off. Use it.

DORCAS. You really are beginning to sound like a teacher!

MIKE. If I ever get a kid who behaves like you in a class I'll send them out. Why do you have to act so thick?

DORCAS. Because I'm a stupid black.

MIKE. You're a fantastic athlete!

DORCAS. Because when I was at school they thought I was thick. So they let me spend all my time out on the track. 'At least she's got something to keep her occupied.'

MIKE. If you want qualifications start taking classes. Work.

DORCAS. I have to train.

MIKE. However much you train there's always going to be the way down. And the rest of your life.

DORCAS. I'll quit at the top. A blaze of glory. People will take me very seriously.

MIKE. Eat.

Scene Five

The track. Mid-day.

SOUND TAPE. Golden Girls Commercial Reel 3, Shot 2, Take 1. And Action!

> *Enter* HILARY *and* THE GOLDEN GIRL. *Enter* TOM. THE GOLDEN GIRL *exits.* HILARY *to* TOM. *She has a cup of coffee. Pause.*

TOM. Put a drop in it for you if you like.

HILARY. It's O.K. This place is very organised. They have a place where you can get coffee.

TOM. They're making a commercial for a firm called Ortolan. They're the ones who've just announced the sponsorship deal for the women's relay team. I'm surprised they haven't pulled out after yesterday.

HILARY. What do you know about the women's relay team?

TOM. On paper they're potential champions. But yesterday was a bloody disgrace. Do you follow athletics?

HILARY. A little.

TOM. They're a national team we could have pride in. Don't you think?

HILARY *nods*.

A sort of identifying process. About the only time you hear the national anthem now. Sports events. The Germans' ll think they're invincible now they're down to forty-one seconds.

HILARY. Records are there to be broken.

TOM. Sure I can't put a drop in there for you?

HILARY. Quite sure. I'm interested. Go on.

TOM. As individuals they're wonderful.

HILARY. As a team?

TOM. They need time together.

HILARY. You sound like a coach.

TOM. Used to do a bit of javelin throwing. I mean — you wouldn't think it now. But I did. Do you know anything about the javelin?

HILARY. Nothing.

TOM. Ruined by the use of steroids. You cheated or you lost or you quit. I'm not a good loser.

HILARY. You were offered drugs?

TOM. They were going to be a miracle. Then they started dope testing and a lot of competitiors declined to take part. There are world champions who are confined to wheelchairs. They didn't realise if they took too much their bones would go.

HILARY. And now?

TOM. They find out somebody's using something — they ban it. Find something else that's harder to detect.

SOUND TAPE. Can we reposition the logo on the running vest?

TOM. The point will come when the drugs are so sophisticated that the tests will become too expensive. The people putting the money in will refuse to pay for them.

SOUND TAPE. Miss Davenport —

TOM. They'll go like the notion of the amateur.

SOUND TAPE. Miss Davenport!

HILARY. Excuse me. I'm wanted.

TOM. Thought you didn't look like an athlete. You use it?

HILARY. Pardon?

TOM. This new shampoo. I wondered if you ever used it?

HILARY. Yes, actually.

TOM. It looks very nice. Your hair.

HILARY. Thank you.

She goes. TOM *watches her. Enter* MIKE *and* LACES. MIKE *with blocks.*

LACES. Try moving them over. (MIKE *does this.*) Not that much. Just a fraction. There!

MIKE. Down?

LACES. Yes O.K. I'll give you the commands and just come up slowly.

Enter NOËL.

NOËL. Mind if I watch?

LACES. Fine by me.

MIKE. No problem.

LACES. One, two three —

MIKE *comes up off the blocks.* THE GOLDEN GIRL *runs across.* MIKE *stops in his tracks. He looks round.* NOËL *and* LACES, *intent on* MIKE, *have not noticed.*

LACES. You could do me the credit of concentrating.

NOËL. His head's too high.

MIKE. Did you —

LACES. It's not in alignment.

SOUND TAPE. Cut!

LACES. Mike!

MIKE. Sorry. (MIKE *walks back and gets on his marks again.*)

LACES. Is that comfortable?

MIKE. Feels O.K.

LACES. Is it comfortable?

MIKE. Start I always use.

LACES *adjusts* MIKE's *head.*

LACES. Feel better?

MIKE. It's going into my shoulders.

LACES. Relax.

MIKE *gets up and shakes himself out.*

NOËL. Have you tried moving his hands forward?

MIKE. I've been through all that.

LACES *has a feel up* MIKE's *spine.*

NOËL. When was the last time you saw a physio?

MIKE. A couple of weeks.

LACES *indicates to* NOËL *to feel* MIKE's *spine.*

NOËL. A few knots.

LACES. He say anything?

MIKE *shakes his head.* LACES *begins to massage it for him.*

LACES. One lap.

NOËL. Loosener? (*They go.*)

Enter TOM. THE GOLDEN GIRL *runs across. Enter* DORCAS.

DORCAS. Is she supposed to be an athlete?

TOM. Apparently.

DORCAS. She's over-striding.

TOM. Shame they can't use Sue Kinder isn't it?

DORCAS. She's not the only one in the squad.

TOM. Bad feeling in the team is there? Personality clashes? Tiffs over boyfriends?

DORCAS. Who do you think you are?

TOM. Did a bit of athletics myself at one time. I know what it's like. There are rumours about you and Mike Bassett. Things not being easy.

DORCAS. Mike's irrelevant.

TOM. Do me a favour?

DORCAS. What?

TOM. I'd like your autograph.

(*She laughs.*)

I believe in you.

HILARY *comes back.*

HILARY. Dorcas . . . Hilary Davenport. I'm responsible for Ortolan's sponsorship.

TOM. Give her the money. Whatever she wants. She'll be worth it. Every penny. She'll get it back for you. (TOM *goes.*)

HILARY. Is that man drunk?

DORCAS. He's from the papers.

Enter THE GOLDEN GIRL.

HILARY. Well done. You must have seen our adverts. This is Anna, our Golden Girl.

DORCAS. If you stand up, you'll breathe better.

THE GOLDEN GIRL. My last job was in a jacuzzi!

HILARY. This is Dorcas Ableman.

THE GOLDEN GIRL. I feel silly. I wish I had your dedication.

DORCAS. I wish I had your money.

SOUND TAPE. Sorry, we have to do it again. Thank you, Anna.

THE GOLDEN GIRL. *Ciao!* (ANNA *and* HILARY *go*.)

   Re-enter MIKE, NOËL *and* LACES.

MIKE. Janet Morris.

JANET (*off*). Track!

LACES. She's supposed to report to me!

   They watch. LACES *starts his stopwatch. They say nothing for 23 seconds. Something extraordinary is obviously going on.* LACES *stops the clock.*

LACES. I don't believe it! Hardly accurate from this distance.

NOËL. You thinking of bringing her into the squad?

LACES. It's crossed my mind.

NOËL. And drop who?

LACES. She's still very young.

NOËL. Tell you who she should go in for.

LACES. If I need your advice on my squad, I'll ask. (*Pause.*) She's never run in an international.

NOËL. She's done 22.18.

LACES. Not officially.

   HILARY *to* LACES.

HILARY. Is that her?

LACES. Yes.

HILARY. She's black.

LACES. Sorry?

HILARY. You didn't say she wasn't white. I sort of assumed —

LACES. Does it matter?

HILARY. Is she special?

LACES. I want to know what goes on in her head. (*To* DORCAS.) Oi! Where were you this morning?

NOËL. I used to tell my Sue she'd make a film star. I always kept her nice. A real little girl, little girl. It used to surprise people. More than coping with what I did.

HILARY. Your daughter is a great runner.

NOËL. She's not at her best. Not yet. Is she?

LACES. Sorry?

NOËL. Sue. Not at her best. Not yet.

LACES. Probably not.

NOËL. Next year. Have her at her peak for Athens.

SOUND TAPE. That's it for today.

HILARY (*to* LACES). We'll speak soon?

LACES. My pleasure.

HILARY. I'll be in touch.

She goes.

NOËL. The power behind the throne?

LACES. You don't bite the hand that feeds you —

NOËL. Miss Davenport — (NOËL *goes after* HILARY.)

MIKE. I thought Pauline was more your sort.

LACES. Leave it out.

MIKE. It was a very strange sequence you dropped people off in last night.

LACES. Let's talk about Janet Morris.

MIKE. Star of Muriel's school. You should ask Muriel.

Enter JANET MORRIS.

JANET. Mr Mackenzie?

LACES. Yes. And Mike Bassett. Not as glamorous as he looks in the running mags, I'm afraid.

JANET. Hi!

MIKE. Congratulations.

JANET. What?

MIKE. Just now. You were pretty impressive.

JANET. You were watching?

MIKE. Sure.

JANET. Mrs Farr tells me off for it.

LACES. Quite right. You aren't doing yourself any sort of favour by showing off.

JANET. Just a bit of fun.

LACES. I'm not interested in fun.

JANET. Then what's the point?

LACES. I don't like messing.

JANET. I don't mess.

LACES. I'd like to have a look at you with weights. When you're ready. (LACES *goes*.)

MIKE. His bark's worse than his bite.

JANET. He's a Scot. (JANET *blows a raspberry*.)

MIKE. Don't let him hear you do that.

Pause.

JANET. I never thought I'd meet you —

MIKE. You'll get over it.

JANET. You were my pin-up when you took the Commonwealth record. I ran away from — from — somewhere I was staying. All I took, your picture and my running things. In the end it got ripped down by a guy I went with. Mike Bassett — white trash — he didn't let me explain it was to do with your running.

MIKE. You'd better see Laces. (JANET *questions*.) Mr Mackenzie.

JANET. The Scots don't half have weird names. Excuse me, I've some strides to do. Then I'll see him.

MIKE. He doesn't like being messed about with.

JANET. Tell him I'm just finishing.

MIKE. O.K. (*He goes.*)

JANET *watches him go.* DORCAS *to her.*

DORCAS. Mike giving you advice?

JANET. He's kind, isn't he?

DORCAS. Mike? You're having a trial for the Golden Girls Squad?

JANET. Yes.

DORCAS. D'you want to be one of us?

JANET. My dream. I want to go horse-back riding. The stuff for that costs a fortune. Have you ever been riding?

DORCAS. I hate horses.

JANET. What do you have to say. To get in?

DORCAS. The more you keep your mouth shut, the better they like you. Just show Laces what you can do. That you're serious. (*Pause.*) You'll do it.

JANET. You really think so?

DORCAS. You're very, very good.

JANET. Mrs Farr says I'm better than she was when she was my age. At school I can beat all the boys. It's their own fault. They don't train. I've got to finish.

DORCAS. See you at the next squad session. (JANET *starts off.*) Hasten slowly young one. (JANET *stops.*)

JANET. Sorry?

DORCAS. Hasten slowly.

JANET. I don't know what it means.

DORCAS. Don't go too far too fast.

Pause.

It's not meant to sound frightening. (DORCAS *goes.*)

JANET. I wanted to be sent away and made to train. When I was a kid I used to whip comics and they had stories of school teams that got kidnapped and forced to train. Baddies wanting them to win because of enormous bets. They grumbled and then escaped. I wanted someone to take me away and tell me I couldn't have chocolates ever again. We got those black pumps for school — the sort with brown bottoms and elastic across the front of your feet. Fitted about four times and then the elastic went all crinkly, fell off your feet all the time. They gave the lads football boots. Because you couldn't be a boy without them. They made me beg to get a proper pair of spikes. Then they were surprised I ran away.

Scene Six

Start in blackout. The multi-gym.

PAULINE, JANET *and* DORCAS *warming up to begin a session* LACES *and* VIVIEN *with clip boards. Enter* SUE *with an empty specimen jar.*

VIVIEN. I want a urine sample in that jar. Try thinking about water. Turn all the taps on and leave the door open.

PAULINE. She doesn't know what running water is.

SUE. We aren't tramps. (SUE *goes.*)

LACES. Oi!

VIVIEN. How much have you got on there? (*She counts it up.*)

JANET. I can do it!

VIVIEN. If you're not careful it will do you. Up. (VIVIEN *adjusts the weights.*) You do nothing until we've worked you out a proper programme.

JANET. Mike Bassett can do it.

VIVIEN. One he's a chap and two he's probably been using weights regularly for the past 10 years.

LACES. What are you doing tonight?

PAULINE. Weights.

LACES. Later?

PAULINE. I'm not interested.

LACES. No one?

PAULINE. Why? Should there be?

LACES. You're attractive.

PAULINE. So?

LACES. I don't understand.

PAULINE. It's not a sacrifice. I don't punish myself.

Enter MURIEL.

MURIEL. Some moron's left all the taps on.

VIVIEN. Most athletes have a sense of timing built into them. Or doesn't yours apply to clocks like the rest of us?

MURIEL. Sorry. George's birthday tomorrow. I had to wait for the cake to be cold enough to put in the tin.

VIVIEN. George or Ortolan. If you're going to take what they're giving, you'd better make sure of what they're getting in return. I want a urine sample in there. I'm not looking for drugs so you can let rip and do a decent amount.

Enter SUE. MURIEL *goes.*

SUE. I couldn't manage any more. Honestly.

VIVIEN. There's a label for it over there. What was Muriel's passing like yesterday.

LACES. Pauline had to move her mark back a bit. Could just be that she's been out of training.

VIVIEN. I can't find anything. Nothing looks wrong when she's moving. She said anything to you?

LACES. I think it's just that she's frightened of doing it again. She say anything to you when you're driving?

PAULINE. Turn right, turn left, stop grinding the gears.

LACES. After that?

PAULINE. You don't have intimate conversations in a 2CV.

VIVIEN. Nothing about how she feels?

PAULINE. If she doesn't do it in Athens, she'll never do it. She knows that.

JANET. You know what they call her at school?

SUE. What?

JANET. Farr-t.

LACES. That's terrible.

DORCAS. Better than being called Wog.

JANET. They've got a new one now.

PAULINE. What?

DORCAS. What?

Pause.

LACES. She'll find out soon enough.

Enter MURIEL.

DORCAS. Did you know you'd got a new nick name?

MURIEL. No.

JANET. Honestly, I wasn't going to tell them Mrs Farr.

MURIEL. What is it?

JANET (*flatly*). So near, but yet so Farr. It's because you always come second. It was the boys that made it up.

VIVIEN. If you want my help in furthering your athletic prowess, perhaps we can get on.

Silence.

One, anybody who has an appointment with me and doesn't keep that appointment without some very good reason isn't going to get very much of my attention. Two, you might not like some of the things you're going to be asked to do but they are in your own interests. I'm not here to turn your bodies into machines, just to make sure that they function at maximum possible efficiency. This afternoon is going to be a list of questions and then an intensive workout to see what you can and can't do. From that we'll work out an interim training schedule to keep you going until the scientific data's been programmed.

DORCAS. I thought we weren't being machines.

VIVIEN. I'm the one that Ortolan pays to be clever. I have just given you a series of forms which are to be filled in every day. Every single day with the number of hours slept and your weight before breakfast . . .

JANET. Excuse me.

VIVIEN. Yes.

JANET. We haven't got no scales.

VIVIEN. Buy some.

JANET. I haven't got any money yet.

LACES. Miss Davenport is coming in this afternoon, she'll sort all that out for you.

VIVIEN. On the other one you write down everything you eat. Not just meals but all the bits and bobs in between as well. Anybody who has sugar in her tea or coffee I want to know how many. The other important thing is exactly how much liquid you're taking in each day. Drinks go on the blue sheet.

SUE. We have a lot of soup. Where does soup go?

VIVIEN. With food but it would be a good idea if you put how much.

DORCAS. How much food as well?

PAULINE. Soup, you idiot.

VIVIEN. The charts are quite self-explanatory once you get the hang of them. Any problems ask me or ask Laces.

DORCAS. How long has this got to go on for?

VIVIEN. Long enough for us to see some overall pattern.

JANET. This is worse than the form I had to get for my passport, Mrs Farr had to help me get that filled in.

MURIEL. This really is rather complicated.

VIVIEN. Is there anyone here who understands it?

One by one they shake their heads.

VIVIEN. Laces and I thought it was —

LACES. Viv, why don't you take them through it?

VIVIEN. Right sit down. I've got time to go through it once so listen. (*To* DORCAS.) How much sleep did you have last night?

DORCAS. Don't know.

VIVIEN. You must have some idea what time you went to bed and what time you got up?

PAULINE. Too much bed, not enough sleep.

DORCAS. Oh, fuck off!

VIVIEN. It doesn't have to be down to the hundredth of a second.

DORCAS. About six hours.

VIVIEN. That all?

DORCAS. I don't need much sleep.

VIVIEN. You put six hours in the column marked Sunday night and so on throughout the week.

SUE. What if you have a sleep during the day?

Pause.

VIVIEN. It had better go in the total for that night. Food. What did you have for breakfast?

JANET. Toast and tea.

VIVIEN. That's not a very well balanced breakfast.

JANET. I have to have whatever Aunty cooks.

VIVIEN. What about protein? Meat, cheese, fish?

JANET. I don't like cheese.

VIVIEN. What about the others?

JANET. They cost a fortune.

MURIEL. When you get some money —

JANET. Got some bacon. Put it in the fridge and Warren ate it all.

VIVIEN. What about the rest of you?

PAULINE. I'm a vegetarian.

VIVIEN. Yes, you would be.

SUE. How come you've got a leather skirt?

PAULINE. It's the idea of dead flesh. Skin's another matter.

LACES. A bit of hush.

VIVIEN. Where it says Monday breakfast you write down toast.

JANET. Ta.

VIVIEN. You put the cups of tea on the other sheet and so on
   for the rest of the day. The incidentals, chocolate bars, any of
   that rubbish go at the bottom of the column for that day's food.

PAULINE. What's this sheet?

VIVIEN. A few personal details. I'll come to them in a minute.

PAULINE. It's the sort of stuff that ought to go in your diary.

SUE. Only if you've got a diary with a lock.

   Enter NOËL. *He has come to return* LACES' *stopwatch.*

VIVIEN. Do you want something?

NOËL. Is all this weights stuff really necessary?

LACES. As far as I'm concerned.

NOËL. Only I've been reading some stuff and it worries me a bit.

LACES. Noël, this isn't really the time or the place.

VIVIEN. Mr Kinder, I'm expected to help these girls get results.
   I have to do that on my own.

NOËL. I won't interfere.

LACES. Please, just go away.

SUE. This is Ortolan stuff Dad. They pay for it. Go on. I'll tell
   you all about it later.

NOËL. Right. (NOËL *gives* LACES *the stopwatch. He goes.*)

SUE. He used to be the only Dad at sports day. He went berserk when I lost the egg and spoon race. Who's going to see this?

DORCAS. Something you don't want your Dad to know about?

VIVIEN. It's strictly confidential between me and Laces.

SUE. Laces, I just don't think we should be asked these questions.

LACES. Vivien's territory, not mine.

SUE. They've got nothing to do with the way we run.

DORCAS (*to* MURIEL). Miss Prim and Proper.

VIVIEN. I beg your pardon but the scientific data would disagree. There wouldn't be scientific data if other girls hadn't answered the same questions.

DORCAS. It's only when you're on, what sort of precautions you take.

VIVIEN. I'm not prepared to put you on continual cycles of the pill so menstruation doesn't interfere with your training, unless they're answered. If you're embarassed because there's a man in the room I'll ask him to leave.

SUE. Are we having an internal examination as well?

VIVIEN. You will do.

JANET. What examinations?

DORCAS. They poke your insides about.

PAULINE. Abortions?

VIVIEN. If any of you get as good as you want to be, that skeleton will probably come rattling out of the cupboard along with a lot of others.

PAULINE. What's it got to do with Ortolan?

MURIEL. Bloody firm. Your body's not your own.

DORCAS. Do you want a list of who, where, when as well?

VIVIEN. Not at this stage. The more details we have —

DORCAS. You don't need this much.

PAULINE. I . . . .

VIVIEN. Perhaps you'll allow me to be the expert.

DORCAS. Ortolan doesn't own us!

LACES. I'm sure in your case Dorcas they'll be very glad to know that.

VIVIEN. I suggest you take these home and decide just how important you think winning is. You all know how to take your own pulse? (*Yes from all of them*.) Does anyone have any objection to having her pulse rate recorded?

(*Nothing from the girls*.) This week before every session, and before means before warm-ups as well, I want you to take your resting pulse rate and record that. Your rate again after maximum effort. Again 5 minutes later. Laces if you'd like to count us through thirty seconds. Then your usual warm up and on to the weights when you're ready.

LACES. O.K. Starting now —

They start taking their pulses.

Enter HILARY.

HILARY. Good news about —

LACES. Shush.

HILARY. Sorry. Everything O.K.?

LACES *nods.*

LACES. And stop. (*The girls work out the results*.) They're just about to start a new session.

HILARY. A quick word that's all. I have to get back to London tonight.

VIVIEN. If it is a quick word. Locums become expensive at night.

HILARY. You're very conscientious about our money.

VIVIEN. Wasn't I expected to be?

JANET (*to* LACES). Will you ask her about my money?

VIVIEN (*to* SUE). Try getting absolutely straight there. That's it.

HILARY (*to* LACES). Is there a problem with money?

LACES. She hasn't got her golden card yet.

HILARY. I've been trying to chase it up for her. Legally she's a minor, big stores won't give them credit. It's very difficult.

LACES. You must have some clout with them.

HILARY. I'm afraid it's going to have to be receipts until your birthday.

LACES. Next month.

DORCAS. Hard luck, Morris Minor.

HILARY. There can't be anything you want that badly. Let me know if there is.

VIVIEN. I can't delay the session for you.

HILARY. Sorry. Is it O.K. if I talk to them while they're doing . . .

LACES. They're quite *compos mentis*.

VIVIEN *claps her hands twice.*

VIVIEN. Come on, sit down.

HILARY. I'd like to spend a few minutes with you on the do's and don'ts of being the Golden Girls squad. We don't believe that sponsors should interfere with their er — there's not really a word for it — those we're sponsoring. But if you work for any organisation there are a few ground rules. I've brought with me several crates of Golden Girls shampoo and from now on I'd ask you only to use Golden Girls. I've brought up your tracksuits and running togs. I know yellow doesn't suit everybody —

SUE. I look dreadful in yellow.

HILARY. But I think our designers have managed to find a shade that will do justice to all of you. We're keen for you to wear these at all times. I know that some of you have certain affinities to various articles of clothing but I hope you'll be able to re-invest those in the Golden Girls kit. No one wants to lay down rules of behaviour to grown women but I think you must all realise that being a Golden Girl has certain responsibilities. Obviously we want winners but if you don't win, don't forget the glory there is to be obtained by being a good loser. The joy of the race is in the running, after all. I think we'd all agree that we wouldn't look up to a heroine who swears like a trooper, even if she has just lost. I need't stress how important it is for you to stress that you are sponsored by us. That as athletes you are assisted by us for the money that allows you to compete and a little that we put into your trust funds but nothing more. No one wants to hear the dirty rustle of five pound notes.

PAULINE. I wouldn't mind, however dirty.

HILARY *allows herself to laugh.*

HILARY. Have I missed out anything Laces?

LACES. Sounds fine to me.

HILARY. One more thing. Any trouble, any sort of suspension or ban and we'll drop you like a hot potato.

DORCAS. Can we drop you if you do something we don't like?

HILARY. What could we possibly do?

SUE. Don't you test shampoo on the eyes of rabbits, things like that?

HILARY. The last thing I want to say is you'll find it difficult in interviews — people will do everything they can to avoid you mentioning the name of the product. But the more accidental slips you make the more you help our sales and consequently what we can invest in you. It can become a little game. We're going to reward you with an extra £100 in your trust funds everytime you manage to mention Ortolan or Golden Girls. Most of all I want you to enjoy the benefits that Ortolan's sponsorship can give you and to put everything you can towards first Gateshead and Crystal Palace and then triumphing in Athens. Do that and we'll see where we can go from there.

Silence.

JANET. Thank you.

HILARY. I think Dr Blackwood wants to get on. I'll explain to Laces about your money.

JANET. Ta.

HILARY. Will you take me out for tea?

LACES. I thought you were in a hurry?

HILARY. I've got half an hour. Or I could take you. It's all Ortolan's money after all.

VIVIEN. I can manage here if Miss Davenport wants a word.

LACES. I'd just like to check the weights. (*He does.*)

MURIEL. How many are we doing?

VIVIEN. I want it all out. Everything you've got. The moment it starts being unendurable stop. And . . .

HILARY. How's it going?

VIVIEN. You don't know until the clock stops.

HILARY. You ran yourself?

VIVIEN. Yes.

HILARY. Why?

VIVIEN. Pleasure.

HILARY. I find it quite extraordinary.

VIVIEN. Wanting to be good at something? You must understand ambition.

HILARY *smiles.*

HILARY. What do you get out of this?

VIVIEN. The chance to do some pure research. There's a chair in medical psychology coming up in about three years time that I'd like to go for.

HILARY. Is that enough time to make a reputation?

VIVIEN. I know a lot about timing my run from the back.

Pause.

HILARY. I want golden girls.

VIVIEN. I'll give them to you.

LACES. Right, they're all set. I'll do the tea. You don't look as if you'll cost me gateau.

HILARY. I might surprise you.

They go.

VIVIEN. I want it all out. Everything you've got.

The girls start to work seriously. It becomes more and more powerful. VIVIEN *watches in a white coat. When you think it's about to become unendurable the lights blackout.*

Scene Seven

VIVIEN'S *room*

Enter LACES. *He prys. Enter* VIVIEN.

VIVIEN. Sorry, I seem to have a locum for the locum.

LACES. I managed to amuse myself.

VIVIEN. They're supposed to be private and confidential.

LACES. You get to know a lot about them, their ups, their downs.

VIVIEN. Dorcas?

LACES. I'm getting there.

VIVIEN. You'll be glad to know a lot of it's better than I expected. On paper the way Janet eats looks like malnutrition. Sue's quite anaemic but that's easy enough to sort out. A few vitamin supplements all round wouldn't really go amiss.

LACES. What about getting them to change their diets?

VIVIEN. I'm not giving cooking lessons.

Pause.

There's something I want to try. Don't look suspicious before you've heard me out.

LACES. It's something you don't think I'm going to like.

VIVIEN. Just hear me out.

LACES. If it's not legal I don't want to know.

VIVIEN. It wouldn't show up in urine tests.

LACES. Blood tests?

VIVIEN. Nowhere.

LACES. Not a drug?

VIVIEN. A drug that no one would ever be able to prove.

LACES. Then it's not ethical.

VIVIEN. You can't be a purist. Sport isn't like that any more.

LACES. An unfair advantage?

VIVIEN. Against whom? The Germans? They'd take anything
that would give them an advantage against the Lynikova's of
this world, if they knew it was safe.

LACES. There isn't anything safe.

VIVIEN. This is.

LACES. They know everything legitimate that's on the market.

VIVIEN. But this is brand new. Hydromel.

LACES. Doesn't Hydromel show up?

VIVIEN. Not if they aren't really taking it. Not if they're really
taking something else.

LACES. A placebo?

VIVIEN. Exactly. There's a pill called Similexon. It's made from
sugar and cornstarch. The stuff turkish delight is rolled in. But
they'll think it's Hydromel. They'd think it gave them a
fighting chance. If there was any other way I could give them
self-belief.

LACES. It's still cheating.

VIVIEN. You'd have no objection to them training at altitude?

LACES. They'd still have scruples.

VIVIEN. Well Dorcas doesn't have them for a start.

LACES. She's asked?

VIVIEN. Not in as many words. Questions about other teams.
What are they on. Where do they get it? Why aren't they

found out.

LACES. Well hardly —

VIVIEN. If other athletes are prepared to take something to win, so is she.

LACES. That's Dorcas, the others?

VIVIEN. Sue would do whatever was necessary to keep up with Dorcas and so on.

LACES. I'm not convinced.

VIVIEN. See this?

LACES. Urine analysis?

VIVIEN. My urine after taking Similexon. Can you see anything that shows?

LACES. No.

VIVIEN. Precisely. There is nothing. But they might — and I'm not saying it's a certainty — they might find themselves a couple of hundredths of a second.

LACES. If they were found?

VIVIEN. There's nothing to find. Think of the future it would give them. I'm a doctor. Trust me.

Scene Eight

The women's locker room.

MURIEL, DORCAS, SUE *and* PAULINE. MURIEL *has made* JANET *a birthday cake.*

MURIEL. Have you got the candles?

DORCAS. No. I've got something else. (DORCAS *takes a toy car from her locker.*)

MURIEL. What?

PAULINE. She's coming. Quick!

MURIEL. What's that?

DORCAS. It's a Morris Minor for Morris Minor.

Enter JANET. *She has just been on her first Ortolan shopping trip and she's bought meat, bathroom scales and running shoes. The others sing her happy birthday.*

MURIEL. You'd better take it off, so we don't have to put Morris Minor down on the diet sheets.

DORCAS. Wish.

JANET *shuts her eyes, wishes and blows.*

SUE. Bet I know what you wished.

JANET. What?

SUE. I know.

JANET. You can't know.

DORCAS. Something about Gateshead?

JANET *is embarassed.*

PAULINE. Presents?

JANET. Stuff we had to buy with our money.

MURIEL *is slicing the cake and handing it round.*

MURIEL. No one's mentioning this, O.K? Or you don't get a slice.

SUE. O.K.

MURIEL. Happy Birthday.

DORCAS. Morris Minor.

JANET. I'm a Morris Major now. (JANET *gets out the scales.*)

MURIEL. That furry stuff'll just get matted.

JANET. I thought they'd be warm. (*She stands on them and watches the dial while she eats her cake.*)

DORCAS. You got your gold card then?

JANET. Yes. It's exciting, isn't it? Just getting things not having to give people any money. This isn't making any difference.

SUE. Did you get anything exciting?

JANET. Four pairs of spikes. And meat. This huge piece of steak. Bigger than the T-bones you get at the Totem.

DORCAS. Is it O.K. for you to come with us tonight?

JANET. Aunty says I'm legally old enough to come home drunk.

PAULINE. And?

JANET. And what?

PAULINE. Other things.

JANET. I didn't need anything else. They had some nice jeans.

SUE. Why didn't you get them?

JANET. They get you jeans?

PAULINE. Why not? They don't want you to go round looking like a frump.

DORCAS. If you like you can come in with us.

MURIEL. She's too young to want all those things.

DORCAS. We have a little system. If there's something one of us really wants, we all go down to Pearts and pool our credit.

DORCAS. That's how we got the settee.

JANET. I thought it had to be to do with running?

DORCAS. I like to put my feet up after a hard day on the track.

SUE. You should have got yourself something new for tonight.

JANET. I didn't know.

DORCAS goes to open her locker.

DORCAS. Like it?

JANET. Great. Mike'll really like it. He likes blue.

Pause.

MURIEL. Front room curtains. (*She takes yards of curtain fabric from her locker.*) I'm going to do them with a triple pleat at the top. And this is for the back bedroom. (*More fabric.*)

SUE takes a water carrier with a tap from her locker.

SUE. For Dad. So he doesn't go on moaning about the one we've got. Have you seen this dress?

JANET *is dazed; she stands on the scales.*

PAULINE (*bringing out a fur coat*). It mightn't be quite Hilary Davenport but — (*The room is strewn with goodies.*)

JANET. I just brought my best jeans.

MURIEL. Put yours on, Dorcas.

DORCAS. Only if you are.

MURIEL. Sue?

They start to get dressed up.

PAULINE. Haven't seen your Dad this week?

SUE. He's trying to fix the move.

MURIEL. Here?

SUE. Where else.

DORCAS. What's he going to do?

SUE. Coach.

DORCAS. I thought you were training with Laces now.

SUE. Only while Dad's away.

PAULINE. He'll never get a part-time job here because there aren't any.

SUE. Dole here or dole there, what's the difference?

MURIEL. Hardly worth buying all that stuff.

SUE. Takes ages to sell houses now at home.

PAULINE *begins to decant some other shampoo into a Golden Girls bottle.*

DORCAS. Oi! What're you doing?

PAULINE. I just don't trust Golden Girls, mine gets ever so greasy using it all the time.

She decants shampoo.

JANET. It's cheating.

PAULINE. Who's to know what's inside. (PAULINE *starts to dress up.*)

An alarm goes off in JANET's *bag.* JANET *rushes to get out her Similexon.*

JANET. Why she couldn't give us ones you have to have with your dinner, not 2 hours after. I keep forgetting. Then I get scared I might have to take two on the same day.

MURIEL. Never, ever. Do you hear me?

JANET. Why not?

PAULINE. Because the dose is one. If two were safe she'd give us two.

SUE. Don't you ever think it's cheating?

DORCAS. A fighting chance.

They are nearly dressed.

DORCAS. Have you got any blusher?

PAULINE. In my bag.

JANET. It really suits you, Dorcas.

DORCAS. Thanks. Do you want to borrow something for tonight? Why don't you try this.

JANET. Ta.

MURIEL. Make you the belle of the ball.

She helps JANET *get changed into* DORCAS's *new frock.*

I hear you've been upsetting Mr Dimond?

JANET. He's a wally Mrs Farr — Muriel — he is honestly.

SUE. What size shoes?

JANET. Six.

PAULINE. You can have these, not the most glamorous but —

Enter HILARY.

HILARY. A party, well, well, well.

JANET. Would you like a piece of cake?

HILARY. I thought this sort of thing was strictly forbidden. Well a little fling. I won't say anything. It's Sue I wanted actually. About this weekend.

SUE. It has to be no.

HILARY. For me?

SUE. One weekend. One weekend on my own.

HILARY. That's hardly the way champions talk.

SUE. It's not a competition.

HILARY. We'll fix everything. There and back, everything.

SUE. Two weeks before Gateshead, it's crazy.

HILARY. No pressure. They just want you to put in an appearance and sign a few autographs. It's quite safe.

SUE. I have to run?

HILARY. People will come to see you run.

SUE. No.

HILARY. There's no risk.

PAULINE. She's got a hamstring problem.

HILARY. Are you saying you know what's best for her.

PAULINE. Some things you can do that are silly.

HILARY. Any strains of any sort I'll get the best physio money can buy. You can take it gently.

SUE. I can't run and take it gently.

DORCAS. We've been working towards Gateshead for a long time.

HILARY. Girls. Don't you think you owe Ortolan a favour. I like to think you understand my position. I have to be accountable. Men in suits and waistcoats. All right, Sue. Come on; I'm sure we can come to some arrangement.

SUE. What?

HILARY. Whatever's reasonable.

SUE. Money?

HILARY. Obviously.

Enter LACES.

What about the practice?

LACES. Practice?

HILARY. If she did the Golden Girls promotion in Manchester?

LACES. You haven't got the first idea. You train very carefully to peak for a race. O.K. she goes to Manchester this weekend and then she loses at Gateshead. Is that fine by you?

HILARY. Do you know how much we've got tied up in this promotion?

LACES. I don't care.

HILARY. If we pull out now —

LACES. Everything you've done so far hinges on four girls and forty-one seconds. It's like floating a needle on water. The tiniest slip and it sinks.

HILARY. Listen to me Sue —

LACES. She's said no.

HILARY. Let's just discuss this in a rational manner. What about you Pauline?

LACES. This weekend is off.

HILARY. It's fixed.

LACES. Unfix it.

HILARY. Your whistles, your stopwatches —

LACES. Have them. (LACES *starts to undress.*)

HILARY. Put them on. I'll find another girl.

LACES. My training schedule's full.

HILARY. I believe Mr Kinder wants to do more coaching.

Pause.

LACES. You all look very good. Big night out?

PAULINE. Janet's birthday. We're going to the Totem. Want to come?

HILARY. Don't you dare let me hear of any of you getting drunk. (HILARY *goes*.)

Pause.

SUE. Thanks.

LACES. Did your Dad want you to do it?

SUE. I didn't ask him.

DORCAS. Go on Laces. Come tonight. Please.

LACES. I'll see. Dorcas, I'd like a word. On your own.

DORCAS. What?

LACES. I'm dropping you for Gateshead.

DORCAS. What?

LACES. You, Sue or Janet and I can only take two.

DORCAS. Drop Sue?

LACES. She's been very consistent in training.

DORCAS. I haven't?

LACES. I have to see what Janet can do.

DORCAS. The reserve.

LACES. If something goes wrong I can't bring her in with no experience. Well can I? You want her to have her chance don't you?

DORCAS. Sue. She hates running the relay. Hates it.

LACES. I thought you'd understand.

DORCAS. My place.

LACES. I'm sorry. It's my only option. The start of the season you expect a bit of chopping and changing.

JANET. What about this, Dorcas?

DORCAS *looks at her*.

DORCAS. Athens?

LACES. The best team I can get at the time.

DORCAS. It's that woman that's behind this isn't it?

LACES. No.

DORCAS. My place.

LACES. She's young. A lot of potential. She deserves her chance, Dorcas.

DORCAS. Not my place.

LACES. Then I'm sorry but you won't be running at Gateshead.

DORCAS. I should have been singing. (*She goes.*)

LACES. I'll see you all on the track tomorrow morning. I want to do some more work on the passing. Sue to Pauline and Muriel to Janet.

JANET. What about Dorcas?

LACES. I'm working the team I want to run at Gateshead.

PAULINE. What about tonight?

LACES. I'm sorry. (*He goes.*)

JANET. I'm running at Gateshead?

MURIEL. Looks like it.

JANET. It's what I wished!

PAULINE. Did you wish you'd win?

Scene Nine

The multi-gym

Sound of fast and furious working. Lights. DORCAS *is driving herself fanatically. Enter* HILARY *in pink with a radio.*

HILARY. It's O.K. I'm not chasing your place. Business lunches. Alcohol. You begin to understand why men get paunchy. Gateshead. I just couldn't face the drive. I thought you'd be up there supporting Mike Bassett.

DORCAS. Things to do here.

HILARY *starts to warm up: an imitation of the athletes.* DORCAS *works properly and hard.*

HILARY. Do you think they can do it?

DORCAS. Don't know.

HILARY. Laces seemed pretty confident yesterday.

DORCAS. The way he operates.

HILARY. Be interesting to see how Janet Morris runs.

DORCAS. What do you get out of it if the squad wins?

HILARY. I prefer to use the word when.

DORCAS. When?

HILARY. I will have proved my point. Women are worth the investment. It'll make an impression.

DORCAS. Not Ortolan. You?

HILARY. Onwards and upwards. A place on the board. I want to be one of the people who make decisions. At some stage I'll quit the company and go for a multi-national. The real big boys, the one's who really do have power.

DORCAS. Do people really buy stuff because we use it?

HILARY. Yes. You're very well known. There's already a response and once the ad's released —

DORCAS. Can I see it?

HILARY. Pardon?

DORCAS. Can I see it?

HILARY. I could bring you a tape, if you know anyone with a video.

DORCAS. Got one.

HILARY. Of course. You must miss a lot of things when you're out training.

DORCAS. Watch myself. How I do. How I can be better. I want a gold. However. I want a gold. Nothing I wouldn't do to be in that squad.

HILARY. I'm told that any four of you is a terrific team. That the disadvantage before has been that there's always been a weak link.

DORCAS. Five of us makes it more difficult.

RADIO. Well, welcome back to Gateshead. Our next event, a very important one, the women's 4 x 100 meter relay. The weather still dull and overcast and that's been reflected in the times on the stopwatch, they've been a little slow. And these girls really looking for a fast time. This is a most important relay for them. They've been training together regularly now and they've got tough opposition in the Czechoslovakians who are drawn in Lane 6. Great Britain drawn in Lane 3. In fact the full line up is Sweden on the inside, then outside them Holland, Spain and the very strong looking Czechoslovakian squad. And the Great Britain squad, well the order, Sue Kinder, Pauline Peterson, Muriel Farr and young Janet Morris the seventeen-year-old orphan girl who came in as a last minute replacement for Dorcas Ableman —

DORCAS. She's eighteen, and she's not an orphan.

RADIO. — a new find for the season — so it must be pretty nerve-racking for her this afternoon. Well Sue Kinder goes to the blocks, thumbs up to Dad, of course, all waiting for that and thumbs up from Dad in return. A very reliable first leg runner, Sue Kinder. Starter's gun is up. Away they go. Sue Kinder running smoothly, chasing hard on the Dutch girl outside her, makes up, oh, about a yard, and then the Spanish girl, the Czechoslovakian's out in front, but that's a good leg by Sue Kinder, running to Pauline Peterson who takes the baton. It's a good exchange. Pauline Peterson's got the wind behind her — she's flowing nicely down the back straight. Running very well indeed. She's taken a yard out of the Czechoslovakian girl. The British squad moving very well and she comes up to Muriel Farr and that's another good exchange. The British squad looking very, very good indeed. Muriel Farr on that bend going hammer and tongs. She's overtaken the rest. It's only Czechoslovakia and they're down and what can Janet Morris do now? She's got the baton safely. Three good exchanges and she's got a yard and a half in front. Now the British squad have really got it together for the first time. Can she hang on to that yard and a half and I'm sure she's going to make it to the line and indeed she does make it to the line. That's a marvellous run.

The British squad really getting it together there and look at the watch! A remarkable forty-one seconds.

HILARY. Is it a remarkable time?

RADIO. A new British record and pretty close to the world record. Now clearly these girls have benefited enormously by getting together day after day in coaching, their sponsorship has paid off.

HILARY. By, by —

RADIO. There really has been a tremendous improvement. What about the seventeen-year-old orphan girl on the last leg? Janet Morris, standing in for Dorcas Ableman.

HILARY. Do you know the number for Gateshead?

DORCAS *is upside down.*

RADIO. Well, it paid off; it really was a remarkable run; a brave run from her. And if these girls show the same form at Crystal Palace in the final trials, I must say this team looks good for medals in Athens.

HILARY. I should have made sure I sent a representative. There must be an area manager or something who could get flowers if he's not playing golf. (HILARY *turns the radio off.*)

DORCAS *begins to cry.*

HILARY. I'm sorry. I know you wanted to run. (HILARY *goes.*)

DORCAS *cries then sings.*

DORCAS. He is the righteous Saviour,
And he shall speak,
He shall speak Peace, Peace,
He shall speak Peace
Unto the heathen.

DORCAS *begins to swallow some pills.*

ACT TWO

Scene One

Heathrow Airport: departure for Athens.

VIVIEN, HILARY, LACES, NOËL, MURIEL, JANET, SUE, DORCAS, PAULINE, TOM, MIKE, THE GOLDEN GIRL.

Flash bulb then lights. The squad are having their photo taken.

PHOTOGRAPHER (*off*). Smile again.

PAULINE. Can't you take one with Split Second in his new outfit?

SUE. They won't let him back in, you know. There'll be a rabies scare.

    Flash.

HILARY. Think that you've already won!

    Flash.

PHOTOGRAPHER. O.K!

TOM. You certainly know what you are doing.

HILARY. It's my job.

TOM. Is the company satisfied with its investment?

HILARY. There's an identification process certainly. People remember the ad. It's been popular. Sue Kinder's quite a star.

TOM. She's blossomed.

VIVIEN. They'll go to pieces if I take it away now. You know what they're like. Any change in their routine.

LACES. I'm twitchy. I accept it works, but I wish we could find an excuse.

VIVIEN. Are you unhappy with all that I've been doing?

LACES. It's been wonderful.

VIVIEN. They could actually win, they should actually win. Dorcas at Crystal Palace. I wish I wasn't the sort of person who had to know where their passport was every five minutes. (*She looks in her bag.*)

HILARY. I like to know what's going on.

TOM. Don't you trust them behind your back?

HILARY. They wear our logo.

TOM. Sponsors have been very cagey since the Milk Race. Drugged cyclist dying.

HILARY. There you are. Do you blame us? We have a lot invested.

TOM. How much?

Silence.

HILARY. A sports journalist.

TOM. I'm thinking of branching out. It's the investigative boys get all the kudos. If I could just find something in Golden Girls which was smelly, nasty. Your track record is so clean.

She smiles at him.

HILARY. Good as gold.

TOM. I need a scandal for my career. You wouldn't like dinner in Athens this evening?

HILARY. That's a scandal?

THE GOLDEN GIRL. O.K.

HILARY. Is this the one with me in?

PHOTOGRAPHER (*off*). Two seconds.

HILARY. They're all fit?

VIVIEN. Barring accidents and tummy bugs.

HILARY. You don't have anything, well, you know — flying. I know it's totally irrational that planes just don't drop out of the sky.

PHOTOGRAPHER. O.K.

HILARY is to have her photo taken.

She is flanked by SUE *and* THE GOLDEN GIRL.

Just bring your hair forward over your shoulder —

NOËL *crosses to brush* SUE's *hair.*

TOM. They say you've worked them out a wonderful diet.

VIVIEN. They've been doing a lot of hard work. A relay team's never had a chance to spend so long together.

TOM. That the secret?

Camera flash.

VIVIEN. It's a technical race. Won or lost on the moment when the baton changes hands. They know the other girls' palms as well as their own. From the touch to the grasp. That and the fact that they're all terrific runners in their own right.

Camera flash.

TOM. You sound as if you've had nothing to do with it.

VIVIEN. I'm a backroom boy.

TOM. What happens while you're on this jaunt?

VIVIEN. Annual holiday.

TOM. For which you're getting paid?

VIVIEN. I won't come home out of pocket.

HILARY (*launching into a speech for the assembled*).

Ladies and gentlemen. If you like to see that you've got a glass. I would just like to say how pleased we are that these girls are running for Britain and for Ortolan —

DORCAS. One hundred pounds.

MURIEL. Can you remember what her total is?

JANET. Can't be anywhere near Sue's.

DORCAS. That's because Sue gets all the interviews.

HILARY. Ortolan —

MURIEL. Two hundred pounds.

HILARY. — is proud to have been able to let these girls have a chance to develop into a team, a real team, and —

P.A. British Airways announces the departure of Flight BA 349 to Amsterdam.

HILARY. And we're just as much in the dark as anyone as to whom the final team is likely to be. Dorcas Ableman's fantastic run at Crystal Palace has really thrown the whole issue into the melting pot. So if you would all like to raise your glasses, I would just like to wish the squad good luck, *bon voyage*, and the Midas touch.

Camera flashes.

VIVIEN. She's had her ginger?

NOËL. She's not bad on planes.

LACES. Got your boarding passes?

NOËL. Mine, Sue's.

LACES. Any more for duty free, do it now.

NOËL. Sue, love, smile.

MIKE. Excited?

JANET. Yes. I want to see it all. All tiny cars.

MIKE. The Alps are spectacular.

JANET. Aunty gave me a St Christopher. Stupid, she doesn't believe in saints.

MIKE. Did you take the toothpaste?

DORCAS. Yes.

MIKE. What am I supposed to use?

JANET. You can have mine.

DORCAS. They do have toothpaste in Greece.

MURIEL. I've left George a quiche; after that he's on his own with the freezer.

JANET. He never comes to watch?

MURIEL. Too busy. Hi-fi firms don't run themselves.

MIKE. Hey, that's our plane. Look.

JANET. Seeing I'm the only one who hasn't flown, do you think they'll let me sit by the window?

TOM. I gather you're buying a house so you can be nearer the centre.

SUE. That's right, Tom.

TOM. Must be quite a difference after the prices up North.

SUE. You're telling me.

TOM. Mortgage?

SUE. I'm not earning.

TOM. Then you still regard yourself as an amateur?

SUE. Aren't I? Who wants to go pro? Tax, accountants, all that sort of hassle.

TOM. So it's more profitable being an amateur?

SUE. Oh no. Just like there are no politics.

TOM. You're a bright girl.

SUE. Just because I've got it in my legs doesn't mean I haven't got it up here.

TOM. Who are they going to drop?

SUE. I beg your pardon?

TOM. I thought that after Gateshead that Dorcas was the obvious one. But after her time at Crystal Palace.

DORCAS *separates* MURIEL *from the rest.*

DORCAS. Have you said anything?

MURIEL. No.

DORCAS. It is discrimination.

MURIEL. You can't prove it.

DORCAS. I've seen the ad. It's all Sue Kinder and the Golden Girl. All we are is little black dots. She signs the cheques. She gets what she wants. And what she wants is four Sue Kinder clones. Since she can't have that, two black, two white is the obvious compromise.

LACES. Boarding passes.

MURIEL. Ta.

LACES. I've assumed you wanted Mike to sit beside you to hold your hand.

DORCAS. We want a word about the squad.

LACES. Nothing is decided.

DORCAS. But you know the team you would like?

LACES. Perhaps not here, Dorcas.

DORCAS. Why's Muriel out?

LACES. No one is out.

DORCAS. Me, Sue, Pauline and Janet — with Muriel as reserve. Isn't that the plan?

LACES. Five into four isn't simple mathematics. A thousand things between then and now. Who's to say what might happen in the individuals?

DORCAS. Sue's a lousy starter.

LACES. She's made a lot of progress this season.

DORCAS. Don't you want a team that will win?

LACES. Any combination of you could. You're all well within the qualifying time. Who says this one won't.

DORCAS. It's the slowest.

LACES. I don't accept that.

DORCAS. What if we go and talk to Madame?

LACES. If you get a sponsor you don't upset them.

DORCAS. So that is what's happened.

LACES. I had to pick some sort of team. A rough list, not a final decision.

DORCAS. You can't just —

LACES. Are you offering to be reserve?

DORCAS. No.

LACES. O.K.

DORCAS. It isn't fair.

LACES. No one ever said it was. I'm sorry Muriel but your times are least consistent.

MURIEL. Since when?

LACES. The team stands. (*He goes.*)

DORCAS. Since when?

MURIEL. He's not going to change it.

DORCAS. He will.

MURIEL. Oh leave it. The longer it's set to work out the change-overs the better.

DORCAS. No.

MURIEL. It's going to look like a personal feud.

DORCAS. If you don't care.

MURIEL. I don't know. I don't want a fuss. It's not that I don't care but —

DORCAS. We're being pushed around.

MURIEL. We can't prove it.

DORCAS. It doesn't need a witness box. What's Sue's personal best this season?

MURIEL. You're pretending you don't know.

DORCAS. At Crystal Palace I wasn't even looking for her.

JANET *returns.*

JANET. If Sue put on all those fancy clothes she'd look just like the Golden Girl.

DORCAS. You have to run.

MURIEL. I've got my own event.

DORCAS. Our event. The team. Sue's not part of it. She never has been. She doesn't belong with us.

MURIEL. Let's forget it. O.K? (*She starts to go.*)

DORCAS. You did the best time in the world last year.

MURIEL. Laces thinks I'm not consistent.

DORCAS. Are you?

MURIEL. Look —

DORCAS. What do you want?

Pause.

MURIEL. I don't know.

DORCAS. You do. (*She holds* MURIEL *threateningly.*)

MURIEL. My last chance. I want to run.

Camera flash.

DORCAS. O.K.

DORCAS *lets go of* MURIEL.

MURIEL. How?

DORCAS. Madame first, I suppose.

MURIEL. She'll just say it's Laces.

DORCAS. We find a reporter. Someone who knows what they're talking about and we talk. Tom Billbow, someone like that. Someone with a mouth they don't mind shooting off.

JANET. We should refuse to run.

DORCAS. What?

JANET. Refuse to run.

DORCAS. We'd be suspended.

NOËL *crosses to* TOM.

NOËL. Will you be using Sue's photo?

TOM *shrugs.*

TOM. Black girls at each others' throats. Which would you use?

NOËL. You a cheque book journalist?

TOM. Why? You got something you want to sell?

NOËL. Just wondered.

TOM. The problem is people sell you the story you're buying.

NOËL. I used to like your column.

TOM. People don't know who I am any more.

P.A. Flight BA 128 for Athens now boarding at Gate Four.

NOËL. Sue.

SUE. O.K. O.K.

    A song from the group as they leave.

LACES. I won't have it.

DORCAS. We weren't fighting.

LACES. Where are your spikes?

JANET. In my case.

LACES. Have you never heard stories of cases going astray and ending up in the middle of nowhere?

MIKE. You'd better pee. There's something about aircraft loos makes it difficult.

LACES. Go on. Before it goes without you.

    JANET *and* MIKE *go.*

PAULINE. Do I have to guess who I'm sitting next to?

LACES . I know Split Second likes to have a window seat.

    PAULINE *goes.*

    HILARY *comes back.*

HILARY. There are already questions. I think it would be an idea for you two to sit together. Nip any rumours in the bud.

MURIEL. It wasn't a fight. (MURIEL *goes.*)

LACES. Even after Crystal Palace you aren't so untouchable that you can't be dropped.

DORCAS. There'd be questions.

HILARY. We'd have answers.

DORCAS. You need me.

HILARY. There's a point where we'd be losing more than we're gaining.

DORCAS. You pick and choose us.

HILARY. I sign cheques. I know nothing about athletics.

DORCAS. Exactly.

LACES. Shall we just see how it goes in Athens?

DORCAS goes.

HILARY. I'm not the one who should have to deal with this.

LACES. I'll sort it out.

HILARY. I hope so.

LACES. There's a lot of tension, they've put in a lot of effort. I don't think you appreciate —

HILARY. I don't like flying. I'd appreciate my hand being held.

She goes.

LACES. What happens to you?

THE GOLDEN GIRL. No one's said. I suppose I just get changed and go. (*She gathers up her things.*)

LACES. I'll give you a hand.

The stage is empty for a few seconds. MIKE and JANET enter.

MIKE. Dorcas is just hyped up, that's all.

JANET. Do you think I should offer to be reserve?

MIKE. No. You're very good.

JANET. You're fabulous.

MIKE. Not the best.

JANET. I believe in you.

MIKE. I'll get a paunch like Laces' in the end.

JANET. You won't. (*They kiss.*)

LACES sees.

LACES. You're a fool.

Pause.

What are you?

MIKE. A fool.

LACES. As if she hasn't got enough.

MIKE. I'm not a machine.

LACES. I don't mean to sound like a school teacher, but the next two weeks are going to need every ounce of your concentration. Kudos, is it? Mike Bassett?

MIKE. She didn't chase.

LACES. Do you think it's clever.

JANET. My life.

LACES. Yes. It could be called unfortunate. Get on that plane.

(*She goes.*)

Mike, there are certain times in your career when you just don't blow it —

MIKE. She believes in me.

LACES. — whatever the temptation. You have to do that for yourself. Have you never learned?

MIKE. I injure badly.

LACES. A hypochondriac looking for excuses. Mike, you won't win in Athens, do you know that?

MIKE. I could win.

LACES. You have to give running one hundred per cent. If you prefer the other, that's your choice; but you are on the way down, Mike.

MIKE. She doesn't think I'm on the way down.

LACES. It's called flattery. It makes you feel important. I'm not denying it feels good, but she's eighteen.

MIKE. She has her own mind.

LACES. And she has to focus it. And what about Dorcas?

MIKE. They can't crack it anyway.

LACES. A good day, the right conditions — forty dead is not impossible. It is just difficult to contemplate, the women as quick as the men.

MIKE. The men's team is lousy.

LACES. The women have always been slower.

MIKE. Laces Mackenzie blows sport wide open!

LACES. Yes. Shush! That relay team. Any combination, magic.

MIKE. You don't believe in magic.

LACES. I believe in them.

P.A. This is the final call for Flight BA 128 for Athens, now boarding at Gate Four.

They go.

THE GOLDEN GIRL *crosses, without the gear she looks drab, dreary and ordinary.*

Scene Two

Greece at night. A terrace above Athens.

JANET. So much to see and they shut you in.

MURIEL. Safety. The Olympics in Munich. And a sporting ideal. Comrades in competition.

JANET. I hate being in there behind that wire. The world cut in little shapes like a jigsaw. You run to be free. Not to share a room and smell other people's pumps at night.

MURIEL. Is there a problem sharing with Dorcas?

JANET. She's got these funny habits. There's a special order she has to do everything in.

MURIEL. It'll happen to you. One big win and you'll start looking for what it was made it happen.

JANET. Never.

MURIEL. She's O.K. Don't try and chat that's all.

JANET. Some of the men are in hotels.

MURIEL. It's been said time and time again.

Some music from the town can be heard.

JANET. I'd like to have a good time. Just let go —

MURIEL. Ruin it for the rest? Just nerves. You'll be O.K. You're a natural. You don't have to think of where you're putting your feet. Just do everything, everything as it always has been.

JANET. I'd like to go in the dark. Just run. See where I was when the morning came.

MURIEL. The countryside?

JANET. Yes. Here's like anywhere else. All those lights on. Could be Liverpool.

MURIEL. It's a good track.

JANET. I thought it would be more special. As a place I mean.

MURIEL. Hot.

JANET. I mean different. Really different. Not Coca Cola. Greece is supposed to be historic. That's what they'll say about us isn't it. If we crack the British men's record. We made history.

MURIEL. Perhaps.

JANET. I'm going to make history, Greece. Do you hear that? (*She raises her arms and shouts.*) Me. Here. History! (*The words echo.*) You see, it knows. (*She lowers her arms.*) I hate the shirts. So sticky.

MURIEL. Team shirts.

JANET. Why do you do it?

MURIEL *shrugs.*

MURIEL. Way of life.

JANET. Really though?

Pause.

MURIEL. I want that tape to come home to. The moment when it breaks. That moment. (MURIEL *slowly lifts her arms. She wraps them round herself.*

She sighs.)

JANET. What?

MURIEL. Lonely, that's all. Lonely inside.

JANET. What?

MURIEL. Nothing.

Enter VIVIEN and HILARY.

HILARY. Look, I'm really starting to catch the sun.

Moment.

VIVIEN. What was supper like?

MURIEL. O.K.

VIVIEN. You eat?

JANET. Yes.

VIVIEN. Good. And it's going to be an early night?

MURIEL. You can't sleep for the noise.

VIVIEN. Do you want something for it?

MURIEL. No.

VIVIEN. I could give you something very mild. Hardly an asprin.

MURIEL. I said no!

HILARY. Surely a good night's sleep —

MURIEL. That racket. If you want a return on your investment you could put us in a hotel where the rooms are sound-proofed.

HILARY. Are you having problems?

JANET. It's all fine. Great! Smashing!

HILARY. Good. And you're feeling confident about the heats?

JANET. Yes.

VIVIEN. Don't go all out.

JANET. You sound like Laces.

VIVIEN. I'm meant to.

MURIEL. She's a natural.

VIVIEN. There's no fun in being too certain.

HILARY. I'm relying on you not to let me down. I want to go to the board next week and put four gold medals on the table and say 'Look, I was right'.

JANET. Our medals?

HILARY. You'll get them back.

JANET. I'm wearing mine. Twenty-four hours a day I'm wearing it.

MURIEL. They're hell when you're trying to sleep.

Pause.

The gold comes off. Did you know that? They're plated. They tarnish.

VIVIEN. Let's get through the heats shall we before we start discussing how long the medals are going to last. Beautiful, isn't it?

JANET. If you look down there you can see the board with the events.

JANET *and* VIVIEN *go.*

HILARY. You must be pleased with your time this afternoon?

MURIEL. The fastest qualifier. A lot of people would see that as an ill omen.

HILARY. Really?

MURIEL. Giving your all before the big race. You are supposed to hold back. Do just as much as necessary.

HILARY. You miss-timed it?

MURIEL. I wanted to be sure I made the final.

HILARY. What do you reckon your chances are there?

MURIEL. Pauline ran just the right race this afternoon, she'll have an advantage over me.

HILARY. Are athletes always pessimists?

MURIEL. So many things to go wrong.

Enter DORCAS.

DORCAS. I bet Barbados is like this. Warm at night. My Ma said there were crickets there, used to cheep all night. Dad says she's just imagining it. He's forgotten which side of the road the cars go on.

HILARY. Cicadas.

DORCAS. Pardon?

HILARY. Cicadas, in the trees, not crickets. In Barbados.

DORCAS. You went there?

HILARY. On holiday once.

DORCAS. What was it like?

HILARY. There was a typhoon. Sand got everywhere. I itched for days.

DORCAS. What side did the cars go on?

HILARY *tries to remember.*

HILARY. I'll tell you when it comes back to me.

DORCAS. My Ma got pregnant with me in Christchurch. Just my luck to get born in Dagenham.

Enter MIKE.

Pause.

HILARY. Bad luck.

MIKE. Thanks.

MURIEL. Still your relay.

VIVIEN. Hilary, come and look at this.

HILARY *goes.*

Pause.

MURIEL. You can see the board above the stadium. (*She goes.*)

Pause.

DORCAS. I can't take it Mike. Not tonight.

MIKE. It's the end.

DORCAS. It's always like that when you lose. Get it together, another race.

MIKE. Lose again. Knowing that they're waiting for it.

DORCAS. I don't want to hear. Not tonight.

MIKE. I want to talk to you. Right? (*Pause.*) I had to win.

DORCAS. You didn't.

MIKE. How many million people saw me with tears running down my cheeks.

DORCAS. Television doesn't show the losers. You start too slowly to get it back trying to accelerate on the curve.

MIKE. Any school coach would tell me that.

DORCAS. Then you know.

MIKE. I want to win and I can't.

DORCAS. English born and bred, you're supposed to be a good loser.

MIKE. Talk to me.

DORCAS. I can't.

Pause.

But I need you there watching me.

MIKE. I lost.

DORCAS. I need you there.

Enter JANET.

JANET. Our toothbrushes are the same. Mine's in the glass. (*She hands* MIKE *a tube of toothpaste.*) She and I can share the toothpaste. Don't let it get to you.

MIKE. Not here.

DORCAS. Shooting stars! (*They look*).

You're supposed to wish. (*They look. Nothing.*)

JANET. Wish me luck.

MIKE. You don't need it.

JANET. Will you watch?

MIKE. I promised Dorcas.

Pause.

JANET. When we get back.

MIKE. I'm not sure.

JANET. You promised.

MIKE. I don't know. Dorcas'll guess.

JANET. I don't care.

MIKE. I don't want her hurt.

JANET. Enough. You said you'd had enough.

DORCAS. There! (DORCAS *points*.)

MIKE. No.

Enter SUE *and* NOËL *with ice creams.*

NOËL. Have you tried the ices?

MIKE. No time.

NOËL. Bad luck. Up to the girls to fly the flag.

MIKE. Yes.

NOËL. I thought I saw a Bee Eater this afternoon. But the bird books here are all in Greek. The sort of place for Night Jars.

MIKE. I thought I heard something up there in the trees.

MIKE *and* NOËL *go.*

SUE. Awful luck with the draw.

DORCAS. The heats are supposed to be even.

SUE. They can't change them now, it would be admitting the draw was wrong. I don't suppose you have a problem with the heat.

JANET. I'm sweating something awful.

SUE. Has Vivien given you some salt?

JANET. No.

SUE. You ought to have some.

JANET. I'll ask her. (JANET *goes*.)

SUE. D'you want a taste?

Pause.

DORCAS. Thanks. (DORCAS *takes a lick of* SUE's *ice cream*.)

Enter TOM.

TOM. How touching.

SUE. You're a sweet man and I know you're very keen but we've a big day tomorrow —

TOM. O.K., I understand.

He creeps off.

DORCAS. Room O.K?

SUE. Never share with a swimmer! It's wet bathing costumes and those horrid little rubber hats everywhere. What's the kid like?

DORCAS. At least she's tidy. You know what it's like with Pauline, stuff everywhere.

SUE. One of these days someone'll put themselves out falling over her junk.

Nervous?

DORCAS. Yes. You?

SUE. Yes. What do you think of the kid's chances?

DORCAS. She's the unknown.

SUE. She's got quite a crush on Mike.

DORCAS. We call her the Lamb.

NOËL (*calling*). Sue!

SUE. I can't see the bloody things hiding in the trees in the daytime let alone the dark.

DORCAS. As far as I'm concerned they're all sparrows or black-birds.

SUE. Once you get obsessed there are different sorts of sparrows.

Enter JANET.

JANET. She says she'll get me some.

SUE. Good.

JANET. If we were film stars we'd have our names up there in lights. Not just our events.

NOËL (*calling*). Sue!

SUE *shrugs to* DORCAS.

SUE. It's like playing I-spy. (*She goes.*)

JANET. Poor Mike eh?

DORCAS. Don't give him sympathy. Make him run for it.

JANET. But crying.

DORCAS. Don't you think you might have something to do with it?

JANET. You what?

DORCAS. It doesn't bother me. Just keep him off my back until after this. And a bit of discretion. I couldn't handle people wanting stories.

Enter MURIEL.

MURIEL. You haven't seen Tom Billbow?

DORCAS. He's sniffing around here somewhere.

Enter MIKE.

MIKE. I thought I'd have an ice. At least I'm not off my food.

JANET. I'm so excited it just disappears. I'm really hungry all the time.

MIKE. Have an ice.

JANET. I think I might. Do they do chocolate?

MIKE. Don't know.

MURIEL. Why don't you go with him and choose your own?

MIKE. Do you want one Dorcas?

She shakes her head.

JANET. Come on. (*JANET and* MIKE *go*.)

MURIEL. Can you remember when it used to be fun like that?

DORCAS. Still is. Isn't it?

MURIEL. The running of the races.

DORCAS. If it isn't you should quit.

MURIEL. I know.

DORCAS. We could get a relay gold.

MURIEL. It's not up to us.

DORCAS. Yes, it is.

Enter HILARY *and* VIVIEN.

HILARY. I'll have to go in. I don't know what they ate before I got here. The cars are the same as at home. I'm almost certain. It's British after all.

VIVIEN. Have you seen Janet?

DORCAS. Buying some ice cream.

VIVIEN. I could never have eaten ice cream the night before my heat.

MURIEL. She has no nerves.

HILARY. I think I'm doing the worrying for her.

Enter NOËL *and* SUE.

NOËL. You're hearing things. Nightingales don't sing at this time of year.

VIVIEN. Early nights?

NOËL. She's on her way.

MURIEL. Pauline went to bed hours ago.

VIVIEN. There'll be plenty of time to savour the atmosphere once the heats are over.

SUE. We'll have the finals.

HILARY. I'm glad someone is an optimist.

MURIEL. Have you seen a phone box anywhere?

HILARY. Is there one in the taverna?

MURIEL (*looking at her watch*). He mightn't be home yet. Still worth a try. (*She goes.*)

HILARY. I'm going to be eaten alive. Coming?

VIVIEN. I'd like to give Janet her salt before she goes to bed.

DORCAS. Give it to me. I'll give it to her.

VIVIEN. Of course, you're sharing.

DORCAS. Night.

SUE. Night.

VIVIEN *and* DORCAS *go*.

HILARY. We don't want bags under those eyes. Not if she wants to be considered as the new Golden Girl. (HILARY *goes*.)

SUE *stands*.

SUE. Why can't she leave me alone?

NOËL. Come on. Bed.

Pause.

SUE. Listen!

Pause.

NOËL. You heard what Miss Davenport said?

SUE. I want to stay.

NOËL. You've a race tomorrow.

SUE. I know. Outside at night and it's warm.

NOËL. I'm not staying up here all night.

SUE. Go.

NOËL. I'm going to get cross.

SUE. Get cross.

NOËL. I'll tell Laces.

SUE. What's he going to do? Come and fetch me?

NOËL. You don't like the dark.

SUE. This isn't dark. Listen!

Pause.

NOËL. I'm going.

SUE. Go. I can do it for myself now, Dad.

She stands her ground. He is forced to go.

A moment. Possibly we hear the bird. Enter MURIEL.

I'd like to stay for the dawn. If I hadn't got a heat. It's so easy running in the sun. The outside as warm as in. Heaven.

MURIEL. Whenever I'm away I want to go home. To go somewhere to be still. To be able to shut the door.

SUE *goes.*

MURIEL *stands for a moment. Enter TOM.*

TOM. Doesn't it worry you? A girl up here on your own? You know what they say about Greek men?

MURIEL. I can look after myself.

TOM *belches.*

TOM. Pardon. Greek wine is filthy but I can claim it is scotch. I was impressed this afternoon.

MURIEL. Thank you.

TOM. Can you do it?

MURIEL. Who can ever say?

TOM. Are you beginning to think of quitting?

MURIEL. Sometimes. (*Pause.*) I wanted a word.

TOM. With me?

MURIEL . Yes, I think so. (*Pause.*) It's a sort of question really. I hope you don't mind.

TOM. I'm flattered to be asked.

MURIEL. It's about Heidi Lynikova.

TOM. Yes.

MURIEL. There are stories in the camp —

TOM. Isn't gossip always rife amongst you?

MURIEL. Please.

TOM. I beg your pardon.

MURIEL. You know she was pregnant when she smashed the record in Oslo?

TOM. Fanny Blankers-Cohen in 1948 all over again.

MURIEL. Did you ever hear about the baby? (TOM *thinks*.) It had everything wrong with it. They say it was a freak.

TOM. Really?

MURIEL. The American girls say it had something to do with some stuff she was taking. I wondered if you knew.

TOM. Why?

Pause.

MURIEL *produces a capsule.*

TOM. Oh!

MURIEL. It's legitimate. At least in the sense that nothing shows up.

TOM. A wonder drug?

MURIEL. We haven't had a bad season.

TOM. I thought it was the presence of Janet Morris amongst you. Youth snapping at your heels. Do you know what it is?

MURIEL. It's called hydro-something.

TOM. It's not cricket.

MURIEL. No. I don't want to stay in this game forever. Even if you want to your body starts to go and lets you down. I want to win here and then children. (*About the drug.*) We're running as fast as some of the men. (TOM *takes it.*) It's not black market stuff. They come from the doctor.

TOM. Paid for by Ortolan?

MURIEL. I suppose so, in a manner of speaking. I thought you might have some way of finding out.

TOM. Hairy chests, anything like that?

MURIEL. It's not a steroid. It's made from rats.

TOM. It could be very messy.

MURIEL. Yes.

TOM. Drug analysis is expensive. The paper's money. They'll expect to be able to make a story.

MURIEL. Yes.

TOM. You'll be pilloried in every paper, every sports club —

MURIEL. Find out what it does. Please. Isn't it what they call a scoop?

TOM. Yes.

Scene Three

At bens.

The team are working on the baton changes. They work in pairs: SUE to PAULINE; MURIEL to JANET; DORCAS on the side lines. LACES watches.

They start with the shout and the change. JANET starts too soon.

LACES. Do that on the day and you'll be out of the box without thinking about it.

JANET. Sorry.

LACES. You've to be absolutely certain of the moment to go. (*The other change-over has gone well.*) Well done.

SUE. Thanks.

LACES. Try moving your mark back — just about a meter.

   JANET does.

MURIEL. Louder shout?

LACES. Give it as much as you can.

   They do it again and it is better but JANET looks back after she has started her run.

LACES. Don't look back.

PAULINE. It's so hot. Dripping off me.

SUE. Think what it will be like with the tension.

PAULINE. Don't.

LACES. If it's sweaty get a dry one on. You can get chills even at this temperature.

SUE. What was that like?

PAULINE. The baton was just too far forward. I'd have had problems on my hand over. (*She demonstrates.*) If you could just take your hand fractionally back along it.

SUE. The problem with that is starting. (SUE *tries to work out her start with the baton in the new position in her hand*.)

PAULINE. Perhaps it's just me. We always did the downward pass at school.

SUE. You see the problem is there. Hang on. (*She goes through several repeats.*)

LACES. O.K. Dorcas, you come in as outgoing runner.

DORCAS. Give me a few.

MURIEL. Hand. (MURIEL *does a few slow motion movements of the baton into* DORCAS's *hand.*)

MURIEL. Hand. My hand's so sticky. Hand.

DORCAS. O.K.

LACES. Ready?

DORCAS. Is this supposed to represent the edge of the box?

LACES. Yes.

DORCAS. Can you put something there so I can see it when I come up to it?

LACES *puts a bit of clothing, or something, there.*

LACES. O.K?

DORCAS. Great. Thanks. (*To* MURIEL.) Right?

MURIEL. Right?

DORCAS *counts back — and makes her mark.*

HILARY *enters.*

LACES (*to* JANET). Watch this.

DORCAS. You giving the go?

LACES *signals to* MURIEL. *The whole thing takes place perfectly.*

HILARY. Was that good?

LACES. About as good as it ever can be.

HILARY. Congratulations.

LACES. Look, whatever it is I don't want to hear here and now. We've only got another 30 minutes.

HILARY. Can I watch?

LACES. Of course.

SUE *and* PAULINE *set up to go again.*

SUE. Hand!

PAULINE *misses the baton.*

PAULINE. Shit!

LACES. What happened?

PAULINE. Slipped.

SUE. Another go?

PAULINE. Do you mind?

SUE. It's O.K.

They go again.

SUE. Hand!

Again PAULINE *drops the baton.*

LACES. Have you gone to pieces?

PAULINE. No.

LACES. Then what?

SUE. I thought you had it.

PAULINE. I did.

SUE. Try spraying your palms with deodorant.

PAULINE. Have you got some?

SUE, *of course, has.*

DORCAS. Can we call it a day?

LACES. You happy with that?

DORCAS. Fine. (*To* MURIEL.) Have you got any problems?

MURIEL. No.

LACES. I'd just like to have a look at Janet to Pauline.

JANET. Fine.

DORCAS *and* MURIEL *stay to watch this.*

LACES. Don't stand there like muffins. Set it out for yourselves. I won't be down there in the heats tomorrow.

JANET *and* PAULINE *go about setting their marks.*

HILARY. Have you finally decided?

LACES. Not yet. Why?

HILARY. It's just that it would be nice if there was the same balance in the team as there is in the advertisement — two black and two white girls.

LACES. I think you'll find you need it further back than that.

PAULINE. You aren't going to be down there on the track tomorrow.

They get ready.

LACES. Just the change. That's all. Ready?

They go.

JANET. Hand!

PAULINE *drops the baton.* LACES *is beside himself.*

LACES. What the hell is the matter with you? (PAULINE *just stands and shakes her head.*) Go. (*The others do.*) And you. (HILARY *goes.*) If it's something I can do. Tell me.

PAULINE. She just doesn't give me enough.

LACES. Janet or Sue?

PAULINE. I've blown it, haven't I?

LACES. Of course not.

PAULINE. Three drops one after the other.

LACES. I don't make snap judgements. I find the reason then decide.

PAULINE. I'd rather just know.

LACES. As soon as I make the decision to drop you, I'll let you know, O.K? So don't stand there and come that with me. I know the screws are on and it's all getting tighter and tighter — are you sleeping?

PAULINE. Yes.

LACES. Even without taking anything?

PAULINE. All that stuff Vivien's done about talking to myself.

Pause.

LACES. Is it that you know and you're not going to say?

Pause.

Something to do with the squad? (*She shakes her head.*)
Are they pressurising you? Dorcas's plan for three black girls together?

PAULINE. They're all better than me.

LACES. Muriel ran a silly race yesterday. She's probably used all she's got. You ran it exactly right. You've got something left over.

PAULINE. Just let me be the reserve, O.K.

LACES. If I think you're good enough to run, you'll run.

PAULINE. I don't want to be picked just because you fancy me. I know I'm not good enough.

LACES. I run you in the relay squad because I think you're good. Because you have technique at your finger-tips.

PAULINE. Butter fingers!

MURIEL *comes back. She protects* PAULINE.

LACES. It's a crisis of confidence. (*Pause.*) I didn't mean to shout at you. I'm sorry.

PAULINE. Shout at me. Tell me I'm no good. Tell me the truth. (PAULINE *cries.*)

LACES. You are a very, very good runner. You have text-book technique. I do like you a lot. But if you think another coach would help perhaps that's what had better happen. (*He goes.*)

MURIEL *stands with* PAULINE.

PAULINE. I'm hopeless.

MURIEL. That's what you say about learning to drive.

PAULINE. He fancies me and Madame wants as many white runners as possible. That's the only reason I'm in. I know I'm no good.

MURIEL. This is silly. I'm not going to listen to it.

PAULINE *gradually calms down.*

Enter TOM.

TOM. Something up?

PAULINE. Sky! Don't want Split Second getting sun stroke. (*She takes Split Second and goes.*)

TOM. I take it we have a team?

MURIEL. Don't jump to conclusions.

TOM. I'd call tears conclusive.

MURIEL. Well?

TOM. Not Hydromel.

MURIEL. What?

TOM. Completely rodent free. (*He hands her a piece of paper.*)

TOM. The Greek analysis.

MURIEL. This is impossible.

TOM. That's what they say it is.

MURIEL. We're turning in results as if we'd got a following wind and this says we're taking the ingredients of a cake mix. It doesn't make sense.

TOM. No. London have their doubts about the Greek labs. They'd like to get some back and get them analysed properly. I have to have some more.

MURIEL. She'd know.

TOM. Five, one off each of you.

Pause.

MURIEL. I'll try.

TOM. You'll get them to me?

MURIEL. Yes.

TOM. You can reach me at my hotel. The Acropolis. It's all reinforced concrete. I could take you out to eat if you like.

MURIEL. No thanks. The butterflies get the better of the menu.

Exit TOM.

At school I was always the fastest runner. From I don't remember when. George would understand boxing. He'd like a boy to be a boxer. I like the tape to come home to. The moment when you dip and no one has to tell you that you've won. When all the waiting and all the effort's been worthwhile. The winning. The peace of it all being over. Then the pain comes back. The tightening of the thighs and pins and needles in the heels. Once I looked at my feet and could see blood coming through my shoes. And you smile and smile because it doesn't matter. Nothing matters. One would do it again and again and not count the cost. Until there was something you wanted more.

Scene Four

Athens. The athletes' camp.

Everyone is bored. It is the morning before the big race; SUE is sun bathing and MURIEL is writing post cards. MIKE is reading about community access to educational sports facilities. NOËL has binoculars and a bird book. JANET is testing PAULINE on her highway code. DORCAS plays solitaire, obsessively, and LACES paces.

SUE. What time is it?

NOËL. Quarter to.

JANET. Blue square, then in the middle of it is like a 'T' and the top of the 'T' is red.

MIKE. It's easy.

PAULINE. I'm thinking.

MURIEL. My road?

PAULINE. Dead end?

JANET. Yes. Red triangle —

    Enter VIVIEN.

VIVIEN. You'll get dehydrated.

    SUE *sips her drink.*

JANET. With white in the middle and sort of rock?

PAULINE. Danger falling rocks.

LACES. Can you have a look at Janet's hamstring? It's a bit tender.

VIVIEN. Of course. (VIVIEN *goes to* JANET.)

LACES (*to* SUE). I just want to talk you through your start.

SUE. Trust my back foot, trust my grip, trust myself.

LACES. Good girl. Are you happy with the change-over to Muriel.

SUE. I have to be.

LACES. You know what you're going to do if she wrong foots?

SUE. She won't.

LACES. But if she does?

SUE. You're giving me something to worry about that I don't need to.

VIVIEN. Is that better?

JANET. A bit.

VIVIEN. There's not much else I can do, I'm afraid. All I can do is promise you some pain killers when it's all over.

LACES *goes up to* DORCAS.

DORCAS. I get the baton and then I run like the wind. O.K?

LACES. Great. (*He watches her play.*) What will you do if it ever comes out?

DORCAS. It won't.

SUE. What time is it?

NOËL. Ten to.

SUE *turns over.*

SUE. Do me a favour.

PAULINE *starts to rub sun tan lotion on* SUE.

VIVIEN. Any more aches and pains?

NOËL. You'll turn them into hyperchondriacs.

VIVIEN. If I can give them one thing less to worry about — I give them a split second's more concentration.

MIKE *to* DORCAS.

DORCAS. I have to have your chain.

MIKE. I lost.

DORCAS. I still have to have it.

He gives it to her.

Thanks . You will come down to the track?

MIKE. Why?

DORCAS. I want you to see me do it.

MIKE. O.K.

>   NOËL *to* SUE.

NOËL. Sue, shall we talk about the start?

SUE. I know what I'm doing.

NOËL. You've got to remember —

SUE. You aren't my coach anymore. (*Pause.*) I'm sorry but I have to have the very best.

NOËL. Him?

SUE. He's taught me things that —

NOËL. I've sold the house. Everything. I'm not asking for thanks but —

SUE. What do you want?

NOËL. I wanted you to have your chance.

SUE. I'm taking it.

>   NOËL *moves away.*

MIKE. She's uptight.

NOËL. I don't like being in the south. I don't belong. I wanted her to have her chance.

MIKE. Once we're all back home.

NOËL. My little girl.

LACES (*to* PAULINE). You O.K?

PAULINE. Don't be nice to me.

LACES. Then I don't know what to say.

PAULINE. It's easy. Don't say anything.

LACES. You couldn't have been selected.

PAULINE. I know.

MIKE. Why did they call you Laces?

MURIEL. Yes, tell us.

LACES. It's silly.

JANET. I thought it was your real name.

LACES. School. One day I forgot my laces. Couldn't keep my shoes on. Couldn't run. The team lost. Put us out of the running for the shield. Every time the gym teacher saw me after that he used to shout 'Remember your laces.' I've been Laces ever since.

VIVIEN. What's your real name?

LACES (*embarrassed*). Lawrence.

DORCAS. Lawrence!

PAULINE. It's no worse than Dorcas.

DORCAS. Dorcas means gazelle.

LACES *looks at his watch.*

LACES. O.K.

The girls start to get up to go.

VIVIEN. Good luck.

DORCAS. We're going to do it. Aren't we? We're going to do it.

The four runners gather in a huddle.

DORCAS. Forty seconds dead!

MURIEL. Forty seconds dead!

JANET. Forty seconds dead!

SUE. Forty seconds dead!

LACES. Let's go!

MURIEL. Come down and watch.

PAULINE. Perhaps.

MURIEL *goes.*

MIKE. I'll be there.

DORCAS. Yes. (*She goes.*)

MIKE (*to* JANET). Don't panic. Wait 'til she hits her mark and then go like the wind.

JANET. Right. (*JANET goes.*)

VIVIEN. Your big day?

LACES. Could be.

VIVIEN. Will be.

LACES. Thanks.

> VIVIEN *goes.*

SUE. You have to give me the thumbs up.

NOËL. Everything Sue.

SUE. You're still my Dad whether you train me or not. (SUE *goes.*)

> LACES *goes.*

VIVIEN. Well we could all have some lunch? Mr Kinder?

NOËL. Might as well. Kill the time. (*They go.*)

> PAULINE *goes back to her highway code.*

MIKE. Going to pass this time?

PAULINE. Better do.

MIKE. What are you going to do now?

PAULINE. Have another shower. Go down to the track. Wave the flag.

MIKE. Back home?

PAULINE. Start training again. Really concentrate. Might change coaches. I've never thought of the future, not before I'm twenty-five.

MIKE. I'll end up shouting at kids like that guy did at Laces.

PAULINE. You're a good runner. You could still get it back.

MIKE. I don't think I want to. I'll see you down there?

PAULINE. Yes.

> MIKE *goes.*

I used to be happy being the best in the street. Then the best in the school, best in Kilburn, London, England, Britain, Europe, the world. You do one of them you think you'll be satisfied. You're still hungry. Do another and it makes you hungrier. Every win you think there'll be a feeling of content. And there isn't. You get up and start all over again. Thinking one day you'll be full.

Enter TOM.

TOM. You can smell the tension.

PAULINE. A lot of people's big day.

TOM. Have you seen Muriel Farr?

PAULINE. Gone down to the track.

TOM. Hell!

PAULINE. Something the matter?

TOM. A few questions about the squad.

PAULINE. There's still me.

Pause.

TOM. What do you know about Hydromel?

PAULINE. Sounds Greek to me.

TOM. It's a drug.

PAULINE. I don't know anything about no drugs.

TOM. Are you sure?

PAULINE. Yes.

TOM. But you've heard of it?

PAULINE. Yes.

TOM. You know what it does?

PAULINE. Supposed to make you run faster.

TOM. Yes. And the side effects?

PAULINE. Why should I know?

TOM *gets out a capsule.*

TOM. You recognise it? (*Pause.*) Vivien Blackwood. She's as hungry that the team do well as you are.

PAULINE. It's because we've got it cracked on the baton changes.

TOM. Why aren't you in the team?

PAULINE. I dropped the baton.

TOM. They tell me Hydromel speeds up the physical processes but not altogether consistently. Co-ordination is affected.

PAULINE. You haven't got any proof.

TOM. A lot of evidence.

PAULINE. Proof!

TOM *indicates the drug.*

PAULINE. You could come in here with anything and pretend we swallow it but unless you can get one of us to piss into a jar for you — (*She picks up* SUE's *glass.*) Do it in here for you if you like.

TOM. O.K. It's not you. But if it's not you, it's one of them down there and where does that leave me?

Enter HILARY.

HILARY. I wanted to be here to say good luck.

PAULINE. They had to go.

HILARY. Did they seem bright?

TOM. Feet of clay.

HILARY. I'm sorry?

PAULINE. I have to have lunch. (*She goes.*)

TOM. You know they're taking something?

HILARY. Who?

TOM. Your team.

HILARY. Of course not.

TOM. Didn't Vivien Blackwood promise you winners? (*Pause.*) Everyone cheats in this game, everyone knows. It's not Ancient Greece any more.

HILARY. Don't you know that girls can win. That men can be surprised? I'm going to go into that boardroom and lay four gold medals on the table.

TOM. They're plate. The gold comes off.

Scene Five

The race.

The runners come down the stage passing the baton sideways between them.

Announcement of the race and the start in Greek etc.

They take their tracksuits off. For the first time we see them all in The Golden Girls running stripe.

The race: as they run each girl has one chant in the rhythm of her race.

SUE. Go! Go! (*She repeats until the baton is passed to* MURIEL.)

MURIEL. For me! For me! (*She repeats until the baton is passed to* JANET.)

JANET. Want to win! Want to win! (*She repeats until the baton is passed to* DORCAS.)

DORCAS. Go for it! Go for it! (*She repeats until she goes through the tape and the clock stops.*)

Jubilation; the sound of the stadium; flash bulbs and a moment while they look at their time.

Enter PAULINE.

PAULINE. You were fucking wonderful.

The official time goes up on the scoreboard: 39.99 seconds.

DORCAS. Yes!

JANET. History!

MURIEL *starts to cry.*

MURIEL. I'm just so happy.

SUE. This year's men's record!

Enter MIKE *and* NOËL.

DORCAS. We did it!

MIKE. You were like the wind. Ten second legs!

SUE. You see that Dad? You see that time?

NOËL *take a photo of her.*

MURIEL. If only George was here.

MIKE. I didn't know you could run like that. I never dreamed.

JANET. I've got a gold medal. Me.

    Enter LACES.

SUE (*hugging* LACES). We did it!

LACES. Well done.

NOËL. Is that all you can say?

    LACES *gives* DORCAS *the dope testing card.*

LACES. Short straw I'm afraid. Ableman, Farr, Kinder, Morris —

JANET (*to* DORCAS). I told you you'd get tested in the end!

    Enter HILARY. *She carries a bust crowned with laurel leaves.*

HILARY. I was so excited. Athena, the Goddess of Victory. We wanted to mark the occasion.

SUE. I must have done ten seconds.

LACES. Now!

    LACES *and* MIKE *chair* DORCAS. *As they carry her off, she seizes the bust from* HILARY.

HILARY. The traditional victor's crown. Everybody'll be wanting pictures, stories — Dorcas! (HILARY *goes.*)

SUE. Take that for me, Dad. Take that!

    NOËL *tries to find an angle to get the shot.*

NOËL. You did it for me. The time of my life. (*He goes in order to get the picture.*)

JANET. Fancy having to piss into a jar at a time like this!

PAULINE. Yes, but it's one in the eye for Tom Billbow.

MURIEL. What?

PAULINE. He just never gives up. He says he can prove we're taking Hydromel.

JANET. Nothing showed yesterday.

SUE. Where's he got this from?

PAULINE. If nothing shows up there is no proof.

SUE. Of course there's no proof. We've been taking it and being tested for months.

Enter VIVIEN.

VIVIEN. Did I tell you all? (*She hugs them.*) You must be thrilled.

JANET. I'm getting a gold medal!

Re-enter HILARY *with the wreath back on the bust.*

HILARY (*to* VIVIEN). Congratulations.

VIVIEN. Couldn't have done it without Ortolan.

HILARY (*gathering them to her*). Our Golden Girls.

TANNOY. The medals ceremony of the women's 4 x 100 metres relay has been suspended pending an official enquiry.

Pause.

HILARY. What?

VIVIEN. Some technical hitch. That equipment is very sensitive.

SUE. That stuff you gave us?

VIVIEN. Pardon?

PAULINE. Dorcas has got caught. Hasn't she?

VIVIEN. No.

SUE. I've got to go and be tested.

VIVIEN. Nothing illegal.

MURIEL. Hydromel's not legal. If it was, you wouldn't have told us to keep quiet.

HILARY. You were giving them drugs?

VIVIEN. Nothing that could possibly disqualify them.

SUE. She's been caught.

JANET. I don't know what I'll do if I'm disqualified.

HILARY. Who gave you permission?

VIVIEN. Look at their results.

HILARY. I thought we had made it quite clear. Play by the rules.

VIVIEN. I did.

MURIEL. You doped us.

VIVIEN. No. Never.

SUE. All those pills?

VIVIEN. There was nothing in them.

MURIEL. You told us it was Hydromel.

Pause.

VIVIEN. What I gave you was something called Similexon. A placebo. Flour and sugar in a gelatine shell.

JANET. What's going to happen to me in there?

PAULINE. Just one of us Tom Billbow said.

VIVIEN. Did he say what?

PAULINE. Hydromel! What you told us it was.

MURIEL. Dorcas?

VIVIEN. If Dorcas is taking something, it's nothing to do with me. It's something she's done on her own. She's always wanted to be brightest and best.

JANET. When I was thirteen she used to be my God.

Enter TOM.

TOM. I thought there'd be a surfeit of smiles. I did try and warn you.

HILARY. One out of five?

TOM. I always suspected Ableman was half crazy.

HILARY. How did you get on to it?

TOM. Women rivalling men. There had to be an explanation.

HILARY. There's still Sue's run. Janet's. Muriel's.

JANET. I did run that fast?

VIVIEN. Yes.

Enter DORCAS.

DORCAS. Why?

HILARY. I knew you were a liability.

JANET. You're a cheat.

VIVIEN. Why Dorcas? Why?

DORCAS. Safe you said. Safe.

VIVIEN. I was pretending.

DORCAS. It isn't a game. It isn't a game.

VIVIEN. What I gave you was safe.

HILARY. Do you know how much money you've just poured down a very dirty drain?

DORCAS. Do you know where I got the money.

TOM. Ortolan?

HILARY. This is nothing to do with us.

DORCAS. What about our accounts? I got all sorts of things. I swapped. Couldn't have got it without your money.

SUE. If you wanted to run faster why didn't you just ask her.

DORCAS. If she'd given me two she could have given you two. (*To* VIVIEN). We had a deal. It was safe. Nothing was supposed to show.

VIVIEN. That's because there was nothing there. Anything else you got is due to your own stupidity.

DORCAS. I'm not stupid.

VIVIEN. You went and got more of what I gave you.

SUE. You did give it to us?

VIVIEN. Of what you thought I gave you.

DORCAS. You gave us stuff. I got more. What's the difference? How was I supposed to know it wasn't real?

VIVIEN. Did it never cross your mind?

DORCAS. No, because I'm stupid. All I wanted was to win.

HILARY. How can you possibly call that winning?

TOM. Feet of clay.

DORCAS. You pathetic little man.

PAULINE. Dorcas!

DORCAS. Sniff, sniff, sniff.

TOM. Nothing to do with me. You were dope tested.

DORCAS. Not for months and months. Why today?

TOM. You can't let the flag go up for someone who doesn't play by the rules.

DORCAS. What fucking rules? No one else has any rules. (*She goes at him.*)

MURIEL. Dorcas, don't.

DORCAS *struggles with* TOM.

MURIEL. Leave him.

DORCAS. I'm going to kill him.

MURIEL. Get him out.

VIVIEN *and* HILARY *rescue* TOM. JANET *starts to scream. The other women hold* DORCAS.

HILARY. I can assure you Golden Girls has no part in any of this.

TOM. I suppose I should be thankful it wasn't steroids.

They take him off.

PAULINE (*to* VIVIEN *as they go*). I could have run. If there was something I could have had to calm me down.

Enter LACES. *He has the others' dope testing cards.*

LACES. They're waiting. It's the rules.

Scene Six

The post-mortem

MURIEL. I was frightened. I had to say. Perhaps I should have waited.

DORCAS. I might have been tested anyway.

PAULINE. No one knows if it's true about Lynikova.

SUE. Rumour and counter-rumour. We wanted her to have cheated. None of us believed she could be that good.

JANET. I really believed in Vivien. She shouldn't have played games with us.

MURIEL. We went along with it . . .

SUE. Of course we did, look at our times.

PAULINE. She told us it wouldn't show up.

SUE. We didn't want to know.

MURIEL. We only thought of getting off the next hundredth.

JANET. We were used!

SUE. Of course we were used.

JANET. Vivien.

PAULINE. Tom Billbow's copy.

MURIEL. Ortolan. I'm sorry. You'll never be the Golden Girl now.

SUE. It's Dad you have to explain to. I wouldn't mind staying here in the sun, forever. If we never had to go home.

JANET. It's going to be horrible going home.

MURIEL. We've still got our silvers and our personal bests.

JANET. We'll be banned.

DORCAS. *You* won't.

JANET. But —

DORCAS. You did it, young one. You did it. All of you.

SUE. What about you?

DORCAS. What about me?

Enter LACES.

LACES. I've tried to keep them off your backs for as long as I could. BBC. They've got ten minutes on the satellite. (*The women go*.) Not you. (DORCAS *stops*.) It'll be for life, Dorcas.

DORCAS. For 5 minutes we were the best. Better than the East Germans. Better than anybody. Better than the men. The most perfect there could be. What I'd always wanted. I was pure gold.

LACES. It's a good feeling, isn't it?

DORCAS. Best in the world.

LACES *and* DORCAS *shake hands.* LACES *goes.* DORCAS *takes the dross of the bust. She sings.*

Speak ye comfortably to Jerusalem,
Speak ye comfortably to Jerusalem,
And cry unto her,
That her warfare,
Her warfare is accomplished,
That her iniquity is pardoned,
That her iniquity is pardoned.